Textile Products

Textile Products
SELECTION, USE, AND CARE

Patsy R. Alexander

The University of Mississippi

HOUGHTON MIFFLIN COMPANY • BOSTON

Atlanta • Dallas • Geneva, Illinois • Hopewell, New Jersey

Palo Alto • London

Copyright © 1977 by Houghton Mifflin Company.
All rights reserved. No part of this work may be reproduced
or transmitted in any form or by any means, electronic
or mechanical, including photocopying and recording, or
by any information storage or retrieval system, without
permission in writing from the publisher.
Printed in the U.S.A.
Library of Congress Catalog Card Number: 76-11955
ISBN: 0-395-20358-9

Contents

Preface xiii

Part One Textile Elements 1

Chapter 1 Fibers and Yarns 3
- NATURAL FIBERS 4
- MANUFACTURED FIBERS 6
  - *Generic Names* 7
  - *General Characteristics of Manufactured Fibers* 10
  - *Selected Characteristics of Manufactured Fibers* 12
- FIBER IDENTIFICATION TECHNIQUES 16
  - *Burning Test* 16
  - *Solubility Test* 17
  - *Microscope Test* 18
- FIBER BLENDS 18
- GLOSSARY OF FIBER TERMS 20
- YARNS 21
  - *Carding* 22
  - *Combing* 23
  - *Spinning* 23
  - *Sizing* 24
- TYPES OF YARNS 25
  - *Simple Yarns* 25
  - *Novelty Yarns* 25
    - Slubbed Yarns 26
    - Looped Yarns 26
    - Knotted or Nubbed Yarns 27
    - Spiral Yarns 27
  - *Textured Yarns* 27
  - *Thread* 28
- GLOSSARY OF YARN TERMS 28
- STUDY QUESTIONS 29
- SUGGESTED ACTIVITIES 30

Chapter 2 Fabrics 31
- FABRICS MADE DIRECTLY FROM FIBERS 31
- FABRICS MADE FROM YARNS 33
- FABRICS MADE FROM NEITHER FIBERS NOR YARNS 45
- MULTILAYER FABRICS 45
- GLOSSARY OF FABRIC NAMES 48
- STUDY QUESTIONS 56
- SUGGESTED ACTIVITIES 56

Chapter 3 Finishes 58
- TYPES OF FINISHES 58
  - *General or Routine Finishes* 58
  - *Special or Functional Finishes* 59

COLOR 64
DESIGN 65
   Structural Design 68
   Applied Design 68
GLOSSARY OF COLOR AND DESIGN TERMS 74
STUDY QUESTIONS 75
SUGGESTED ACTIVITIES 76

Part Two   Care   77

Chapter 4   Care Characteristics   79
FIBER PROPERTIES AND YARN STRUCTURE 79
FABRIC CONSTRUCTION 83
FABRIC FINISHES 86
CARE AWARENESS SHOPPING 89
STUDY QUESTIONS 89
SUGGESTED ACTIVITIES 90

Chapter 5   Consumer Protection   91
LABELING 91
   Wool Products 91
   Fur Products 91
   Fiber Content 93
   Permanent Care 94
     Apparel 95
     Piece Goods 95
     Upholstery Fabrics 97
FLAMMABILITY 98
   Care Instructions 102
STUDY QUESTIONS 102
SUGGESTED ACTIVITIES 103

Chapter 6   Laundering and Stain Removal   104
LAUNDRY PRODUCTS 106
   Soaps and Detergents 106
   Pretreatments 106
   Bleaches 107
   Starch 108
   Fabric Finish 108
TEMPERATURES 108
   Water 108
   Drying 110
STAIN AND SPOT REMOVAL 110
AN ENVIRONMENTAL CONCERN 114
STUDY QUESTIONS 117
SUGGESTED ACTIVITIES 117

Part Three Selection 119

Chapter 7 Textile Consumption 121

   DEVELOPMENTS OF THE TWENTIETH CENTURY 122
      Textile Technology 124
      International Trade 124
   CURRENT TRENDS IN FIBER AND FABRIC CONSUMPTION 128
   CHANGES IN USE OF TEXTILES 129
      Wool Fiber 129
      Cotton Fiber 131
      Manufactured Fibers 132
      Considerations for the Consumer 133
      Clothing Recycling 133
         Restyling 136
         Renovating 136
         Patchwork 136
   STUDY QUESTIONS 137
   SUGGESTED ACTIVITIES 138

Chapter 8 Consumer Satisfaction 139

   BEAUTY 139
      Fiber Properties 140
      Yarn Processes 140
      Fabric Construction Methods 140
      Finishes 142
   HAND 144
      Fiber Properties 144
      Yarn Processes 144
      Fabric Construction Methods 145
      Finishes 145
   SERVICEABILITY 146
      Fiber Properties 146
      Yarn Processes 147
      Fabric Construction Methods 148
      Finishes 148
   COMFORT 148
      Fiber Properties 149
      Yarn Processes 149
      Fabric Construction Methods 149
      Finishes 150
   CARE 152
      Fiber Properties 152
      Yarn Processes 152
      Fabric Construction Methods 154
      Finishes 154
   STUDY QUESTIONS 154
   SUGGESTED ACTIVITIES 155

Chapter 9 Textile Properties in Home Sewing 156
- FABRIC AND PATTERN COMPATIBILITY 157
- FABRIC PREPARATION 159
- STITCHING OPERATIONS 162
- PRESSING TECHNIQUES 165
- STUDY QUESTIONS 165
- SUGGESTED ACTIVITIES 166

Chapter 10 Stores, Sales, and Credit 167
- TYPES OF STORES 168
  - *Specialty or Exclusive Shops* 168
  - *Department Stores* 168
  - *Chain Stores* 170
  - *Variety Stores* 170
  - *Second-hand Stores* 171
  - *Mail-order Houses* 171
  - *Supermarkets* 171
  - *Discount Stores* 171
- HOW TO SHOP AT SALES 173
  - *Preclearance Sales* 174
  - *Clearance Sales* 174
  - *Preinventory Clearance Sales* 176
  - *Special Item Sales* 176
- CREDIT 176
  - *Determining the Need for Credit* 177
  - *Types of Credit* 177
    - Charge accounts 177
    - Credit cards 178
    - Personal loans 178
    - Check-credit plan 178
  - *Consumer Credit Protection* 178
- SHOPPING TIPS 179
- STUDY QUESTIONS 180
- SUGGESTED ACTIVITIES 180

Chapter 11 Guidelines for Purchasing 181
- DECISION MAKING 181
  - *Values* 183
  - *Needs* 184
  - *Value Clarification* 185
- SELECTING TEXTILE PRODUCTS 185
- QUALITY IN FABRIC AND CONSTRUCTION 185
  - *Fabric* 186
  - *Garment Construction* 187
- TRADEMARKS 189
- METRIC MEASUREMENT 192
- STUDY QUESTIONS 193
- SUGGESTED ACTIVITIES 194

Part Four Family Clothing 195

Chapter 12 Preferences in Clothing 197
   CLOTHING VALUES 204
     A Scale for Identifying Values in Clothing Buying 205
       Directions 205
   FIT IN READY-MADE CLOTHING 210
     Size Standards 212
   STUDY QUESTIONS 213
   SUGGESTED ACTIVITIES 213

Chapter 13 Clothing the Individual 214
   BASIC HUMAN NEEDS IN CLOTHING 214
     Physiological 214
     Sociological 216
     Psychological 216
   CLOTHING FOR CHILDREN 216
   CLOTHING FOR ADOLESCENTS 219
     Early Adolescence 219
     Adolescence 222
     Desirable Clothing Properties 222
   CLOTHING FOR ADULTS 224
     Desirable Clothing Properties 226
   CLOTHING FOR THE ELDERLY 227
     Desirable Clothing Properties 230
   CLOTHING FOR THE PHYSICALLY HANDICAPPED 231
   CLOTHING FOR THE BLIND 231
   STUDY QUESTIONS 232
   SUGGESTED ACTIVITIES 233

Chapter 14 Apparel for Children 234
   SIZING 235
   THE INFANT 235
   THE TODDLER 236
   THE PRESCHOOL CHILD 236
   THE SCHOOL-AGE CHILD 240
   STUDY QUESTIONS 244
   SUGGESTED ACTIVITIES 244

Chapter 15 Apparel for Men and Boys 246
   SIZING 247
   SUITS, JACKETS, AND SLACKS 247
     Fabric 247
     Construction 250
     Fit 252
   OVERCOATS AND TOPCOATS 253
   SHIRTS 256
     Styles 256
     Fabrics 257

  Sizes   258
  Construction and Fit   258
 JEANS   259
  Construction   259
  Style   260
  Care   261
 LEATHER APPAREL   261
 SWEATERS AND JERSEYS   262
 SOCKS   263
 UNDERWEAR   264
 PAJAMAS   265
 STUDY QUESTIONS   265
 SUGGESTED ACTIVITIES   266

Chapter 16 Apparel for Women and Girls 267
 COATS   276
  Construction   277
  Fit   279
 SUITS   280
 DRESSES   281
  Fit   282
  Construction   284
 PANTS   284
 BLOUSES   286
 SWEATERS   286
 FOUNDATION GARMENTS   287
  Fabric   288
  Size   289
  Styles   289
  Construction and Care   290
 NIGHTCLOTHES   290
 HOSIERY   290
  Size   291
  Construction and Care   291
 STUDY QUESTIONS   292
 SUGGESTED ACTIVITIES   293

Chapter 17 Shoes 294
 PARTS OF THE SHOE   294
 SHOE MANUFACTURE   296
  Sewing   296
  Cementing   296
  Molding   296
   Vulcanizing   297
   Injection Molding   297
   Slush Molding   297
 SHOE MATERIALS   298

 PURCHASING SHOES 298
  Checking Fit of New Shoes 298
  Fitting Clues from Old Shoes 300
  Quality 300
 SHOE CARE 301
 LEATHER TERMS 302
 STUDY QUESTIONS 303
 SUGGESTED ACTIVITIES 304

Part Five Textiles in the Home 305

Chapter 18 Home Furnishings 307

 UPHOLSTERED FURNITURE 309
  Framework 309
  Construction 310
  Outer Fabric 312
  Care 312
 RUGS AND CARPETS 315
  Fibers 315
  Quality 316
  Construction 317
  Care 317
 INDOOR-OUTDOOR CARPETING 318
 CURTAINS AND DRAPERIES 318
  Size 319
  Styles and Fabrics 320
  Serviceability 322
  Care 322
 STUDY QUESTIONS 322
 SUGGESTED ACTIVITIES 323

Chapter 19 Household Linens 324

 BEDROOM 324
  Sheets 324
   Shape and Size 325
   Fabrics 325
  Pillowcases 328
  Mattress Covers and Pads 328
  Blankets 329
   Size 329
   Fabrics 329
   Bindings 331
   Colors and Patterns 331
  Bedspreads 331
  Comforters 331
 BATHROOM AND KITCHEN 332
  Towels 332

      Sizes 332
      Fiber 333
      Construction 333
        Colors and Patterns 334
   Bath Mats or Rugs 335
   Shower Curtains 335
DINING ROOM 335
   Sizes 335
      Purpose and Suitability 336
      Durability 337
STUDY QUESTIONS 337
SUGGESTED ACTIVITIES 338

Bibliography 339

Trade Associations 344

Index 345

Preface

THIS BOOK PRESENTS the basic concepts of textiles and relates them to consumer satisfaction in using textile end products. It sets forth the simple facts about fibers, yarns, fabric construction, and finishes in language understandable to the individual who has had no previous formal instruction in textiles or science. I have included only those textile science concepts that appear relevant to the average consumer. In this respect, the scholar seeking a book with a highly scientific textile science orientation will most likely find this one inadequate. Many excellent textile science books are already on the market; this text does not belong in such a category.

This book may be used by any individual—whether student, instructor, or average consumer, of any age—who is interested in specific, practical details on making an informed selection of textile products. The text is directed toward specific end uses, and it presents instructions on maintenance and care of textile products to ensure maximum consumer satisfaction. It also provides guidelines for evaluating products—especially items of clothing, household linens, and home furnishings—to help the consumer make intelligent decisions in shopping, and includes a brief review of textile laws and legislation that have been passed to protect the consumer. The presentation on clothing for the family is concerned with stages in the family life-cycle that present special problems for the consumer, and it deals with aspects of developmental needs that relate to clothing, and, more specifically, to textiles. This section suggests ways in which these needs may be met through selection of the appropriate textile fibers, yarns, fabrics, and finishes.

The author and the publisher are grateful for the assistance of those who made professional reviews of the manuscript. Reviews at different stages of manuscript development provided valuable assistance in shaping the final form of the book. These reviewers, to whom we give thanks, were Emma Briscoe, Emeritus, University of Montana; Dr. Imogene Ford, North Carolina Central University; Juanita Ford, Montclair State College (New Jersey); Wendy Ann Morck, Grossmont College (California); Mary Rile, Monterey Peninsula College (California); Rebecca Sisk, Pensacola Junior College (Florida); Patricia Stockebrand, Hutchinson Community College (Kansas); and Betty Tweten, University of Nebraska, Omaha.

Many other individuals have contributed immeasurably to this book. To my students at both Eastern Illinois University and The University of Mississippi, who helped me develop and continually evaluate the consumer textiles course, I am deeply grateful. They offered many suggestions in both content and teaching methods that helped determine the scope of the book.

The several years spent in actually writing the book would have been tedious ones without the encouragement and assistance generously given by friends and coworkers at The University of Mississippi. I wish to extend my personal appreciation to Dr. Porter L. Fortune, Jr., Chancellor, Dr. Arthur DeRosier, Jr., Vice Chancellor for Academic Affairs, and Mary N. Duvall, Administrative Assistant to the Chancellor, for their general encouragement to me to engage in professional writing; to Dr. Joseph Sam, Dean of Graduate School, for financial assistance for special photography work; to Dr. Maeburn Huneycutt and Dr. Gerald Walton, Deans of the College of Liberal Arts, for financial assistance in duplicating copies of the manuscript; to Dr. George Street, Director of University Relations for much valuable legal advice; to Dr. Edwin Meek, Director of Public Relations, for media releases; to Dr. William H. Norman, Professor of Biology, and William C. Martin, Biological Consultant-Photographer, for the specialized photography of fabric swatches; and to Annie Elizabeth Mills, Documents Librarian, for assistance in researching materials.

I am also grateful to Betty M. Fulwood and Laverne S. Hellums, professors in the Department of Home Economics, who served as consultants in writing the chapters on selection of home furnishings and consumer buying, respectively; to Dr. Paul Hendershot, Professor in the School of Business, who assisted by providing materials used in writing the chapter on textile consumption; to Dr. Louise Burnette, Chairman, and Dr. Willie Price, Professor in the Department of Home Economics, who proofread portions of the manuscript in the early stages of writing; to Jayne Ozier, professor in the School of Home Economics, Eastern Illinois University, who challenged me to attempt to write the book; and to Mrs. John Pilkington and Mae Stone, who carefully typed the manuscript. A special note of thanks goes to the Springs Mills Consumer Division, Springmaid Sheets and Pillowcases, for permission to use a part of their Newburyport pattern on the cover. We would also like to thank the Educational Bureau, Coats & Clark, Inc. for the use of one of their diagrams as the basis for the part opener to Part One.

These acknowledgments would be incomplete if I did not express appreciation to my brothers and sisters and their families for their encouragement throughout the entire writing process.

A very special appreciation is extended to my sister Mrs. C. B. (Sydney) Gray and her family for their sustaining strength and continued support throughout all of my professional and personal endeavors, and specifically in accomplishing this particular goal, which entailed some discouraging and frustrating moments. It is to Sydney that I dedicate this book.

Patsy R. Alexander

Part One
Textile Elements

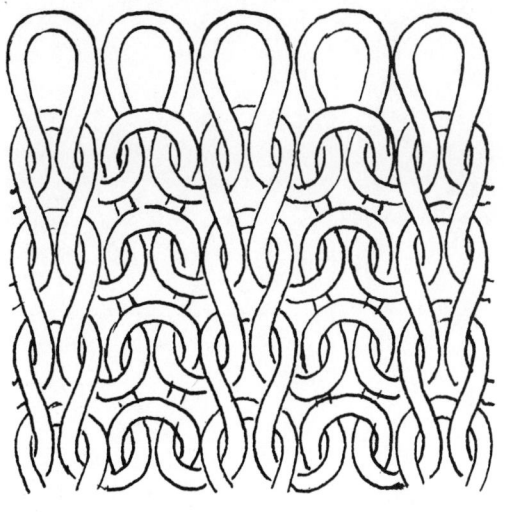

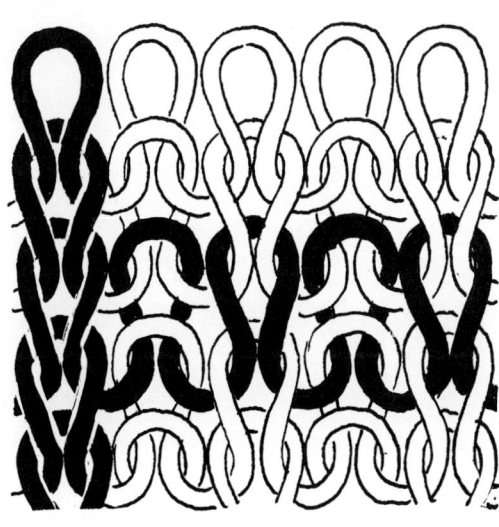

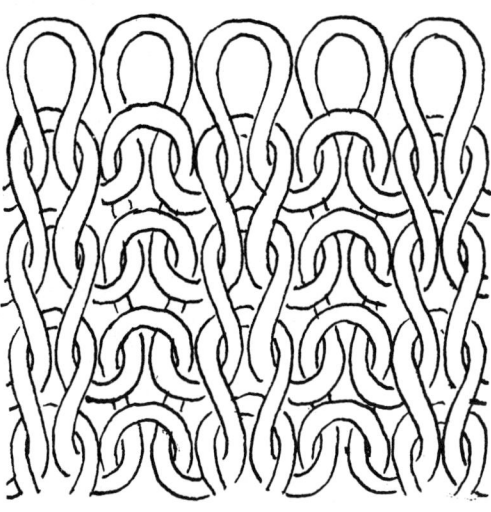

Chapter 1

Fibers and Yarns

TECHNOLOGICAL developments in recent years have so revolutionized the textile industry that today textiles are a highly scientific area of study. The average consumer, however, does not look for an in-depth, science-oriented body of knowledge about textiles, but does need to know enough facts about textiles to obtain maximum satisfaction from the many products on the market. Since consumer satisfaction is derived primarily from end-product qualities such as beauty, serviceability, comfort, and ease of care, an adequate basic knowledge of textiles and textile products will enable the consumer to evaluate products in terms of these qualities.

The textile goods themselves are the end results of several intermediate processes, beginning with the basic textile unit, the *fiber*. The particular physical and chemical properties of different fibers largely determine the characteristics of the products made from them. These properties are affected by all the processes involved in manufacturing—spinning the fiber into yarn, making the yarn into fabric, finishing the fabric, and constructing the fabric into the end product. This chapter will outline the essential facts about textile fibers and yarns, so the reader may understand how they contribute to product satisfaction.

Fibers are the smallest visible units from which fabrics and other textile products are made. They are derived from specific substances, are usually of a definite length and diameter, and possess identifiable microscopic, physical, and chemical characteristics. To be suitable for use in textiles, fibers must have greater length than diameter and be flexible and strong to withstand the strain of the various manufacturing processes. They must be inexpensive, easily available, and constant in supply. In addition, a fiber should be pleasing to the touch in both temperature and texture, absorbent enough to accept dyes, comfortable to wear, and cleanable by some method. Generally, fibers are classified according to their origin, as either natural (from sources existing in nature) or manufactured (developed by people in some way).

Natural Fibers

The natural fibers most commonly used to make textile products are cotton (Figure 1-1), flax, jute, silk, and wool.

FIGURE 1-1 *A cotton boll as it comes from the cotton plant.* (Courtesy of American Textile Manufacturers Institute)

Other natural fibers used include hemp, ramie, kapok, angora, cashmere, feathers, mohair, and vicuña. Many natural fibers are not used for textile fabrics because they lack the properties that make a fiber spinnable into a yarn used to make cloth, namely, length, pliability, strength, and cohesiveness. The origin of natural fibers may be cellulosic (plant), protein (animal), rubber, or mineral. Seed hairs, stalks, leaves, and nut husks supply plant fibers such as cotton and flax, wool fibers are animal hairs, and silk fibers are secretions from silkworms.

Cellulosic fibers such as cotton (Figure 1–2) and flax (Figure 1–3) have several properties in common which affect their use in textile products. Because they absorb moisture and conduct heat well, they make cool, sheer fabrics, which provide comfortable clothing for hot weather. Fabrics made from them will withstand high temperatures, can therefore be sterilized in boiling water and demand no special precautions in ironing. However, because of their low resiliency, such fabrics wrinkle badly unless they are finished to control this factor. These fibers can be made into compact yarns and high-count fabrics that are durable and strong. Their high density makes fabrics that feel heavier than some others. Since they are good conductors, they do not build up static electricity to "shock" the wearer. They are harmed by mineral acids, and fruit stains must be removed immediately from a garment to prevent setting. Storage is simplified because of resistance to moths, but mildew, which attacks damp, soiled articles, can be a problem. Cellulose fibers will ignite quickly and burn freely, so that filmy or loosely constructed garments should not be worn near an open flame. These fibers are only moderately resistant to sunlight: fabrics exposed to direct sunlight for long periods of time may fade and rot unless they are protected.

Protein fibers, for example, wool and silk, similarly have certain common properties that are important to consumers (Figures 1–4 and 1–5). Because of their resiliency, fabrics made from them resist wrinkling and hold their shape well. Those wrinkles that do form tend to hang out between wearings. Their hygroscopicity (ability to absorb and retain moisture from the air) adds to their comfort when worn in cool, damp climates and prevents brittleness in carpets. Protein fibers are considerably weaker when wet and must be handled carefully during cleaning. They generally weigh less than cellulosic fibers of the same thickness and thus produce lighter-weight fabrics. They are flame-resistant and self-extinguishing and make products with some degree of safety.

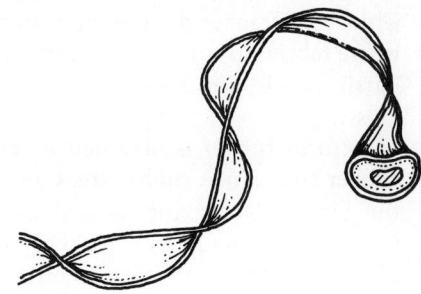

FIGURE 1-2 *The cotton fiber, as shown in this enlarged drawing, has a flat, ribbonlike appearance. The twist at irregular intervals, known as a convolution, is a distinguishing characteristic of the cotton fiber. Different types of cotton plants grow fibers of different lengths, ranging from $\frac{3}{4}$ to $1\frac{1}{2}$ inches. The longer fibers, called long-staple, are of finer quality but are produced in smaller quantity.* (Nancy G. Harries and Thomas E. Harries, Textiles: Decision Making for the Consumer, McGraw-Hill Book Company, New York, 1974)

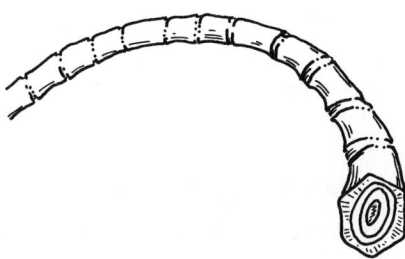

FIGURE 1-3 *A greatly enlarged flax fiber, showing the joints or nodes that give the fiber its resemblance to bamboo. A flax fiber consists of a bundle of cells, and fiber length varies.* (Nancy G. Harries and Thomas E. Harries, Textiles: Decision Making for the Consumer, McGraw-Hill Book Company, New York, 1974)

Chlorine bleaches damage protein fibers and sunlight causes white fabrics to turn yellow. Dry heat causes wool to become harsh, brittle, and scorch easily; steam must be used when pressing it.

Natural rubber is obtained by coagulating latex from the rubber tree. Since rubber trees are not extensively grown in the United States, the natural latex now used is imported from tropical countries. Rubber is an elastomer, or elastic fiber, with the capacity for being stretched many times its length. When the tension is released, it returns instantaneously to its original length. Rubber does not dye well and has very poor resistance to aging, sunlight, oil, and perspiration. It should be washed with much care because it is damaged by heat, chlorine, and dry-cleaning solvents. Most of the latex used in textile products today is chemically produced and is more accurately classified as a manufactured fiber.

Asbestos, the only natural mineral fiber, is found in certain rocks. Chrysotile, a fibrous form of serpentine rock, is the source of asbestos used in textile products. It has good strength, flexibility, toughness, low conductivity, and is of adequate length to be spinnable into yarns. Asbestos is highly resistant to damage by chemicals and is not flammable or damaged by heat. It is difficult to dye and usually is left in its natural color unless it is painted or printed. The principal uses for asbestos in the home are ironing-board covers, insulation materials, filters, and heat protectors.

Manufactured Fibers

The natural beauty of the silk fiber, and its high cost, inspired scientists as early as the eighteenth century to experiment with ways to produce a similar fiber more economically and easily in the laboratory. Fabrics made of rayon and cellulose acetate and called *artificial silk* were exhibited at the World's Fair in 1890, at about the same time that viscose rayon and acetate fibers were being developed. Rayon, acetate, and triacetate are all cellulosic fibers chemically treated to produce fibers with controllable properties. In the early years of this century research was devoted to improving these few new fibers. During the 1940s the trend in research was to produce many new kinds of fibers. Today, most of the emphasis is again on modifying existing fibers for extended uses, rather than developing more new fibers.

Manufactured fibers are all some form of a polymer, the result of combining simple molecules into a large complex

FIGURE 1-4 *A wool fiber, enlarged to show the scale appearance of the outside. Because different breeds of sheep grow wool in different lengths and widths, wool fibers vary in dimension.* (Nancy G. Harries and Thomas E. Harries, *Textiles: Decision Making for the Consumer*, McGraw-Hill Book Company, New York, 1974)

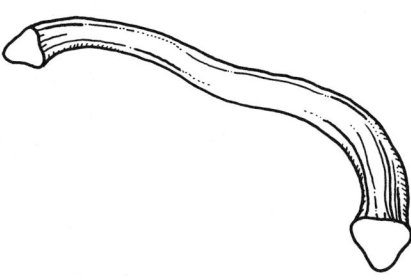

FIGURE 1-5 *A silk fiber, enlarged. To obtain silk fibers, the cocoon of the silkworm is soaked in warm water to loosen the gum that holds it together. The cocoon then is unwound; if the strand of silk is uncut, it may be up to 1,000 yards long.* (Nancy G. Harries and Thomas E. Harries, *Textiles: Decision Making for the Consumer*, McGraw-Hill Book Company, New York, 1974)

molecule by a process called polymerization. Because natural fibers are inherently arranged as polymers, polymerization is the scientist's attempt to simulate this natural occurrence as a means of achieving an equivalent product. Manufactured fibers are produced from fiber-forming substances, which may be (1) polymers synthesized from simple chemical compounds, (2) natural polymers that have been modified or transformed, or (3) glass. In all cases, the fiber-making process involves liquefying the fiber substance, forcing it through a spinneret (which resembles a shower head), and allowing the solution to solidify in filaments (Figure 1-6). The properties of manufactured fibers can be controlled by selection of the substances used, and the fiber diameter and length are determined by the spinneret (Figure 1-7).

GENERIC NAMES

The successful production of manufactured fibers and their growing consumer acceptance in textile products led to a competitive trend within the industry which threatened to result in a proliferation of fibers with identical or very similar characteristics. In order to minimize the confusion, the Federal Trade Commission established a system for grouping and naming manufactured fibers that are basically similar but are produced by different manufacturers. Each new fiber produced is chemically analyzed to determine whether it actually is different from or similar to already existing fibers. All fibers that are similar in chemical structure are assigned the same generic name. The use of a new generic name is authorized only when the fiber in question is completely different in its chemical structure from already existing generic classifications. To date, twenty-one approved generic names are used to classify manufactured fibers (others are waiting for approval): acetate, acrylic, anidex, aramid, azlon, glass, lastrile, metallic, modacrylic, novoloid, nylon, nytril, olefin, polyester, rayon, rubber, saran, spandex, triacetate, vinal, and vinyon. Of these, azlon, lastrile, nytril, and vinal are currently not being produced in the United States.[1] Each producer of a manufactured fiber may designate its own trademark under which the fiber is registered and retailed.

FIGURE 1-6 *A spinneret, which has small holes through which the manufactured substance is sent to produce filaments of the desired shape and thickness.* (Courtesy of American Textile Manufacturers Institute)

---

1. Man-Made Fiber Producers Association, Inc., *Man-Made Fiber Fact Book*, Man-Made Fiber Producers Association, Inc., Washington, D.C., 1974, p. 4.

1 / Fibers and Yarns

a

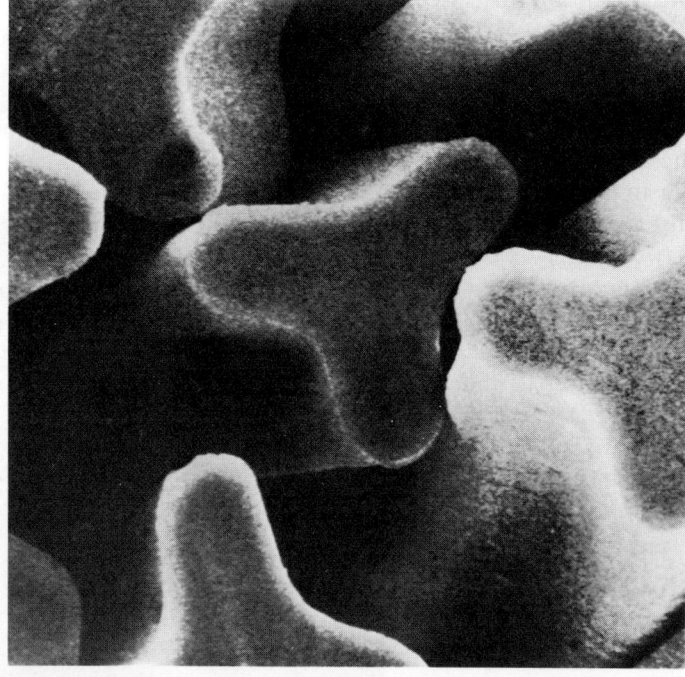

b

FIGURE 1-7 *A group of manufactured fibers typical of those used for rugs and carpets: (a) Antron® nylon filament in a shape that holds its new look longer than other shapes; (b) nylon filament and cut lengths of filament in a trilobal shape; (c) Dacron® polyester, cut lengths in another trilobal shape; (d) cut lengths of Antron® nylon filament. These photographs represent enlarged fibers. (Courtesy of E. I. du Pont de Nemours & Company)*

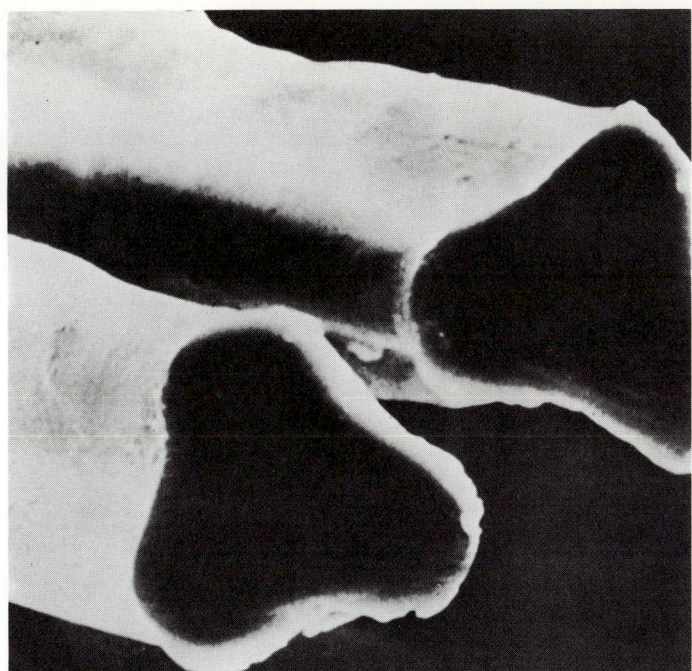
c

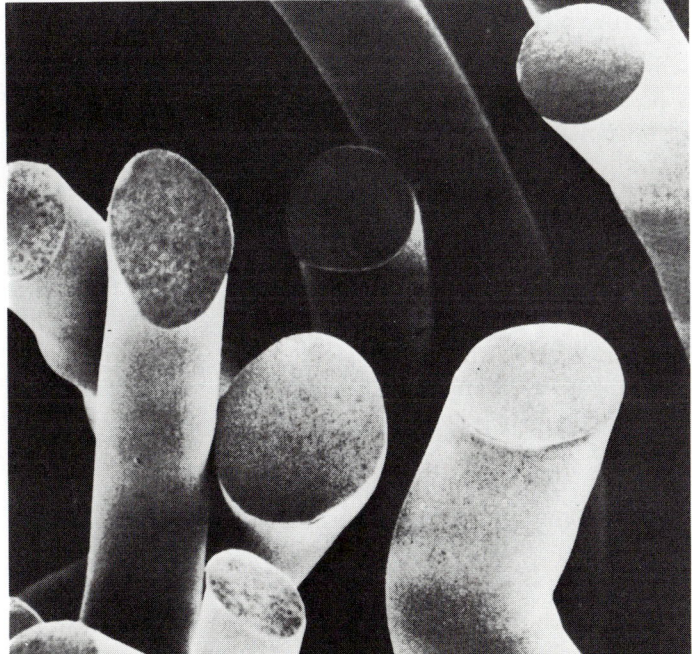
d

1 / *Fibers and Yarns*

In earlier years, advertisers for manufactured fiber products frequently used only the trademark, since the fiber manufacturing company assumed the advertising expense. This practice led to more confusion for the consumer, who, for example, might be vaguely familiar with the generic name of polyester and its first trademark, Dacron, as manufactured by E. I. du Pont de Nemours & Company, Inc., but might fail to associate Encron (produced by American Enka Corporation) or Kodel (of Eastman Kodak Company) as belonging to the same generic group. As a means of trying to bring order out of chaos, the Textile Fiber Products Identification Act was passed by Congress on September 3, 1958. This act required fiber-content labels to include both the generic name and the manufacturer's trademark for all fibers occurring in the textile product.[2]

The term "generic," in connection with fibers, usually refers to the various classifications of manufactured fibers and their manufacturers. Technically, each natural fiber is a generic name, although trade names are not generally used to denote their manufacturer. Table 1–1 lists the more commonly used natural fibers and manufactured fibers, with examples of trade names.

GENERAL CHARACTERISTICS OF MANUFACTURED FIBERS

Each manufactured fiber has its own specific characteristics, but there are several properties possessed by all, including thermoplasticity; abrasion resistance; relative nonabsorbency; resiliency; high strength; dimensional stability; resistance to damage by sunlight, mildew, and moths; resistance to nonoily stains but retention of body oils that penetrate the fiber; a tendency to accumulate static electricity in cold, dry weather; and good washing and drying qualities.

Thermoplasticity (becoming softened or glazed when subjected to heat) is a characteristic common to all manufactured fibers used in textile products, except rayon. This heat sensitivity enables fabrics to be *heat-set*, or take and hold a "set" shape or size during construction of end products. This property may be both an advantage and a disadvantage to the consumer. Embossed designs, pleats, and

---

2. Additional information on this and other textile laws is provided in Chapter 5.

TABLE 1-1 *Generic and Trade Names of Selected Textile Fibers*

Natural Fibers

Protein	Cellulose
wool	abaca
silk	cotton
Specialty hair	flax
alpaca	hemp
angora	jute
camel	kapok
cashmere	pineapple
mohair	Mineral
vicuña	asbestos
	Rubber
	latex

Manufactured fibers

Generic name	Trade names
Cellulose	
acetate	Estron, Celanese
rayon	Bemberg, Avril, Avisco
triacetate	Arnel
Noncellulose	
acrylic	Orlon, Creslan, Acrilan
anidex	
aramid	
azlon	
glass	Fiberglas, Beta
lastrile	
metallic	
aluminum	Lurex
gold	
silver	
modacrylic	Dynel, Veral
novoloid	
nylon	Antron, Cantrece, Enka, Qiana
nytril	Darvan
olefin	Vectra, Herculon
polyester	Dacron, Kodel, Fortrel
rubber	Lastex
saran	Saran, Rovana
spandex	Lycra, Vyrene, Spandelle
vinal	Kuralon
vinyon	Vinyon HH

shapes become permanent, size can be stabilized, and pile is made crush-resistant. Knits require little or no blocking and, during wear, clothing may resist wrinkling. However, care must be taken in laundering or ironing to prevent formation of unwanted heat-set wrinkles, which are then difficult to remove. It is also difficult to remove heat-set creases when garments need alterations.

In addition to being heat-sensitive, manufactured fibers as a group are hydrophobic, or water-repelling. They often are uncomfortably warm to wear in hot weather for this reason. This hydrophobic property also caused considerable difficulty in dyeing yarn and fabric until the recent development of new processes that work quite satisfactorily. Because they do not withstand high temperatures, these fabrics cannot be sterilized by boiling, and special precautions in all phases of laundering are necessary. They are medium to high in resiliency, which minimizes fabric wrinkling. They are poor conductors of electricity and build up static in cold, dry weather. As a result, people often feel a shock when they touch such fabrics. They are relatively low in density and produce lightweight clothing, but they can be texturized so that they have improved warmth-giving properties of bulk and loft without added weight.

Although a few general common characteristics of manufactured fibers can be mentioned, each one must be regarded individually in relation to end-product usage. The reason for this is that manufactured fibers can be tailored for specific purposes. The following are only a few of the properties that can be engineered into fibers: increased or decreased luster, improved touch or hand, increased moisture absorbency, modified dyeability, increased loft and bulk, reduced static electricity, improved whiteness retention, reduced or eliminated pilling, improved flame retardance, and fiber moldability.

SELECTED CHARACTERISTICS OF MANUFACTURED FIBERS

The chemical properties of each manufactured fiber make it different from all the others and qualify it to bear a separate generic name. No attempt will be made here to explain the chemical formulas for each fiber, as defined by the Federal Trade Commission, since this information is available in any of the textile science books listed in the Bibliography. However, the facts about each manufactured fiber generic group given in Table 1–2 may be of interest to consumers.

TABLE 1-2 *Characteristics of Manufactured Fibers*

Generic name	Characteristics	Major uses
Acetate	Is luxurious in feel and appearance, can be made in a wide range of colors and lusters, has excellent drapability and softness, dries relatively fast, is economical and resistant to shrinkage, moths, and mildew.	Blouses, dresses, foundation garments, lingerie, linings, shirts, slacks, sportswear, fabrics (brocade, crepe, double knits, faille, knitted jerseys, lace, satin, taffeta, tricot), draperies, upholstery, cigarette filters, fiberfill for pillows, comforters, mattress pads, jackets, and other quilted products
Acrylic	Is soft, warm, lightweight, shape-retentive, resilient, quick-drying, and resistant to sunlight, weather, oil, and chemicals.	Dresses, infant wear, knitted garments, skirts, slacks, snow and ski wear, socks, sportswear, sweaters, work clothes, face fabric in bonded fabrics, fleece and pile fabrics, blankets, carpets, draperies, scatter rugs, upholstery, hand-knitting yarns
Anidex	Imparts permanent stretch and recovery properties to fabrics, which are retained even after repeated laundering and dry cleaning, improves fit and comfort in apparel and home-furnishing fabrics, provides good shape control, has excellent resistance to gas fading, oxidation, sunlight, oils, and to chlorine bleach.	Athletic wear, blouses, career apparel, dresses, foundation garments, hosiery and half-hose, jackets, lingerie and underwear, linings, rainwear, shirts, slacks, sportswear, suits, sweaters, work clothes, slipcovers, upholstery, lace fabrics
Aramid	Has no melting point, high strength, and low flammability, is unaffected by moisture.	Hot-air filtration fabrics, protective clothing, tires and helmets, and bulletproof vests
Azlon	Is no longer produced in the U.S.A. The fiber-forming substance is composed of any regenerated naturally occurring proteins.	
Glass	Has high strength and resistance to heat, flame, and most chemicals, does not absorb moisture, has little stretch, and can be made into soft and flexible fabrics.	Curtains, reinforcements for molded plastics in boats and airplane parts, batting for insulation in buildings, railway cars, boats, and airplanes
Lastrile	Has never been commercially produced.	

Table 1-2 (cont.)

Generic name	Characteristics	Major uses
Metallic	Is a manufactured fiber composed of metal, plastic-coated metal, metal-coated plastic, or a core completely covered by metal. When adequately coated for protection, does not tarnish.	Decorative purposes in apparel and military uniforms, braids, draperies, laces, ribbons, table linens, and upholstery
Modacrylic	Is soft, resilient, easy to dye, abrasion-resistant, flame-resistant, quick-drying, resistant to acids and alkalies, retains shape well.	Deep-pile coats, simulated furs, wigs, fleece fabrics, knit pile-fabric backings, blankets, carpets, flame-resistant draperies, scatter rugs
Novoloid	Is flame-resistant, nonmelting, has minimum shrinkage when exposed to flame, is acid- and alkali-resistant, insoluble in any organic solvent, easily laundered.	Garments to protect against flames, air filters, protective clothing for race-car drivers and pit crews
Nylon	Is exceptionally strong, elastic, abrasion-resistant, lustrous, easy to wash, resistant to damage from oil and many chemicals, resilient, low in moisture absorbency, can be dyed in many colors.	Blouses, dresses, foundation garments, hosiery, lingerie, raincoats, bedspreads, carpets, draperies, upholstery, air hoses, conveyor and seat belts, parachutes, racket strings, ropes and nets, sleeping bags, tarpaulins, tents, thread, tire cord
Nytril	Is no longer produced in the U.S.A. Is soft, resilient, very heat-sensitive, shrink-resistant, and retains shape well.	In sweaters, pile fabrics, and in blends with wool for shrinkage resistance and shape retention
Olefin	Has good bulk and cover properties, is abrasion-resistant, quick-drying, resistant to deterioration from chemicals, mildew, perspiration, rot, or weather, heat-sensitive, soil-resistant, strong, has wicking properties (ability to carry body moisture from skin through the fabric to the outer surface), which make it comfortable, is the lightest of all fibers.	Knitted sports shirts, men's half-hose and knitted sportswear, sweaters, carpets, carpet backing, slipcovers, upholstery, dye nets, filter fabrics, laundry bags, sandbags, nonwoven felts, ropes and cordage, sewing thread
Polyester	Is strong, resistant to stretching and shrinking, easy to dye, resistant to most chemicals, quick-drying, crisp and resilient when either wet or dry, wrinkle- and abrasion-resistant, retains heat-set pleats and creases, is easily washed.	Blouses and shirts, career apparel, children's wear, dresses, half-hose, insulated garments, lingerie and underwear, permanent-press garments, slacks, suits, carpets, curtains, draperies, sheets and pillowcases, fiberfill, fire hose, power belting, ropes and nets, sewing thread, tire cord, sails

Generic name	Characteristics	Major uses
Rayon	Is highly absorbent, soft and comfortable, easily dyed, versatile, economical, makes fabrics that drape well. Main types of rayon are called viscose, high wet modulus, cuprammonium, and saponified.	Accessories, blouses, coats, dresses, jackets, lingerie, linings, millinery, rainwear, slacks, sports shirts, suits, ties, work clothes, bedspreads, blankets, carpets, curtains, sheets, slipcovers, tablecloths, industrial products, medical/surgical products, nonwoven products, tire cord
Rubber	Has many of the physical properties of thermoplastic manufactured fibers and almost instantaneous stretch recovery. Is especially damaged by direct heat, bleach, and strong detergents, and tends to lose its elasticity after a period of being used.	In the past, in garments designed for body constraint or support, such as elastic hose, girdles, and corsets. Almost completely replaced by other elastomeric fibers for these types of garments
Saran	Wears well, resists common chemicals, sunlight, staining, fading, mildew, and weather, fabrics can be easily washed with soap and water and are nonflammable, but are too heavy in weight for apparel.	Upholstery in public conveyances, deck chairs, and garden furniture
Spandex	Is lightweight, soft and smooth, resistant to body oils, stronger, more durable, and more powerful than rubber (can be stretched repeatedly and return to its original length, and can be stretched over 500 percent without breaking), resists abrasion, is not damaged by perspiration, lotions, or detergents.	Any articles where stretch is desired, athletic apparel, bathing suits, delicate laces, foundation garments, golf jackets, ski pants, slacks, support and surgical hose
Triacetate	Is shrink- and wrinkle-resistant, resists fading, is easily washed, retains heat-set pleats.	Apparel in which pleat retention is important, dresses, shirts, sportswear
Vinal	Is no longer produced in the U.S.A. Softens at low temperatures but is highly resistant to chemicals.	Certain industrial uses
Vinyon	Softens at low temperatures but has high resistance to chemicals.	Industrial applications as a bonding agent for nonwoven fabrics and products

Source: Adapted from *Man-Made Fiber Fact Book*, Man-Made Fiber Producers Association, Inc., Washington, D.C., 1974, pp. 16–24. The description of rubber has been added by the author.

Fiber Identification Techniques

The adoption of the Textile Fiber Products Identification Act in 1958 and the new Federal Trade Commission regulation of July 3, 1972, requiring care labeling on all textile products,[3] made it less important for the consumer to know how to identify fibers found in textile products. However, the consumer may wish to confirm or check the information on the label of some items, for which the burning test and some simple solubility tests may be used. The student of textiles or the consumer with access to a microscope may find microscopic testing of interest and benefit as well.

BURNING TEST

The chemical composition of a fiber generally can be identified as cellulose, protein, mineral, or manufactured by burning a few yarns from each side of a piece of fabric. Observations should be made as the yarns approach the flame, when they are in the flame, and after they have been removed, and on the ash formed and the odor emitted. Cellulose fibers of cotton, flax, and rayon do not fuse or shrink from the flame, but they do burn when in the flame, have an afterglow when removed, leave a gray ash with a feathery smooth edge, and have an odor of burning paper. Protein fibers of silk and wool fuse and curl away from the flame, burn slowly, are sometimes self-extinguishing, leave a crushable black ash, and smell like burning hair. Acetate and acrylic fuse away from the flame, burn with melting, continue to burn and melt when removed from the flame, and leave a brittle, hard black bead. Modacrylic fuses away from the flame, burns very slowly with melting, is self-extinguishing, and leaves a brittle, hard black bead. Nylon fuses and shrinks away from the flame, burns slowly with melting, continues burning after being removed from the flame but usually is self-extinguishing, leaves a hard gray bead, and smells like celery. Olefin fuses and shrinks away from the flame, burns with melting, continues burning, but is self-extinguishing, and leaves a hard tan bead. Polyester fuses and shrinks away from the flame, burns slowly with melting and a black smoke, is usually self-extinguishing, leaves a hard black bead, and has a sweetish odor. Saran fuses and shrinks away from the flame,

---

3. Federal Trade Commission, *Care Labels Can Save You Money and Trouble*, Buyer's Guide no. 10, U.S. Government Printing Office, Washington, D.C.

burns very slowly with melting, is self-extinguishing, and leaves a hard black bead. Spandex fuses but does not shrink from the flame, burns with melting, continues to burn with melting after removal from the flame, and leaves a soft black ash. A summary of the burning reactions of several fibers is given in Table 1-3.

SOLUBILITY TEST

Through use of solubility tests the textile scientist may identify manufactured fibers by generic class and double-check natural fibers. Most of the chemicals used for fiber identification are very dangerous and should be limited to use in a chemical laboratory properly equipped with exhaust hoods, gloves, aprons, and goggles. However, since some of these chemicals are found in commonly used household products, they are mentioned here to warn consumers of the potential danger to both users and textile products, and the need for care in their use.

A 5 percent solution of sodium hydroxide will disintegrate or damage wool and silk fibers. Sodium hydroxide, commonly sold as lye, is found in both drain and oven cleaners. Chlorine, often found in household bleach, weakens both wool

TABLE 1-3 *Identification of Fibers by Burning*

Fiber	Approach to flame	In the flame	Removed from flame	Ash	Odor
Cellulose					
Cotton	Do not fuse or	Burn	Afterglow	Gray and	Burning
Flax	shrink from flame	rapidly		feathery	paper
Rayon					
Protein					
Silk	Fuse and curl	Burn slowly	May be self-extinguishing	Crushable	Burning
Wool	away			black ash	hair
Acetate and Acrylic	Fuse away	Burn with melting	Continue to burn and melt	Hard black bead	
Modacrylic	Fuses away	Burns very slowly with melting	Self-extinguishing	Brittle black hard bead	
Nylon	Fuses and shrinks away	Burns slowly with melting	Continues to burn but may be self-extinguishing	Hard gray bead	Celery

Source: Reprinted with permission of Macmillan Publishing Co., Inc. from *Textiles*, 4th ed., by Norma Hollen and Jane Saddler, p. 15. Copyright © 1973 by Macmillan Publishing Co., Inc.

and silk fibers. Phenol, found in some types of disinfectants, may be damaging in varying degrees to rayon, wool, acetate, modacrylic, nylon, and polyester. Some fingernail-polish removers contain acetone, which, in the appropriate strength and at the right temperature, will dissolve both acetate and modacrylic. Some deodorants and antiperspirants contain aluminum chloride, which may cause damage to and discoloration of acetates.

MICROSCOPE TEST

When viewed under a microscope, each of the natural fibers appears different in its physical structure and these distinguishable differences contribute to the uniqueness of each as a textile fiber. Cotton has convolutions or twists which form a natural crimp, and hence cohesiveness, making it one of the most spinnable fibers. However, since dirt collects in the convolutions, cotton products require vigorous washing action to remove it. Flax is characterized by nodes or joints resembling those of a stalk of cane and produces yarns and fabrics that have a thick-and-thin appearance. Wool fibers have scales, which are responsible for wool's unique felting property. When the fibers are subjected to agitation, friction, and pressure in the presence of heat and moisture, they move about without returning to their original location. While this property allows fabrics to be made directly from wool fibers by felting, it also makes the washing of wool fabrics more difficult because of shrinkage and matting. The fine rodlike appearance of the silk fiber is responsible for its luster and smoothness. It is the only natural *filament* (long threadlike fiber) and may vary in length from 300 to 1,800 yards. The straight, fine fibers give silk fabrics their resilience, suppleness, and drape.

It is more difficult to identify man-made fibers positively under the microscope because some of them look alike or their appearance may be changed by variations in the manufacturing process. As a group, they resemble silk somewhat, especially when viewed lengthwise, having a similar rodlike structure, luster, and smoothness.

Fiber Blends

No textile fiber is perfect: all fibers have some desirable and some undesirable qualities. Blending is a process by which staple fibers of different characteristics are combined and spun into a yarn, so that the good qualities are emphasized and the poor qualities are minimized for each fiber in the blend. There are several reasons why fiber blending improves consumer acceptance of fabrics and textile products.

Not all fibers can be dyed with the same types of dyes, but fibers that have different dye affinities are often blended together. When the fabric piece is dyed, sometimes more than once, attractive cross-dyed or other color effects are achieved, such as the heather look.

Natural fibers are self-blended in order to improve the uniformity of the fiber. This improves spinning, weaving, and finishing efficiency and results in a more uniform final product.

Fiber blending can improve fabric texture, hand, and appearance. For example, a small amount of rayon may be blended with cotton to increase its luster and softness. Less-plentiful, expensive fibers are often blended with more plentiful ones to extend the expensive fibers and reduce cost. Cashmere-and-wool blends cost less than all-cashmere fabrics.

Fabric performance may also be improved through blending. When nylon or polyester is blended with cotton or wool, the fabric's durability, strength, and abrasion resistance may be improved. In durable-press garments, for example, polyester/cotton blends are more durable than all-cotton fabrics.

An important clue to the performance of fabrics made from fiber blends is the percentage by weight of each fiber present in the blend. According to the Textile Fiber Products

TABLE 1-4 *Fiber Properties*

Property	Cotton	Rayon	Wool	Acetate	Nylon	Polyester	Acrylic	Modacrylic	Olefin
Bulk and loft	−	−	+++	−	−	+++	+++		
Wrinkle recovery	−	−	+++	++	++	+++	++	++	++
Press (wet) retention	−	−	−	+	++	+++			
Absorbency	+++	+++	+++	+	−	−	−	−	−
Static resistance	+++	+++	++	+	+	−	+	+	++
Resistance to pilling	+++	+++	+	+++	+				++
Strength	++	+	+	+	+++	+++	+	+	+++
Abrasion resistance	+	−	++	−	+++	+++	+	+	+++
Stability	++	−	−	+++	+++	+++	+++	+++	+++
Resistance to heat	+++	+++	++	++	+	+	++	−	−

Key: +++ excellent; ++ good; + fair; − deficient

Source: Hollen and Saddler, *Textiles*, p. 105. Copyright © 1973 by Macmillan Publishing Co., Inc.

Identification Act,[4] this information must by law be included on the labels attached to all textile products at the time of purchase.

Table 1–4 rates various properties for several fibers. Imagine what properties would result from the equal blending of various combinations of fibers. For example, cotton blended with polyester is less absorbent but recovers from wrinkling more easily, while polyester becomes less heat-sensitive in such a blend.

Glossary of Fiber Terms

ABRASION RESISTANCE The degree to which a fiber is able to withstand surface wear and rubbing.

ABSORBENCY The degree to which a dry fiber absorbs moisture and holds it in its pores.

COHESIVENESS A fiber's ability to cling together while being spun. More important for staple fibers than for filaments.

CONVOLUTION The twist and folds found in some fibers, especially cotton.

COVER A fiber's ability to take up space for protection and concealment.

CRIMP A fiber's waviness. Usually can be seen only with a microscope.

DIMENSIONAL STABILITY The degree to which a fiber (yarn, fabric) holds shape and size after it has been worn and cleaned.

DYEABILITY The degree to which fibers can be colored by dyes.

ELASTICITY The degree to which a stretched fiber returns immediately to its original size and shape.

ELECTRICAL CONDUCTIVITY The ability to transfer electrical charges.

FIBER The smallest visible unit from which textiles are made.

FILAMENT A single fiber extruded to an indefinite length.

FLAMMABILITY The capacity to catch fire and burn.

FLEXIBILITY Pliability, ability to bend.

HAND The way a fiber feels—hard, soft, wet, dry, firm, limp, silky.

HEAT CONDUCTIVITY The ability to conduct heat from the body to the surrounding air.

HEAT SENSITIVITY A fiber's potential for softening, melting, or shrinking when subjected to heat.

HYDROPHILIC Refers to a fiber (yarn, fabric) that absorbs water and is sensitive to moisture.

---

4. See Chapter 5 for more information on this act.

HYDROPHOBIC   Refers to a fiber (yarn, fabric) that does *not* absorb water and is *insensitive* to moisture.

HYGROSCOPICITY   Ability to absorb moisture from the air.

LOFT   A fiber's ability to spring back to its original thickness after it has been squeezed.

LUSTER   The shine or glow reflected from the surface of a fiber or fabric.

MONOMER   The simple chemical constituents of polymers.

PILLING   Small collections of fiber ends on fabric surfaces, forming balls.

POLYMER   Many monomers, joined together into a larger unit.

POLYMERIZATION   Procedure for converting monomers into polymers, used in producing manufactured fibers.

RESILIENCY   Ability to spring back to original shape and size after being compressed.

STAPLE   Short fiber measured in inches or fractions of inches.

STIFFNESS   A fiber's resistance to compression.

STRENGTH   A fiber's ability to resist stress, strain, and wear.

SUNLIGHT RESISTANCE   Ability to resist breakdown in fiber or color from direct sunlight.

SYNTHETIC   A fiber made from chemicals: *man-made* or *manufactured* are the terms generally used.

THERMOPLASTICITY   A substance's ability to become soft or moldable when heated.

TRADEMARK   A symbol used to identify merchandise (fibers or fabric) with a specific manufacturer.

TRADE NAME   The name a manufacturer gives to a product to distinguish it from other products.

Yarns

Yarns are the substances from which most fabrics are made. They are continuous lengths of fibers or filaments, which have been twisted or grouped together to make a strand that can be used in weaving, knitting, or other processing into fabric.

Generally speaking, fibers are either comparatively short, like cotton, or very long, like silk or the manufactured filaments. Filaments can be used as they are, because of their extreme length, but the shorter fibers, called *staple* fibers, must be put through a spinning operation to obtain sufficient length. (Filaments may be cut into staple lengths and spun, if certain effects or characteristics are desired.)

Many processes are carried out in preparing fibers for the different spinning systems currently used. For details on all the processes, the reader who has a special interest is referred to any of the textile science books listed in the Bibliography. Here, only two processes, carding and combing, will be discussed.

CARDING

Natural fibers are shipped to textile plants just as they were gathered up by the producer. The wool from one sheep, called a fleece, is bundled up with other fleeces and shipped. Cotton is simply baled together and shipped. The fibers may be dirty, with pieces of leaves and stems or other foreign matter mixed in, and they are jumbled together in masses, unsuitable for processing.

After cleaning, the fibers must be carded to remove foreign matter that may still stick to them and to separate them.

FIGURE 1-8 *Tissue-weight wool flannel made into a two-button blazer and bias-cut skirt. The soft, light fabric lends itself to crisp tailoring and to the easy flare of the skirt. If this same style were made up in a worsted fabric like serge, the jacket would be much stiffer, and the skirt would have a very heavy look.* (Courtesy of The Wool Bureau, Inc.)

Carding also separates the short fibers from the long ones, and it partially straightens the fibers so they lie more evenly, somewhat parallel to one another.

COMBING

The combing process continues the cleaning and sorting started in carding. The fibers are straightened out, so they lie parallel (i.e., all in one direction).

As a rule, only the better-quality, longer fibers are combed, for use in very smooth, even yarns. Depending upon the fabric for which the yarn is intended, long-stapled fibers may be combed more than once, to increase their smoothness and evenness.

The short-stapled fibers that are dropped out in carding and combing are not wasted, but are made into yarns which need not be as smooth as those made from long-staple fibers.

The terms "carded" and "combed" on textile products usually refer to yarns made from cotton. Combed yarns, made of longer, stronger fibers, produce fabrics of better quality, fine but strong, with a smoother surface.

Wool fibers are always carded, but not all wool fibers are combed. If they are to be used for woolen yarns, they are only carded; for worsted yarns, they are both carded and combed. Woolen yarns are shorter and fuzzier than worsted yarns, which have been straightened out in the combing process, and woolen fabrics are relatively soft, with the somewhat fuzzy surface found on flannel and tweed (Figure 1-8). Worsted fabrics, like gabardine, serge, or crepe, are usually smooth and have a crisp feel.

SPINNING

During spinning operations, staple fibers are twisted together to form a yarn that will hold together and be strong enough to be subjected to later handling in making the fabric. The yarn may be twisted to the left (the S-twist) or to the right (Z-twist), as shown in Figure 1-9, or the direction of twist may be alternated, according to the type of yarn desired.

The amount of twist varies for different types of yarn, and it depends on the degrees of hardness, strength, and tightness wanted in the yarn. Up to a certain point, the more the yarn is twisted, the stronger it becomes; twisted beyond that point, the yarn can break.

The amount of twist is usually measured by the number of turns in a given length, frequently an inch. Figure 1-10

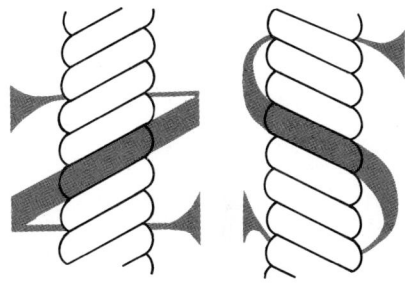

FIGURE 1-9 *The right-hand (Z-) twist and left-hand (S-) twist used in spinning yarns.*

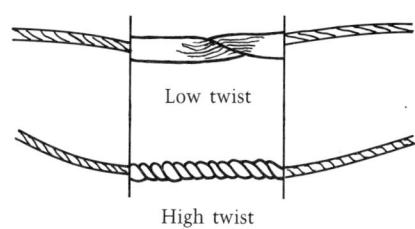

FIGURE 1-10 *Low and high twist in yarns.*

1 / Fibers and Yarns

shows examples of low and high twist, and there are many variations between. For example, a woolen yarn to be handknitted into a soft sweater would have less twist than a worsted yarn designed to weave a tight, firm fabric like gabardine or twill for a uniform. Crepe fabric, which has surface irregularities, is made from a yarn twisted so tightly that it kinks; the rough surface of the fabric results from this very tight twist rather than from a later manufacturing process.

Once a yarn has been twisted, it is described on the basis of the number of strands that have been combined in the spinning process. A *single* yarn is one length of fiber that has been twisted by itself. A *ply* yarn consists of two or more single yarns that have been twisted together. Yarns made of manufactured fibers are described as monofilament (made of one filament) or multifilament (made of several filaments twisted together). Ply yarns generally are firmer and stronger than single yarns.

SIZING

Sizing different types of yarn is confusing, because the same system of measuring is not used for all fibers. In spun yarns, the number, size, or count is based on the weight and length of the yarn.

Cotton yarn is numbered according to the number of hanks (840 yards) needed to weigh one pound. Thus, yarn No. 1, requiring only one hank to weigh one pound, is coarser than No. 10, which requires 8,400 yards to weigh one pound. In other words, as the diameter of the yarn increases, the number decreases.

Spun silk sizing is also based on the 840-yard hank, but flax and wool use a 300-yard hank. The sizing of worsted yarns is based on a 560-yard hank.

Manufactured filament yarn size is determined by size of the holes in the spinneret as well as the rate at which the

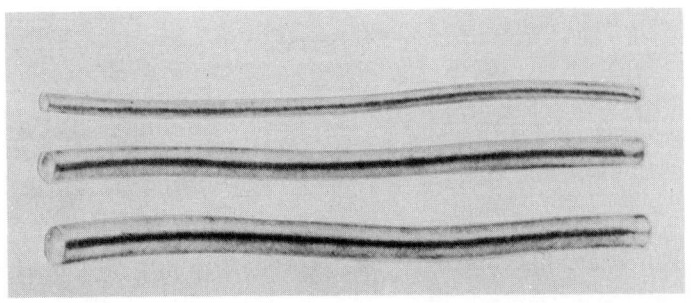

FIGURE 1-11 *Three different deniers of manufactured filament yarn.* (Courtesy of E. I. du Pont de Nemours & Company)

solution is forced through the spinneret. Denier ("den-yer") is the term used for filament yarn size, which is measured in terms of weight per unit of length (Figure 1–11). In this system, the unit of length stays the same; the finer the yarn, the smaller the number used. For example, stockings of 15-denier nylon are made of finer yarn than a pair made of 30-denier nylon.

Types of Yarns

Yarns are generally considered to belong in one of three categories: simple, novelty (or complex), and textured. Many variations are possible within these categories, and only basic information will be given here.

SIMPLE YARNS

A simple yarn is the least complicated type. Although it may be made either of all one fiber or of mixed fibers, it has the same amount of twist along its entire length and appears fairly smooth and even. A fabric made of one simple yarn of one size and fiber content in an even weave would be comparatively smooth; its surface would have little variation.

However, differently twisted simple yarns, or simple yarns of different fiber contents, may be combined to weave fabrics which have varying surface effects. Many combinations are possible, with resulting variation in fabrics.

NOVELTY YARNS

Novelty yarns are usually plied, although some of the special effects can be achieved in single yarns. A typical novelty yarn is made up of two or more singles. One single acts as the "base" or "core" on which the others are twisted, a second single carries the special effect, and the third holds the other two together. A typical novelty yarn is shown in Figure 1–12.

Whereas simple yarns are intended to be smooth and even, novelty yarns are planned to be irregular or uneven in some way, to produce an unusual appearance or texture. While novelty yarns result in very attractive, interesting fabrics, these fabrics tend to wear less well than those with a smooth surface. The loops in bouclé, for instance, can snag and tear, and the higher places made by slubs or knots tend to show wear sooner than the even background fabric. Knotted or

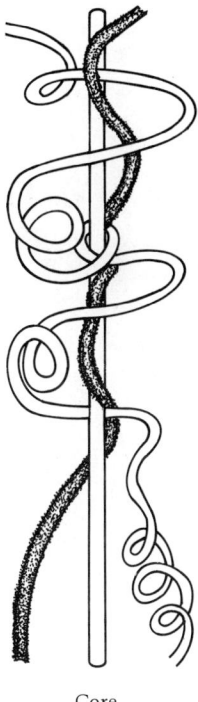

Core

FIGURE 1-12 *A typical three-ply complex yarn.*

slubbed fabric can be difficult to stitch evenly and firmly, since these constructions resist the sewing machine.

Many variations of novelty yarns are possible, but those most commonly found are slubbed, looped, knotted or nubbed, and spiraled.

SLUBBED YARNS A slub yarn is made by changing the degree of twist used, so that a single yarn shows a softer lumpy place. In a ply yarn, the slub may be formed in one single, and the other single is used to hold the slub down. The yarns used in shantung are slubbed, and the uneven surface of the fabric is made by the yarn slubs. Two types of slub are shown in Figure 1-13. Figure 1-14 shows a garment made with slubbed yarn.

LOOPED YARNS This type of yarn is made with a full loop at regular intervals. Bouclé is a common type of looped yarn,

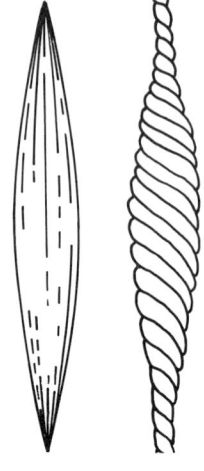

FIGURE 1-13 *Two types of slubbed yarns.*

FIGURE 1-14 *The slubbed 70 percent cotton/30 percent polyester yarn used in fabric for this knitted beach cover-up gives the garment surface a nubby look.* (Courtesy of Cotton Incorporated)

used for women's apparel. The very uneven surface of the fabric results from the closeness of the loops when the yarn is woven into fabric.

KNOTTED OR NUBBED YARNS   Such yarn is made by adjusting the spinning machine so that it will wind the yarn over and over itself in one place, making a knot or nub. Sometimes yarns of two colors are used, and the knot or nub is made in only one color. Fabrics woven from such two-color yarns will appear to have colored spots on a solid ground.

SPIRAL YARNS   A spiral yarn can be made by twisting two yarns of different thicknesses together. Usually the finer yarn has a higher twist than the coarser, and the coarser yarn winds around the finer one. Variations are possible, depending upon the effect wanted in the fabric to be made.

TEXTURED YARNS

The majority of the textured yarns are produced from thermoplastic fibers (fibers that can be set in shape by heat applied in the manufacturing process). Since manufactured fibers are particularly adaptable to heat treatments, many textured yarns are made of them.

The reader will recall that yarns are combed to straighten them, so they will lie smoothly in one direction. In textured yarns, the fibers are deliberately disarranged, so that they lie unevenly. Textured yarns may be looped on one or both sides, curled, bent or crimped (Figure 1–15), or fluffed out (to give bulk). Heat may be applied at any selected point in manufacture, depending on the texture desired in the yarn. A yarn can even be knit into fabric, treated with heat, and

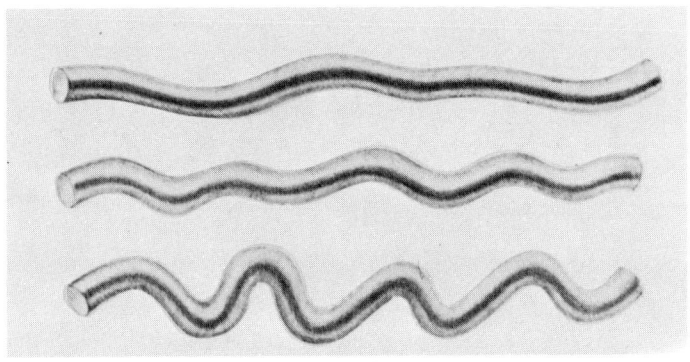

FIGURE 1-15 *Three different types of crimp used in manufactured yarns.* (Courtesy of E. I. du Pont de Nemours & Company)

then unraveled; the resulting yarn will have the shape it took in the fabric, and this shape will affect the texture of the fabric ultimately made from it.

THREAD

Thread is a special type of yarn developed for hand or machine sewing. Because it may be used either on a sewing machine with its even tension or in hand sewing with uneven tension, thread must be very smooth and even. It must be strong enough to hold the seam, yet flexible enough to give when the garment is worn or cleaned.

Thread is produced in a wide range of fibers and must always be selected specifically for the fabric to be handled. Further comments on various kinds of thread will be found in Chapter 9.

Glossary of Yarn Terms

BASE OR CORE YARN   The single yarn on which the other components of a complex yarn are wound.

BOUCLÉ   A novelty yarn of looped construction, which gives a ringed or looped appearance to the face of fabric made from it.

BULK YARN   A type of textured yarn, fluffed out to appear bulky.

CARDING   A cleaning and straightening process applied to fibers on receipt at a textile plant.

COMBING   A manufacturing process which separates short-stapled from long-stapled fibers and straightens fibers to lie in one direction.

DENIER   The term used for filament yarn size, which is measured in terms of weight per fixed unit of length.

FLEECE   The mass of wool as it is sheared from the sheep.

KNOTTED OR NUBBED YARN   A yarn made by causing it to wind over itself at certain intervals, forming a knot or nub.

LOOPED YARN   A yarn made with a full loop, such as bouclé.

MONOFILAMENT YARN   A yarn made of one filament.

MULTIFILAMENT YARN   A yarn made of two or more filaments.

NOVELTY OR COMPLEX YARN   A yarn that is plied to produce a special effect.

PLY YARN   A yarn made of two or more strands twisted together.

SIMPLE YARN   A yarn which has the same amount of twist throughout its length; not plied.

SINGLE YARN   A yarn that has not been plied.

SLUBBED YARN   A yarn that is irregular in diameter and contains uneven sections made by varying the tension during twisting.

SPINNING   The final operation in yarn manufacture, to make a continuous length which can be processed into fabric.

S-TWIST   The left-hand twist used in spinning.

TEXTURED YARN   Yarn, usually produced from thermoplastic fibers, which has been heat-treated to take a shape other than smooth and even in final contour.

THERMOPLASTIC YARN   Yarn made of manufactured fiber, which is affected by use of heat in manufacturing processes.

THREAD   A special type of yarn for use in machine or hand sewing.

TWIST   The turn applied to a fiber in spinning, to make it into yarn.

WOOL YARN   Yarn made from wool fibers.

WOOLEN YARN   Yarn made from short wool fibers that have been carded.

WORSTED YARN   Yarn made from long wool fibers that have been carded and combed.

YARN   Fibers or filaments, natural or manufactured, twisted together to form a continuous length.

Z-TWIST   The right-hand twist used in spinning.

Study Questions

1. Name five natural fibers commonly used in textile products.
2. Give the generic name for at least fifteen manufactured fibers.
3. Explain the difference between a fiber's trade name and its generic name.
4. For each of the following chemicals, (a) state a common household product in which it is found, and (b) name one fiber that may be damaged by it in some way: acetone, phenol, sodium hydroxide, aluminum chloride, chlorine.
5. Why are the combing and carding processes used?
6. Explain the purpose of twist in yarn.
7. Explain the difference between a ply and a simple yarn.
8. Explain the construction of a novelty or complex yarn.
9. Name three types of complex yarns.
10. Explain the difference between woolen and worsted yarns.
11. How is size determined in manufactured filament yarns? What term is used in connection with it?
12. Why are textured yarns usually made of manufactured fibers?

Suggested Activities

1. Prepare slides of various fibers and observe their physical characteristics under a microscope. Make a sketch of each fiber observed and write a description of it.
2. Visit a fabric, clothing, or furnishings store and list the generic and trade names found on the labels of the textile products.
3. Conduct an experiment on the reaction of several different fibers to chemicals such as acetone, phenol, sodium hydroxide, aluminum chloride, and chlorine.
4. Stretch a rubber band between thumb and forefinger and twist a piece of paper between the rubber band. What happens when the band is relaxed? Try the same activity with a piece of heavy string.
5. Find swatches of fabric made from interesting or unusual yarns. Ravel some of the yarns and look at them under a pick glass or magnifying glass. What kind of yarns are they?
6. Observe a polyester or nylon filament and a wool or cotton spun yarn under a magnifying glass. What differences do you see?
7. Write a newspaper story on: (a) the properties of two or three textile fibers and their importance to consumers; or (b) an explanation of the difference between trade and generic names. Submit the story to the college public information service or to a local newspaper.
8. From pieces of fabric, make a card display of yarns, one yarn to a card. Enter on the card the fiber content, the ply count of the yarn, and the name of the fabric woven from the yarn.

Chapter 2

Fabrics

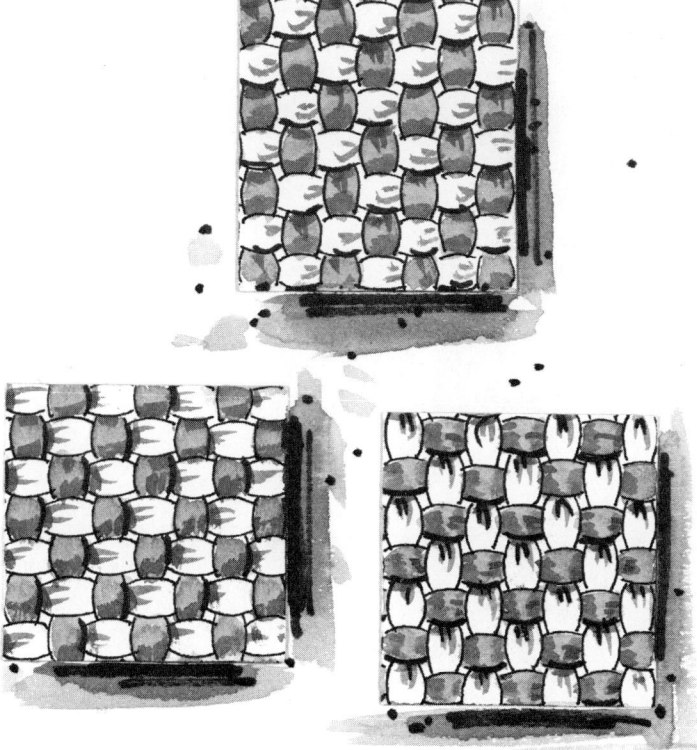

MOST FABRICS on the market today are made either directly from fibers or yarns or by special processes which utilize neither. The latter group will be mentioned only briefly, since it is of less importance than the other two. This chapter will deal with the basic methods of fabric construction and the different design effects that can be created in fabrics.

Fabrics Made Directly from Fibers

Felts and nonwoven fabrics are the most widely known fabric types made directly from fibers. The oldest method of constructing fabric is *felting*, which depends on the property of wool fibers to permanently lock themselves to one another (Figure 2–1). True felt contains all wool, or at least a large percentage of wool, fibers. In earlier years all felts were made only of animal fibers, but with increased demand nonfelting fibers have been blended with wool to produce a lower-cost product. Acceptable fabrics can be made by blending wool with as much as 50 percent of a nonfelting fiber; rayon fibers

FIGURE 2-1 *A sample of felt fabric, in which the wool fibers are locked together.* (The University of Mississippi)

FIGURE 2-2 *A nonwoven fabric of a type commonly used for interfacings in apparel.* (The University of Mississippi)

FIGURE 2-3 *A length of braid.* (The University of Mississippi)

are frequently used. The many desirable properties of felts make them widely used for both industrial purposes and consumer goods. Felt fabrics have excellent resiliency and are good shock absorbers. They absorb sound well and provide good insulating properties with warmth. They are easy to shape and do not ravel, so edges require no finish. Although fibers may pull apart, the fabric will not tear. Felts can be finished to be mothproof, water-repellent, fireproof, and resistant to fungi. Felt fabrics are not strong and garments must be loose to be durable. Holes cannot be repaired invisibly. Felt will not return to its original shape after it is stretched or deformed because it has little or no elastic recovery.

One of the newest construction techniques is used to make *nonwoven* fabric (Figure 2-2). This term usually refers to materials made primarily of textile fibers held together by an applied bonding or adhesive agent or by the fusing of thermoplastic fibers. Most of the fibers used in nonwovens today are of a good quality and such products utilize almost any type or combination of fibers. Since no yarn spinning is involved in the process, fibers of different lengths and chemical composition can be combined successfully in a single product. Nonwoven fabrics are used to make many products including items of clothing and home furnishings. Many of these are designed to be discarded after a single use, but often they may be laundered or dry cleaned with care. Nonwoven fabrics, when used as interfacings or underlinings for garments of woven or knitted fabrics, present a problem. Such fabrics tend to be firm, rather stiff, and without the strength desired in interfacings. Furthermore, they lack good draping qualities and hand and may cause the interfaced pieces to be stiffer than the rest of the garment.

Fabrics Made from Yarns

This group includes fabrics made by the processes of braiding, lacing, netting, knitting, weaving, tufting, and knit-sewing.

In *braided* fabrics, three or more yarns are interlaced lengthwise and diagonally (Figure 2-3). Plain braided fabrics are used for shoelaces, tapes, electrical cord coverings, wicks, and trimmings, while fancy braiding is limited primarily to trimmings. The braiding process is complicated by increased width and therefore these fabrics are narrow. They may be either flat, rectangular, or circular. They stretch considerably

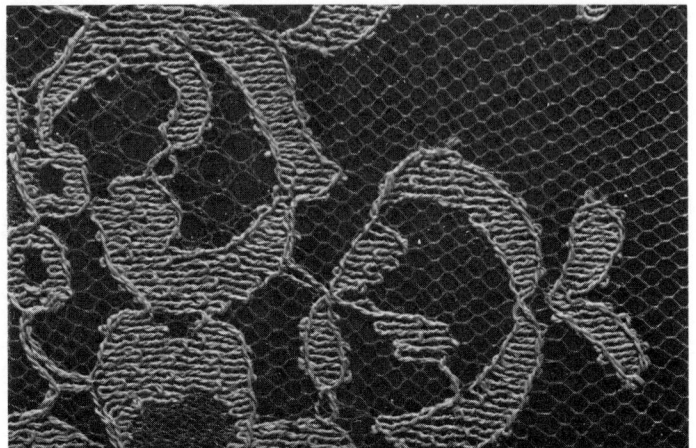

FIGURE 2-4 *Lace*. (The University of Mississippi)

in length and to some degree in width, a characteristic that makes the application of braided trims difficult at times. Besides yarns, strips of any flexible material can be formed into fabrics with varied appearance.

Lace making began as an Italian fine art during the fourteenth century. It was first made by machine in the nineteenth century, and today most lace is machine-made. Lace is recognized as a fabric of decorative design on an open-mesh background (Figure 2-4). It is usually made from threads rather than yarns, but, if yarns are used, they are stronger and twisted more firmly than those used in other fabrics. Lace made from manufactured fibers such as nylon is stronger and wears better than laces made of natural fibers. The main purpose of lace is to add a decorative appearance to textile products. It is available in widths suitable for garments or narrow enough to be used as trimmings. Compared with fabrics made by other methods, lace is fragile and must be handled with care.

Laces and *nets* are similar in that both are open-mesh fabrics, but net may be constructed from either threads or yarns and is without any design, while lace is usually made from threads and has a decorative design. Nets have large geometrically shaped open spaces between the yarn interlacings, which in earlier days were knotted at the points of intersection. Knotting produces nets with a relatively large mesh that will not slip or spread. Before 1800 all net fabrics were made by hand; in 1809 a machine was developed that duplicated the net construction so precisely that only an expert could distinguish the handmade from the machine-made fabric. Today, both laces and nets are readily available at moderate prices and care is simplified because of the use

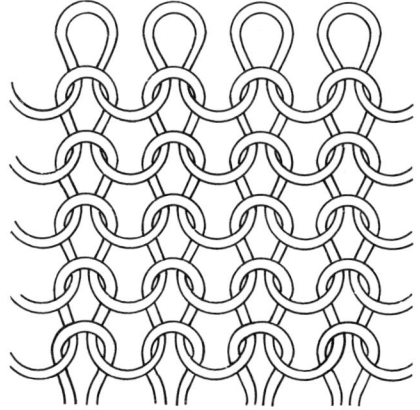

FIGURE 2-5 *Diagram of filling knitting.*

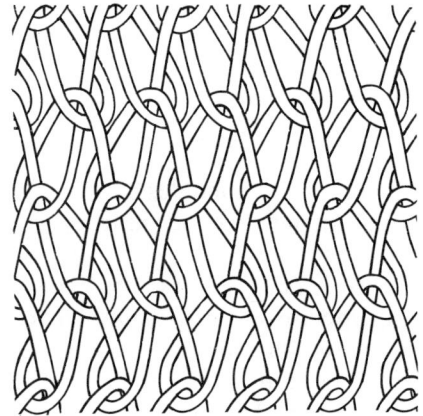

FIGURE 2-6 *Diagram of warp knitting.*

Part One / Textile Elements

of manufactured fibers. Price and quality are determined by factors such as the fiber used, the complexity of the design, whether the fabric is made by hand or machine, and whether it is imported or domestic.

Knitted fabrics are made by interlocking a series of loops of one or more yarns, either by machine or by hand. There are nine basic knitting stitches used in the various types of garment constructed by this process. Jersey flat is used in making full-fashioned sweaters and pullovers, and jersey circular is found in underwear and seamless hosiery. Collars, cuffs, and trims are made by rib flat stitch, and the rib circular is a popular stitch used in double-knit fabrics. Purl flat is commonly used in making cardigans, and purl circular knit makes possible cut-and-sewn sweaters, dresswear, and men's socks. Tricot knit is found primarily in underclothing such as slips, and raschel knitting produces open lacy fabrics, both rigid and stretch; Milanese knit uses several sets of yarns to produce a diagonal effect that is highly run-resistant. There are three main methods of making knitted fabrics: with the loops running across the fabric, called *weft* or *filling* knitting (Figure 2–5); with the loops running the length of the fabric, known as *warp* knitting (Figure 2–6); and with the use of two sets of needles, creating the fabric known as *double knit*[1] (Figure 2–7).

The quality and serviceability of knitted fabrics are determined by factors such as the type of knitting stitch used, the fiber, the yarn fineness and quality, closeness of the knitting, and the dimensional stability (shrink or stretch resistance) of the finished product (Figure 2–8). In general, knit

FIGURE 2-7 *Diagram of a double knit.*

FIGURE 2-8 *A knit fabric, showing the lengthwise interlocking loop formation and a crosswise stripe.* (The University of Mississippi)

---

1. American Home Economics Association, *Textile Handbook*, 5th ed., AHEA, Washington, D.C., 1974, pp. 45–46.

FIGURE 2-9 *Two steps in preparing to produce knitted fabric. Top: A pattern of the fabric is being developed on a computer. When the pattern is completed, the computer will control the knitting machine in the background, issuing directions for the machine to follow. Bottom: Packages of yarn are placed for feeding into the knitting machine at center, which produces fabrics used for women's dresses and blouses.* (Courtesy of American Textile Manufacturers Institute)

fabrics are comfortable because of their stretch and wrinkle-resistant features, both of which are results of the knitting process (Figure 2–9). Double-knit fabrics tend to have more body and durability than single knits. Also, double knits are less likely to sag and retain their shape better, but snagging is a major problem with them. Knit fabric manufacturers and producers of knitted garments are working to minimize, if not eliminate, this property. One of the more recent efforts combines an antisnag finish with knitting techniques that increase the yarn's recoverability.

Woven fabrics are generally considered to be more expensive to make than knits, because of the time and labor involved (Figures 2–10 and 2–11). However, such factors as cost of basic materials used and the complexity of design also

FIGURE 2-10 *A worker adjusts threads on a modern loom. This loom uses darts to carry the filling threads rather than the conventional shuttle.* (Courtesy of American Textile Manufacturers Institute)

FIGURE 2-11 *A roll of cloth is inspected by eye before it is shipped to the customer.* (Courtesy of American Textile Manufacturers Institute)

enter into production costs. Woven fabrics are made by a process of interlacing two or more sets of yarn at right angles to each other. One set of yarns, the warp, runs lengthwise of the fabric, and the other set, the filling, runs crosswise. The two *directions* in which the yarns lie are called the "grain" or "grainline."

Woven fabric has little or no stretch in either the warp or the filling direction, but the *bias* stretch is comparable to that found in knit fabric. True bias cuts across both the warp and filling yarns at a 45-degree angle, and at this angle the stretch is greatest. Any line along the fabric that does not follow either lengthwise or crosswise yarns precisely is "off-grain," and the fabric will stretch at least a little along this line.

The basic weaves are the plain, twill, and satin. All other weaves, and there are many variations, are based on one of these three weaves. The *plain weave* is the simplest of all weaves (Figure 2–12). It alternates one warp yarn over and one warp yarn under the filling throughout the cloth construction (Figure 2-13). Some plain-weave fabrics are taffeta, shantung, organdy, and muslin (Figure 2–14). The basket

FIGURE 2-12 *Diagram of the plain weave.*

FIGURE 2-13 *An example of the plain weave, alternating one warp yarn over and one warp yarn under each filling yarn. This interweaving is particularly clear at the sides of the illustration, where the darker-colored warp yarns appear.* (The University of Mississippi)

a

FIGURE 2-14 *Other examples of the plain weave: (a) linen; (b) burlap; (c) three weights of unbleached muslin. Although all these fabrics are plain-woven, different surface effects are achieved by variations in yarn thickness and in the closeness of the yarns to each other.* (The University of Mississippi)

b

c

weave (Figure 2–15) is a variation of the plain weave, in which two or more yarns are used in both the warp and filling directions; examples of basket-weave fabrics are monk's cloth and hopsacking (Figure 2–16). In the rib-weave variation, the filling yarns are larger in diameter than the warp yarns. Broadcloth, poplin, faille, bengaline, grosgrain, and ottoman are rib-weave fabrics (Figure 2–17).

In the *twill weave* (Figure 2–18), diagonal ridges are formed by yarns which are exposed on the surface, slanting to the right, to the left, or in both directions to form a chevron. Twill weave is found in flannel, denim, serge, and gabardine (Figure 2–19). A common variation is the herringbone, a broken twill weave with a zigzag effect, produced by alternating the direction of the twill to produce a chevron design.

The smooth, shiny surface of the *satin weave* (Figure 2–20) is produced by floats of warp over the filling yarns, or vice

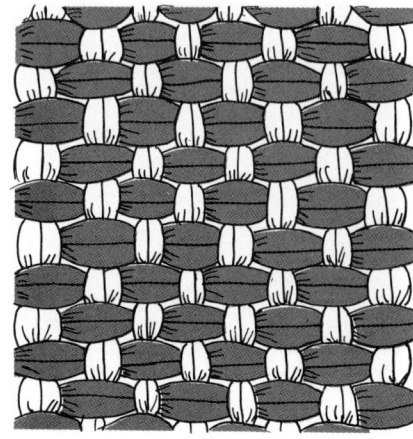

FIGURE 2-15 *Diagram of the basket weave.*

FIGURE 2-16 *An example of the basket weave, a variation of plain weave.* (The University of Mississippi)

FIGURE 2-17 *Broadcloth, a rib-weave fabric. Because the yarns used are fine and even, the surface of the fabric is very smooth.* (The University of Mississippi)

Part One / Textile Elements

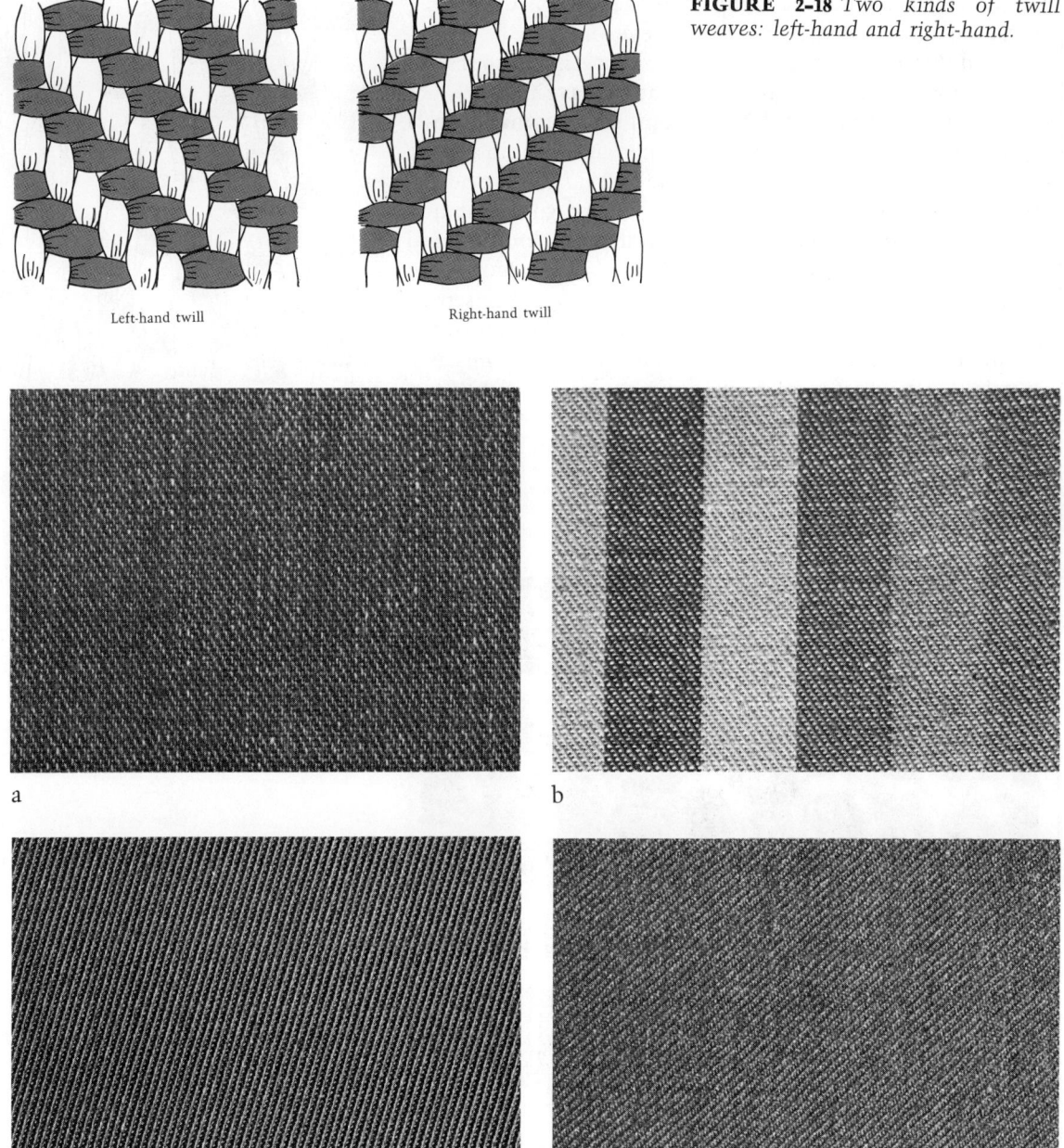

FIGURE 2-18 Two kinds of twill weaves: left-hand and right-hand.

FIGURE 2-19 Twill-weave fabrics: (a) solid-color denim; (b) yarn-dyed striped denim; (c) gabardine, made with a finer yarn, so that the twill effect is clearer; (d) serge, a softer fabric than either denim or gabardine. (The University of Mississippi)

versa. Diagonal lines are formed on the face of the fabric; these are not visible to the naked eye but can be distinguished through a pick glass or magnifying glass. Slipper satin and cotton sateen are examples of satin-weave fabrics.

Marquisette is produced by the *leno weave*, which uses a special attachment that manipulates the warp yarns in a figure eight around each filling yarn (Figure 2–21). Fabric made in this way is usually open and sheer, but of good stability.

Elaborate patterns like those seen in damask, brocade, and tapestry are woven on *Jacquard* looms. These looms are complicated and require a good deal of preparation in setting up to weave. For some patterns, this time may be measured in months. Additionally, weaving on Jacquard looms is a much slower process than on ordinary looms. These two factors are reflected in the higher cost of fabrics so produced, but the beauty and intricacy of patterns result in exceptional fabrics.

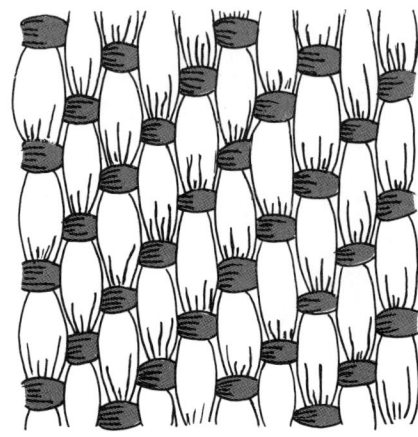

FIGURE 2-20 *Diagram of a satin weave.*

FIGURE 2-21 *The leno weave, with its characteristic figure-eight twist of warp yarns around filling yarns shown at top, produces open fabrics like the marquisette shown at bottom. (The University of Mississippi)*

FIGURE 2-22 *Terry cloth, a fabric with uncut looped pile yarns.* (The University of Mississippi)

Smaller designs, like those found in bird's-eye and huck, are produced by the *dobby weave*. These smaller patterns are combinations of the basic weaves and are made by using a dobby attachment on the loom.

In *pile woven* fabrics, extra yarns form the pile (a one-way effect on the face), which may be either cut or uncut. Terry cloth is an example of uncut pile and corduroy of cut pile (Figures 2-22 and 2-23). Some fabrics, such as velvets, are woven with extra sets of yarns, so that two layers of fabric are woven at the same time, then cut apart.

Tufted fabrics were first made by hand in the early colonial days, as an art limited to fabrics for special uses. At the beginning of the twentieth century, machines were developed to produce tufted fabrics at high speeds. The process produces pile fabrics by inserting loops into a background fabric that is already woven. Although the background fabric and tuft yarns may be of any fiber, most of the tufted fabrics made today are on a base of cotton, linen, or jute woven fairly closely, with the tuft yarns of cotton, rayon, wool, acrylic, polyester, nylon, and acetate. Needles are used to insert the pile loops, which may be either cut or uncut on the face. A special coating is applied to the back to hold the inserted tufts in place, or the tufted yarns are untwisted and the base fabric shrunk. Usually tufted fabrics are less expensive than comparable woven products. Bedspreads, carpets, and blankets are textile products frequently made by this method.

Knit-sewing is a recent development in fabric making, in which either yarns or fiber webs are locked together by using needles such as those used in knitting. Some Malimo fabrics are formed by the use of a three-yarn system in which a filling and warp are held together by a tricot-knit stitch to form

a

b

c

FIGURE 2-23 *Three examples of corduroy, a cut-pile fabric: (a) pinwale; (b) medium wale; (c) wide wale.* (The University of Mississippi)

a ravel-free fabric. Others are made by stitching only the filling yarns together, or by stitching the filling to a background fabric. This technique can also be used to produce pile fabrics.

Fabrics Made from Neither Fibers nor Yarns

Paper, plastic film or sheets, and polyurethane foams are among fabrics found in this group. Technically, paper may not be considered a textile fabric, but in recent years it has been used increasingly as a substitute for fabrics in textile products. Disposable paper items are available for a number of furnishing and apparel purposes, including draperies, laboratory uniforms, medical examination gowns, tablecloths, napkins, and even academic gowns. When choosing between paper and cloth for textile products, the consumer should keep in mind comparative costs such as initial purchase price, anticipated length and type of use, cost of upkeep, storage, and aesthetic factors. Most of these items are designed for a short time of service and are useful only where long wear and continued service are secondary concerns. They eliminate care and storage problems since they probably will be discarded soon after they have served their intended purpose. It is important that they be treated for fire resistance.

Plastic films are made from the same chemical substances as those used for making fibers, except that they are extruded in flat, continuous sheets of film, instead of filaments. These film fabrics may be very thin and transparent, such as cellophane or plastic wrap, or they may be heavy enough to be used for drapery materials, vinyl coats, or even boots. The heaviest such fabrics may resemble leather or heavy woven upholstery materials. Films may be either unsupported or supported by a woven or knitted fabric base which makes them more durable.

Much of the foam used for textile products is found either as fabric laminates (for example, in all-weather coats) or as backing for tufted carpets. Flexible sheets of foam are used for furniture cushions, rug pads, and mattresses.

Multilayer Fabrics

Some fabrics are constructed so that they are really two or more layers of fabric permanently held together to make one piece.

Double-cloth is made by using two sets of warp and filling yarns at the same time to weave two layers of fabric with one on top of the other. A fifth set of yarns interlaces both layers, holding them together. True double-cloth can be separated by removing the threads that hold the layers together. Another type of double-cloth is made by using only four sets of yarns woven into two separate cloths on the same loom. At intervals, according to the design of the fabric, the warp and filling of one cloth exchange places with those of the other cloth. The two layers of cloth are locked together by the crisscrossing of yarns. They are, however, completely separate and can be pulled apart between the crisscross points, if the threads holding the two layers together are cut. *Double-faced* fabrics are made by using three sets of yarns, which may be either one warp and two fillings or vice versa. This process is often used to make blankets and satin ribbon.

Quilted fabrics are made from two layers of fabric with a layer of wadding or batting sandwiched in between. The three layers are then fastened together by machine or hand stitching (Figures 2–24 and 2–25). When thermoplastic materials are used for the layers, they can be fused by heat or adhesives. Quilted fabrics may be heavy or light in weight, depending especially on the weight of the middle layer. Cotton wadding or batting makes heavier quilted fabrics than does either foam or fiberfill (usually acetate or polyester). Most quilted fabrics are now machine-made because it is less time-consuming and more economical than quilting by hand. However, hand quilting is still done as a craft by people throughout the United States who enjoy displaying their products.

Bonded fabrics are made by fusing one layer of fabric to another. Thermoplastic fabrics can be fused together by heat, while an adhesive is needed for nonthermoplastic layers. Almost any type of fabric is used for the face side and knits usually as the backing. The face fabrics may be backed by foam in a heat process, which partially melts the foam so that it adheres to the face fabric. A face fabric may be bonded to a layer of foam, then backed by a third layer, which is usually some type of knit. Some authorities differentiate between these processes by applying *bonding* to fabric-to-fabric backing and *laminating* to fabric-to-foam backing.[2]

Table 2-1 summarizes the different methods used in making fabrics.

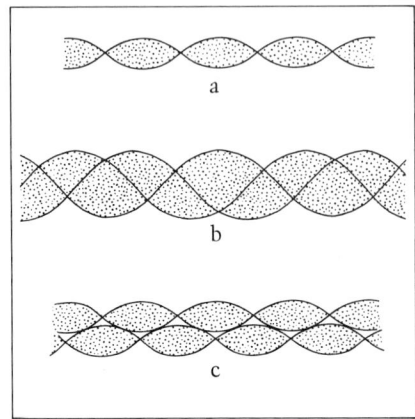

FIGURE 2-24 *Diagram of three types of quilted fabric: (a) filling between two layers of fabric, with stitching evenly spaced overall; (b) thicker filling between the fabric layers, with stitching in lines that distribute the filling evenly; (c) two layers of the first type, stitched together to create air pockets between the layers.* (Reprinted, by permission, from Marilyn J. Horn, *The Second Skin*, 2nd ed., Houghton Mifflin, Boston, 1975, p. 305)

---

2. Dan River, Inc., *A Dictionary of Textile Terms*, Dan River, Inc., New York, 1971, p. 13.

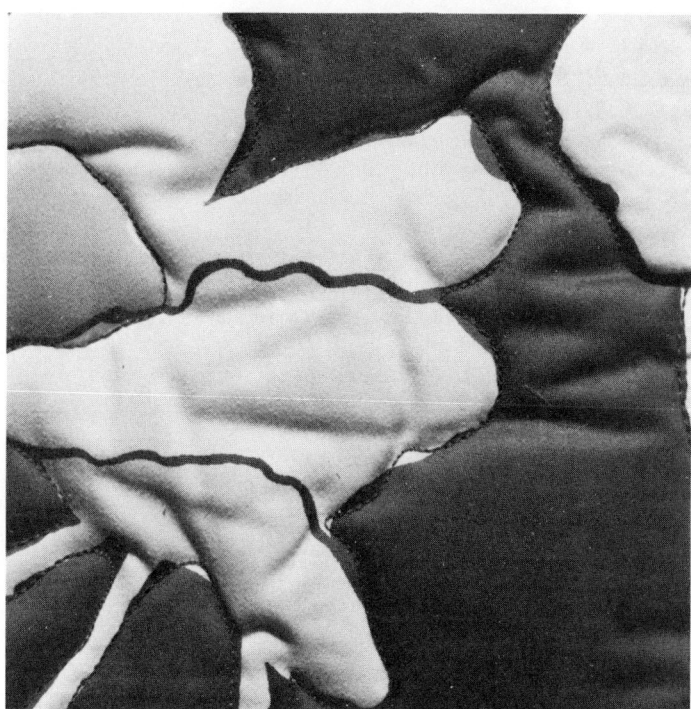

FIGURE 2-25 *A quilted fabric in which the quilting outlines the design in a way that causes the filling to "puff" up the design.* (The University of Mississippi)

TABLE 2-1 *Summary of Fabrication Methods*

Type of fabric	Method of fabrication
1. Fabrics made directly from fibers	
a. Felts	Fibers permanently locked together in manufacture
b. Nonwovens	Fibers held together by applied bonding or adhesive agent, or by heat fusing
2. Fabrics made from yarns	
a. Braids	Yarns laced together lengthwise and diagonally
b. Laces	Yarns knotted, interlaced, interlooped, or twisted
c. Knits	One or more yarns formed into series of interlocking loops
1. Warp knits (tricot; Milanese; raschel)	Machine-made, loops run lengthwise of fabric
2. Filling (weft) knits	Hand- or machine-made loops run crosswise of fabric
3. Double knits	Machine-knitted with a double stitch to provide double thickness
d. Woven fabrics	Two or more sets of yarn, interlaced at right angles to each other
1. Plain	One warp over and one warp under filling throughout fabric
2. Twill	Warp yarn goes over and under different numbers of filling yarns to form a diagonal effect on fabric surface; may be left or right diagonal, or in chevrons

Table 2-1 (*cont.*)

Type of fabric	Method of fabrication
3. Satin	Warp yarns "float" over and under different numbers of filling yarns, unevenly, without surface pattern
4. Pile	Extra warp or filling threads are used to create a thick effect; pile may be cut or uncut; basic fabric holds pile in place
5. Leno	Warp yarns are paired and half- or full-twisted to form a figure eight around filling yarns
e. Tufting	Yarns are forced through premade fabric to form cut or uncut loops
f. Knit-sew	Warp and filling yarns are placed on top of each other, then locked together with a chain stitch
3. Fabrics made from neither fibers nor yarns	
a. Paper	Substitute for textiles; produced as paper, then made into the end product
b. Films	Fiber solutions extruded through narrow slits
c. Foam	Substitute for textiles; air cells are incorporated into solutions extruded as for films
4. Multilayer fabrics	
a. Double-cloth	Three or more sets of yarn used on one loom to produce two separate cloths held together by yet another set of yarns; or two separate cloths held together by criss-crossed yarns between the cloths; or double-faced cloth made with three sets of yarns
b. Quilted	Two outer layers of fabric with a layer of filling in between, stitched or fused together
c. Bonded	Two or more fabric layers fused together by heat or adhesive
d. Laminated	Two or more layers of fabric fused by heat or adhesive; one layer is made of foam

Glossary of Fabric Names

AWNING CLOTH   A durable cotton such as canvas or duck made with a plain weave, often in solid colors or woven or painted stripes. Used for awnings, beach and lawn umbrellas, outdoor furniture covers.

BARATHEA   Closely woven fabric with pebbly weave. Used for apparel.

BARK CLOTH   Durable, plain-woven cotton fabric, with uneven surface. Used for draperies and slipcovers.

BATISTE   Sheer, very fine, lightweight, plain-weave fabric of cotton, rayon, wool, silk, or manufactured fibers. Used for apparel and curtains.

BEDFORD CORD Firm, warp-ribbed cotton or wool fabric; stuffing yarns make a raised cord. Used for apparel and uniforms; heavier qualities for draperies and slipcovers.

BENGALINE Sturdy, warp-faced fabric with characteristic crosswise ribs formed by bulky, coarse-plied yarn. Used for apparel and some draperies.

BIRD'S-EYE Cotton or linen cloth woven in small geometric pattern, with a center dot like a bird's eye. Made on a special loom, with heavier filling yarns loosely twisted to make fabric more absorbent. Used for some apparel, towels, and diapers.

BOBBINET Lacelike fabric, varies from sheer to coarse, with open weave. May be natural or manufactured fiber. Used for curtains.

BOUCLÉ Fabric woven or knitted from a looped or knotted yarn; may be wool, rayon, cotton, silk, flax, or manufactured fiber. Used for apparel and some upholstery.

BROADCLOTH Tightly and plain-woven, lustrous cotton fabric with fine crosswise rib; finest qualities are made of combed Pima or Egyptian cotton. Wool broadcloth has a glossy, napped face and a twill back. Different weights are used for different items of apparel.

BROCADE A rich Jacquard-weave fabric with an all-over interwoven design made clearer by contrasting surfaces and/or colors; face of fabric can be distinguished from back; of natural or manufactured fibers, sometimes with a gold or silver yarn. Used for apparel and upholstery.

BROCATELLE Tightly woven, stiff, elaborate fabric made with Jacquard figure weave; warp yarns form design that stands in high relief from the ground; area not raised is backed with extra yarns. Used for slipcovers, upholstery, and wall coverings.

BUCKRAM Heavily sized and stiffened fabric made by gluing together two fabrics—a low-count, open, plain-weave fabric and a much finer plain-weave fabric. Used as interlining in cloth and leather apparel and drapery headings.

BURLAP Heavy, plain-woven fabric made of jute, hemp, or cotton. Has become a fashion fabric for skirts, tunics, and handbags, and is used for draperies and wall hangings.

CALICO Lightweight, plain-weave cotton cloth with gay printed design; printed cloths may be called calico when a small, overall, floral design is used in dark or bright colors. Used for apparel, sometimes for curtains.

CANVAS Heavy, closely woven, plain-weave fabric, rather stiff; of cotton, linen, or manufactured fibers; various weights. Used in awnings, slipcovers, linings, some footgear.

CASEMENT CLOTH A class of lightweight, sheer, open-work or opaque fabrics; various fibers. Used chiefly for curtains.

CHALLIS Soft, supple, lightweight fabric, usually printed with delicate floral patterns; pure wool, rayon, cotton, or blends. Used for apparel and linings.

CHAMBRAY Plain-weave fabric with a white frosted appearance caused by the use of white yarns in filling, colored yarns in the warp. May be heavy or light. Used for women's apparel, men's shirts, sportswear.

CHEESECLOTH Soft, loosely woven, plain-weave, cotton cloth. Used for curtains and ladies' apparel.

CHIFFON Soft, sheer, plain-weave fabric; in silk, rayon, or manufactured fibers with soft or stiff finish. Used for ladies' evening wear and lampshades.

CHINA SILK Sheer, lightweight, plain-weave silk. Used for linings of dresses and suits, lingerie, and scarves.

CHINCHILLA CLOTH Heavy woolen cloth with spongy texture; has a nap produced by machine. Used for coats.

CHINTZ Large group of gaily colored, highly glazed, cotton fabrics. Some glazes are permanent, some will wash out. Unglazed chintz is called *cretonne*. Used for ladies' summer apparel, draperies, and slipcovers; sometimes for unlined curtains.

CORDUROY Cotton or blended cut-pile fabric, with or without wide or narrow wales, plain or twill-weave back; also available in manufactured fibers. Used for apparel and furnishings.

COVERT Closely woven, twill fabric, usually wool. Used for coats, suits, and sports clothing, mostly for men.

CRASH Rather loosely woven fabric, made from irregular yarns of cotton, linen, rayon, or jute, in various weights. Used for upholstery, draperies, and slipcovers.

CREPE Fabric with a crinkled or puckered surface, achieved by the use of embossing, weave, twisted yarns, or chemical treatment; may be of silk, rayon, cotton, wool, manufactured fibers, or blends. Crepe-back satin has satin face and is reversible. Used for ladies' apparel.

CRÊPE DE CHINE Very sheer, lustrous silk or manufactured fabric; soft, drapy. Used for ladies' apparel.

DAMASK Firm, glossy, patterned Jacquard-weave fabric, similar to brocade but flatter; in cotton, rayon, flax, silk, or blends. Used for tablecloths, napkins, draperies, upholstery, and ladies' evening dresses.

DENIM Twill-weave cotton fabric made of coarse, hard-twisted yarns; warp yarns may be colored and filling yarn white, or fabric may be piece-dyed; smooth or napped finish. Used for apparel, slipcovers, and draperies.

DIMITY Sheer cotton with fine corded, striped, or checked effect; may be plain or printed. Used for aprons, pinafores, dresses, and art needlework.

DOTTED SWISS Open-weave, sheer, crisp, plain-weave cotton fabric with woven or flocked dots. Used for ladies' apparel and for curtains.

DOUBLE-CLOTH Fabric made by weaving two cloths together, using four or five sets of yarns; of natural or manufactured fibers; often reversible. Used for coats, jackets, suits, and sports garments.

DOUBLE KNIT Firm knit fabric, often of interlock stitch or variations, made by a two-needle method. Has less stretch and more durability than jersey. May be of natural or manufactured fibers, patterned or plain. Used extensively for apparel.

DRILL Heavy, firm, twill-weave cotton, sized and pressed to yield a compact fabric; found as khaki cloth, middy twill, and jean cloth. Used in sportswear, men's work clothes, curtains, slipcovers.

DUCK Tightly woven cotton or linen fabric resembling canvas, with plain or rib weave; various weights. Used for coats, jackets, and some footwear.

DUVETYNE Twill fabric with a short nap and velvety feel; usually of wool. Used for suits and coats.

FAILLE Soft but firm ribbed-weave fabric with light, horizontal ribs or cords; of silk, rayon, cotton, or manufactured fibers. Used for ladies' apparel and handbags.

FAKE FUR Woven or knitted plush pile fabric made to look like fur; may be of wool, silk, mohair, rayon, or manufactured fibers; fabric is finished to imitate the animal fur. Used for coats, jackets, and other heavy apparel.

FELT Heavy, compact, nonwoven fabric made from wool, hair, fur, or certain manufactured fibers. Can be found in various weights. Used for some apparel and sometimes for table covers.

FILET A type of lace, usually coarse, with square mesh knotted at corners; of natural or manufactured fibers. Used for curtains.

FLANNEL Plain- or twill-weave fabric of wool or cotton. Has softly napped surface, in various weights. Used for apparel and blankets.

FLANNELETTE Soft, plain- or twill-weave fabric of cotton, lightly napped on one side. Used for lounging and sleeping garments and for shirts.

FLEECE Fabric with deep, napped surface or a pile fabric; also, the effect obtained by napping. Used for outer garments.

FRIEZE Fabric of looped-pile construction, with loops cut or uncut; of natural or manufactured fibers; heavy, ribbed, and durable. Used for upholstery.

GABARDINE Tightly woven, twill-weave fabric, with fine, close, diagonal lines that run from left to right; lines not noticeable on wrong side of fabric; of cotton, wool, rayon, or mixture of fibers. Widely used in men's and women's garments.

GAUZE Sheer, open plain-weave fabric. Used for curtains, dress trimmings, and some ladies' apparel.

GEORGETTE Sheer, dull-textured fabric, heavier than chiffon, of twisted yarn in both directions, to give a pebbly, crepelike effect. Used for ladies' apparel.

GINGHAM Yarn-dyed, plain-weave, cotton fabric, striped, plaided, and checked; firm finish with some luster. Used for apparel, curtains, draperies, and bedspreads.

HARRIS TWEED Fabric of virgin wool made only on the Outer Hebrides, off the west coast of Scotland. Rough surface; usually small patterns with color effects obtained by use of different-colored fibers. Used for coats and suits.

HOMESPUN Plain-weave fabric, loosely woven from uneven, tightly twisted yarns; hand-woven appearance; of cotton, linen, or wool. Used for heavier apparel, draperies, and slipcovers.

HONEYCOMB OR WAFFLE CLOTH A type of piqué fabric. Rough-textured fabric with raised square or diamond-shaped pattern made by floating warp and filling yarns to form ridges along the float lines. Used in apparel, bedspreads, and draperies.

HOPSACKING Open, basket-weave fabric, made of coarse cotton or woolen yarns. Used for some apparel and draperies.

HUCK OR HUCKABACK Linen or cotton fabric with small-figure weave; warp yarns float on top side and filling yarns on the back. Makes very absorbent, durable towels.

JEAN Cotton-twill or chevron-twill fabric similar to denim, with firm, clear-surfaced texture. Used for work clothes, children's clothes, and slipcovers.

JERSEY Single-knit fabric, patterned or plain; in natural or manufactured fibers and blends. Stretches more crosswise than lengthwise, and often is slippery. Widely used in apparel.

LACE Delicate fabric with decorative patterns and open spaces created by the threads used; can be hand- or machine-made; in natural or manufactured fibers. Used for trims and evening gowns.

LAMÉ Brocade, brocatelle, or damask in which metallic yarns are interspersed throughout the fabric. Used for ladies' evening apparel and for decorative purposes.

LINEN Strong, lustrous fabric made of smooth-surfaced flax fibers; available in different weights and varieties of weave. Used for apparel, household articles, and embroidery work, depending on fineness and weave of fabric.

MARQUISETTE Lightweight, open-mesh cloth made in leno weave; sheer but relatively strong; in cotton or manufactured fibers; may be soft or crisp; recognized by a figure-eight interlacing of warp and filling yarns. Used in apparel for women and in curtains.

MATELASSÉ Soft, double-cloth or compound fabric with a quilted surface look; in silk, wool, cotton, rayon, or manufactured fibers; may look blistered, puckered, quilted, or wadded, depending on construction. Heavy weights used for coverlets, draperies, upholstery; lighter weights for ladies' clothing and trimmings.

MELTON Thick cloth, usually made of wool, with a dull, soft finish. Different weights; use depends on specific weight. Chief use is for overcoats, uniforms, and jackets.

MOHAIR Originally goat hair, now frequently a blend of cotton and wool; may be woven into fabric or used to knit sweaters. Weaves vary. Used for apparel and for draperies.

MOIRÉ Plain-woven fabric which has been given a watermark finish; finish is not permanent on nonthermoplastic fabrics such as rayon or cotton; made of natural or manufactured fibers. Used for women's apparel and draperies.

MONK'S CLOTH Loosely woven, basket-weave cotton fabric; plain color or may have stripes or plaids woven in. Heavy weight used for hangings, slipcovers, and draperies.

MUSLIN A large group of cottons ranging from light to heavy weights; may be bleached, unbleached, or partially bleached; solid-colored or patterned. Used for apparel and household purposes, depending on weight and finish. It is the basic fabric from which others such as batiste, cambric, chintz, and organdy are made.

NEEDLEPOINT Hand embroidery technique, now imitated by machinery, in varied fibers, patterns, and colors. Used for women's handbags and apparel, and for upholstery.

NET Even-meshed, lace-type fabric of natural or manufactured fibers; may be sheer and soft or crisp, depending on fiber and finish. Used for ladies' evening dresses and for curtains.

NINON Thin, sheer fabric of natural or manufactured fiber; smooth, with luster. Used for ladies' evening dresses and for curtains.

ORGANDY Sheer, transparent, wiry cotton with crisp finish; may become crushed in wearing but ironing restores its stiffness. Used in women's apparel, curtains, bedspreads, and artificial flowers.

OSNABURG Rough, strong, plain-weave cotton fabric; uneven yarns produce rough texture; weight may vary. Used for sportswear, curtains, slipcovers, and draperies.

OTTOMAN Heaviest of ribbed-weave fabrics; has large, heavy, pronounced cross rib; fibers vary. Used for coats, dresses, sportswear, curtains, and upholstery.

OXFORD CLOTH Plain-weave or basket-weave fabric of cotton or manufactured fiber; ranges from lightweight to heavyweight; soft, with silklike luster. Used for men's and women's shirts, sportswear, and dresses.

PEAU DE SOIE Originally always a silk fabric, but usually now made of manufactured fiber; either single- or double-faced construction; very smooth and silky with semi-dull appearance; much heavier than most satin-weave fabrics. Used frequently for bridal gowns and ladies' evening dresses.

PERCALE Firm, smooth, plain-weave, cotton fabric with little luster; usually piece-dyed. Used for dresses, shirts, curtains, and bedspreads.

PIQUÉ Group of ribbed-weave fabrics, medium to heavy weight; varied surface textures formed by raised ribbing or wales running lengthwise; may be of bird's-eye, pinwale, or waffle designs. Used for ladies' clothing.

PLISSÉ Fine cotton fabric with puckered stripes, patterns, or all-over blistered effect created in weaving or by chemical process; may be made of manufactured fibers. Used for dresses and nightwear.

PLUSH Woven fabric with cut pile; pile may have designs clipped in; usually of cotton or manufactured fiber. Used for apparel if lightweight; for upholstery, if heavyweight.

POINT D'ESPRIT Type of bobbinet, with dots; usually of manufactured fiber. Used for curtains.

POLISHED COTTON Plain-weave cotton fabric with lustrous finish. Used for apparel, sometimes for curtains.

PONGEE Originally made of wild silk in plain weave, from irregular yarns. Imitations made of natural and manufactured fibers. Used for women's apparel and for draperies.

POPLIN Plain-weave fabric with fine cross ribs, similar to broadcloth; of silk, cotton, wool, or manufactured fibers. Used for apparel.

REP Ribbed, plain-woven, sturdy fabric of natural or manufactured fiber. Used for apparel and for draperies.

SAILCLOTH Heavy, very strong, plain-weave canvas fabric; of cotton, flax, jute, or manufactured fibers in different weights. Used for sails, sportswear, and slipcovers, depending on weight.

SATEEN Cotton fabric of either a warp or filling satin weave; may be mercerized and pressed to produce high luster. Used for women's apparel, draperies, bedspreads, slipcovers, comforter covers, and linings.

SATIN Smooth, lustrous, satin-woven fabric, originally made of silk fiber and now usually made of a manufactured one; weights vary; sturdy if made of manufactured fibers. Used for ladies' evening dresses, draperies, and upholstery, depending on weight.

SEERSUCKER Alternating crinkle-stripe fabric made by slack warp tension in alternate yarn groups (which distinguishes it from plissé crepe, produced by printing process or finish); of cotton or manufactured fibers. Used for sportswear, shirts, dresses, housecoats, bedspreads, and curtains.

SERGE Firm, twill-woven fabric, originally made of wool; now may be of blends of natural and manufactured fibers, or of all manufactured fibers; durable, hard-wearing. Used for heavy coatings and draperies.

SHANTUNG Plain-weave fabric with heavier, irregular filling yarns; may be of cotton, silk, or manufactured fibers; imperfections in yarn give it a rough, nubby surface. Used for women's clothing.

SHARKSKIN May have smooth, shiny surface; if wool, has twill weave with yarns of two colors, characterized by small dot effect; wool or manufactured fibers, but sometimes of silk or cotton. Used for men's and women's clothing, depending on fiber and weight.

TAFFETA Fine, plain-weave fabric with heavier filling yarn, giving fine-ribbed look; usually has sheen on its surface. Used for ladies' dresses and some linings.

TAPESTRY Jacquard-weave fabric, made from multicolored cotton or wool yarns; rough texture. Characterized by its distinctive tapestry pattern, which in wall hangings may be large and pictorial. Used for upholstery, draperies, and wall hangings.

TERRY CLOTH Cotton toweling fabric with loops on one or both sides; water-absorbent. Used for towels, slipcovers, and apparel such as bathrobes or beach robes.

TICKING A large group of cotton and flax fabrics made by twill, herringbone twill, satin, or Jacquard weave. Used for mattress and pillow covers and work clothes, depending on weight.

TWEED Rough-surfaced fabric, usually of wool, with homespun look; distinctive patterns are obtained by weaving dyed yarns. Used for all types of coats and, in light weights, for suits.

TWILL, sometimes called CAVALRY TWILL Strong, durable fabric, usually of wool; twill-woven, it has a definite raised diagonal cord. Used for uniforms, coats, and sportswear.

VELOUR Smooth, cut-pile, woven fabric of natural or manufactured fibers; weights vary. Used for apparel and draperies, depending on weight.

VELVET Short-cut, thick pile fabric with a smooth, rich surface; often woven double. May be of natural or manufactured fibers. Called plush if the pile is more than $\frac{1}{8}$ inch high. Used for clothing, upholstery, and draperies.

VELVETEEN Pile fabric of cotton or manufactured fibers; pile is in filling of the cloth and not as erect as that of velvet; surface is lustrous. When made of cotton, can be mercerized; is washable. Used for apparel, hangings, and draperies.

VOILE Sheer, transparent, plain-weave, light fabric made of highly twisted yarns; of wool, cotton, silk, or manufactured fibers. Used for women's clothing, curtains, and bedspreads.

WEBBING Very stout fabric woven of jute, cotton, or manufactured fibers; natural color or dyed; widths vary. Jute webbing is used in upholstered furniture to hold springs; manufactured fiber webbing is used in lightweight, outdoor furniture.

WHIPCORD Twill-woven fabric with clear diagonal cord, usually of wool; durable and long-wearing. Used for uniforms and sportswear.

ZIBELINE Woolen fabric with a high napped surface, with long fibers lying in one direction on the fabric. Used for ladies' coats.

Study Questions

1. What is the oldest technique for making fabric? How does it differ from other methods? Does the resulting fabric have the same qualities as those made by other methods?
2. Explain the basic differences between knitting and weaving as methods of making fabric.
3. Explain briefly how you might recognize fabrics made by each of the following weaving methods: plain, twill, satin, leno, pile.
4. Name ten useful items that are made of nonfibrous fabric.
5. Explain the differences between bonded and laminated fabric.
6. List twenty fabric names, with brief descriptions of each fabric.
7. List four fabrics that might be used for curtains or draperies. State whether they are light or heavy fabrics.
8. List ten fabrics that are used for clothing, giving type of fiber and describing the fabric briefly. State the type of garment usually made from each fabric.

Suggested Activities

1. Make a collection of fabric swatches that represent different methods used in weaving. Mount each swatch on cardboard and label.
2. Make a very simple loom that can be used for weaving fabric. Use a small box for the base, and devise a way to hold the warp yarns taut while you weave in the filling yarns. Make samples of the plain, twill, satin, and leno weaves.
3. Check to see whether there is a weaving department on your campus, or in your town or city. Investigate the various sizes of looms used, and the range of yarns and fibers the weaver(s) use on the looms.
4. Put as many fabric swatches as you can find in a box. Mix them up, then have group or class members remove

them one by one and identify the fiber, the fabric, and other details of manufacture.
5. Make a poster or display of swatches of fabric. Give the name of the fabric, the fiber it is made from, and the garment(s) that might be made from it.
6. Observe people in your town or city and note the fabrics used in their clothing. Make a list of the different fabrics you see. Which are most common? Were you able to tell whether the fibers used for these fabrics were natural or manufactured?
7. Check your own wardrobe and make a list of the fabrics used in the garments. Are they made of natural or manufactured fibers?
8. Check your wardrobe again. Can you tell the different design methods used in the manufacture of the fabrics?

Chapter 3

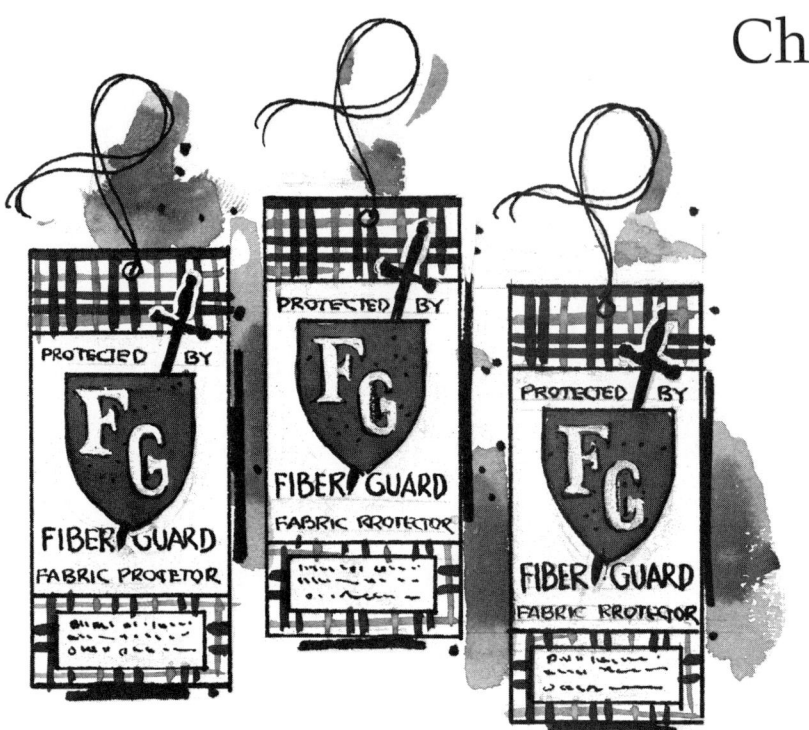

Finishes

ALL PROCESSES that follow fabric construction are regarded as finishes. They contribute immeasurably to the final properties and appearance of the fabric. In particular, consumer choices are frequently based on the appeal of specific finishes. Some finishes are applied routinely to fibers, yarns, or yard goods, and others provide added functional qualities desired in a particular fabric.

Types of Finishes

GENERAL OR ROUTINE FINISHES

Linen or cotton cloth is *beetled*, which flattens the fibers and yarns, giving the fabric a soft, full appearance. Impurities in fabrics may be removed while they are being whitened by use of peroxide or chlorine bleaches. Circular brushes may be run over the surface of a fabric to raise short fiber ends, creating a nap. When fabrics are pressed between rollers they become smooth and glossy; this finish is called *calendering*. Wool fabric may be set permanently by treating the fabric with boiling water, a finish called *crabbing*, which helps prevent creasing and other forms of uneven shrinkage in the finished product. Wool fabric is subjected to a combination of moisture, heat, friction, and pressure to bring about a felting that causes the fabric to appear fuller or more closely woven. Silk contains a natural gum, which must be removed in a hot soap solution. Rayon yarns have a natural luster that may be reduced or eliminated by adding certain chemicals to the solution before the yarns are made (Figure 3–1). Heat and pressure are sometimes used to add luster to yarns and/or cloth. Sometimes sizing is added to fabric to increase strength, smoothness, stiffness, or weight (Figure 3–2).

SPECIAL OR FUNCTIONAL FINISHES

The reader may recognize the trade names of some of these finishes that are applied to fabrics and products (see pages 63–64 for a summary of functional finishes). Fabric may be

FIGURE 3-1 *Taffeta is frequently made of rayon filament and may be chemically treated with delustrants to reduce its shine.* (The University of Mississippi)

FIGURE 3-2 *Buckram is a fabric that has been heavily sized to make it stiff and durable.* (The University of Mississippi)

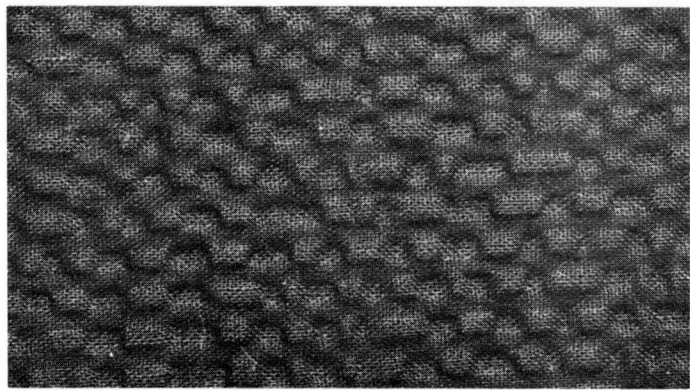

FIGURE 3-3 *The crinkly effect in plissé is made by using chemicals that cause some areas to shrink. The unshrunken areas then pucker in adjusting to the shrinkage.* (The University of Mississippi)

FIGURE 3-4 *Chintz is given a permanent glazed finish by application of resins and heat.* (The University of Mississippi)

made resistant to bacteria by chemical treatments such as Sanitizing and Cyana Purifying. Cotton, rayon, or nylon sheers can be made permanently crisp by adding finishes such as Fresh-Tex, Cransheen, or Cranpress. These finishes also help prevent the rolling of corners on sheer fabrics. Chemicals can also be used to cause some areas of a fabric to shrink, as in plissé (Figure 3–3). The tendency for hydrophobic manufactured fibers to accumulate static electricity can be reduced by special finishes such as Anti-static and Negastat. Acetates and triacetates are especially susceptible to color changes caused by atmospheric chemicals, and such fabrics can be treated to reduce or prevent atmospheric fading. The application of resins and heat gives a permanent glazed finish to some fabrics (Figure 3–4).

Flame-retardant finishes[1] are important to the safety of garments that might be exposed to fire (Figure 3–5). They do not keep fabrics from catching on fire, but affect the rate

---

1. "Retardant" and "resistant" are terms that are used interchangeably.

Part One / Textile Elements

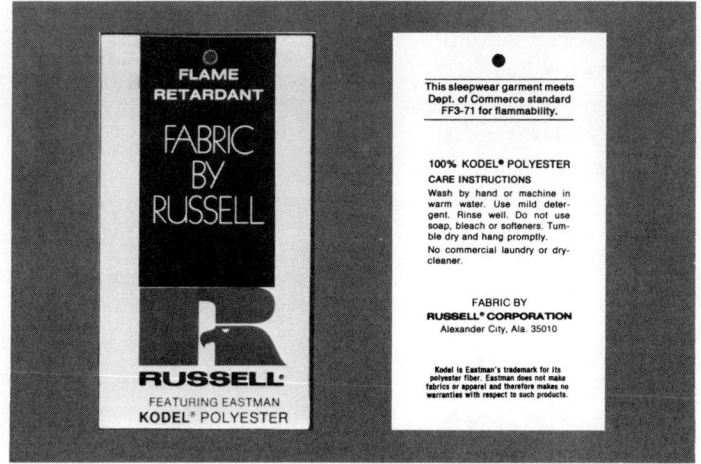

FIGURE 3-5 *The front and back of a typical hangtag found on a garment that has a flame-retardant finish.* (Courtesy of Eastman Chemical Products, Inc.)

at which they burn and help the fabrics extinguish themselves when removed from the flame. This tends to reduce the amount of physical harm that an individual may suffer when wearing such a garment, should it ignite. Today's finishes provide effective protection after many washings, but may lose their usefulness if laundered in soap or nonphosphate detergents (see Chapter 6 for a discussion of this).

Flammable fabrics tend to continue burning even after they are removed from the flame and flame-retardant finishes can help prevent this. Such finishes, however, do not necessarily make fabrics fireproof. A temporary flame-retardant solution can be made by the consumer and applied at home. It is made by mixing 7 ounces of borax and 3 ounces of boric acid in 2 quarts of hot water and can be applied to cotton fabrics without a permanent-press finish. This treatment washes out when the article is laundered and must be reapplied. Since this solution cannot be used on rayon and permanent-press cottons, another solution must be made for these fabrics by mixing 12 ounces of diammonium phosphate with 2 quarts of water. This finish is also temporary, requiring reapplication after laundering.

Cotton fabric may be *mercerized*—treated with a sodium hydroxide solution while the fabric is held under tension. Mercerization makes cotton fabric stronger and more lustrous. If the fabric is mercerized without being held under tension, it acquires some stretch properties.

Fabrics such as rayon, cotton, and linen, which are subject to mildew damage, may be treated with mildew-resistant finishes. Wool fabric is protected from damage by moths and carpet beetles when a finish such as Woolgard is applied to it. The tendency of cotton and linen fabrics to shrink can be reduced by the Sanforization process, which guarantees any subsequent shrinkage to be less than 1 percent.

Durable-press fabrics may be damaged by oil-based stains. Soil-release finishes help prevent the penetration of oil stains into these fabrics. Zepel and Scotchgard (Figures 3–6 and 3–7) are finishes that resist both water- and oil-based stains, while Hydro-Pruf (Figure 3–8) and Syl-Mel protect against water-borne stains only. Water-repellent finishes, for example, Cravenette, Hydro-Pruf, and Lovely On, do not make fabrics waterproof, but they do make them resistant to wetting. Fabrics may be treated so that they resist wrinkling extremely well when dry and have excellent wrinkle recovery when wet, with finishes such as Sanforized-Plus, Belfast, Everglaze, BanCare, Minicare, Perma-Pressed, Tebilized, and Wrinkl-Shed; fabrics so treated are often called "wash-and-wear." Other trade names such as Koratron, Coneprest, Dan-Press, Pen Prest, and Perma-Prest indicate similar fabric finishing.

The characteristics of fabrics for clothing and home furnishings have been changed by recent developments in fabric finishing. These new finishes can mean longer wear, easier care, improved appearance, and greater personal safety. However, some consumers become dissatisfied with textile products because they do not understand the terms, such as "permanent-press," "soil-release," "soil-resistant," and "flame-retardant," used to identify specific fabric finishes.

"Permanent-" or "durable-press" are terms used interchangeably to refer to fabrics that can be expected to keep

a

b

c

FIGURE 3–6 *There are three labels for this finish: (a) for rainwear and outerwear fabric; (b) for polyester fabric other than rainwear and outerwear; (c) for all other types of apparel. (Courtesy of E. I. du Pont de Nemours & Company)*

FIGURE 3–7 *Home-furnishing items with this soil- and stain-resistant finish have tags or labels like these. (Courtesy of Minnesota Mining & Manufacturing Company)*

their shape and pressed appearance after extended use and laundering, including tumble dryings (Figure 3–9). The finish works well on fabrics made from cotton, rayon, and flax fibers, helping them retain their shape and any applied creases and pleats for the lifetime of the article. It is also applied to fabrics that are blends of cotton, rayon, or flax with manufactured fibers such as nylon, polyester, acrylic, or triacetate. In blended fabrics, those containing a higher percentage of manufactured fiber such as nylon or polyester, for example, may be expected to last longer. The reason is that the finishing process weakens the cellulose fibers, causing them to wear out faster. A blend of 50 percent cotton with polyester or nylon has good durability.

Soil-resistant and *soil-release* finishes help in the care of durable-press fabrics. Soil-resistant finishes help keep the stain or soil on the surface of the fabric and often an immediate wiping away prevents any permanent staining. The finish keeps the soil from reaching the durable-press finish. Soil-release finishes are especially beneficial in the removal, during laundering, of oil stains that have been picked up by the durable-press finish, or by the fiber itself. Prewashing spot-treatments are often helpful in cleaning durable-press shirt and blouse collars and the soil-release finishes help the detergent work during actual laundry processes. Cleaning fluids work well to spot-clean, but may cause rings when they dry. Liquid detergent or a paste of dry detergent and water, applied before the cleaning fluid dries, may prevent the formation of a ring.

Soil-resistant finishes can be applied to all fabrics and are available on both clothing and home-furnishing items. They may be applied at the textile mill, but can also be added by a dry cleaner, furniture retailer, or at home (Figure 3–10). The home-applied finish might not be quite as effective as one professionally applied.[2]

FIGURE 3–8 *These labels appear on garments with the Hydro-Pruf finish.* (Courtesy of Arkansas Company, Inc.)

Summary Outline of Types of Functional Finishes

1. softeners: modify stiffness or harshness; used on all types of fabrics
2. bodying agents
    a. starches: stiffen and fill cotton goods
    b. modified starches and gums: modify hand of cellulosic and man-made fibers
    c. weights: give weight to silk and special purpose cotton and acrylic fabrics

---

2. Norma Hollen and Jane Saddler, *Textiles*, Macmillan, New York, 1973, pp. 231–235.

Summary Outline (*cont.*)

    d. resin reactants, durable press: provide crease resistant properties, glazed finishes, shrinkage control for rayon and cotton, assist in water repellency, flame-retardancy, wool shrinkage, etc. adhesives in making nonwoven type fabrics, coatings
3. water repellents:
   a. non-durable: provide excellent temporary water repellency
   b. durable: provide finish permanent through several cleanings; may retain soil
4. flame retardants:
   a. non-durable: provide temporary protection to cellulosic fabrics
   b. durable: laundry resistant flame proofing; improves hand of cotton and polyester
5. mildew and rot proofers and bactericides: prevents damage by bacteria, perspiration-caused odors
6. shrinkproofers: shrinkage control or reduce shrinkage; also may reduce felting in wool
7. antistats: increase electrical conductivity; may soften fabrics; used on man-made fibers
8. no-soil:
   a. soil retardants: reduce tendency of man-made fibers to soil
   b. soil releases: enable release of soil from polyester and blends and durable press fabrics
9. mothproofers: protect wool fabrics against moth attack
   a. non-durable
   b. durable
10. antislip: keeps smooth yarns of rayon and man-made fibers from slipping and becoming distorted during use
11. delusterants: used on man-made fiber fabrics to reduce luster
12. gas-fading inhibitors: reduce the tendency of blues and greys in acetate fabrics to become dull or pink
    a. non-durable
    b. durable

Source: Byron L. Richardson, "Guide to Textile Finishes," *Textile World,* December 1973, p. 45. Copyright 1973 by McGraw-Hill, Inc.

Color

Color plays an important role in making fabric attractive to consumers. The science of seeing color is somewhat technical and will not be discussed here. Anyone interested in a more detailed coverage of the subject should consult any of the textile science books listed in the Bibliography. In this section, fabric color will be dealt with primarily from the aspect of color-application techniques.

Color can be applied to textiles at several different stages during the manufacturing process—to the fibers, yarns, or fabrics. With natural fibers such as wool, there is the possibility of deep penetration of the dye into the fiber, resulting in uniform color and greater colorfastness. Color can be added to the chemical solution of manufactured fibers before it is forced through the spinnerets. This method usually ensures even dyeing and colors that are an integral part of the fiber, resulting in greater colorfastness. This is known as *solution* or *dope dyeing.*

Yarns may be dyed in packages or in skeins. This procedure costs less than fiber dyeing, but *yarn-dyed* designs are limited to the patterns that can be achieved by using dyed yarns in manufacturing the fabric. Manufacturers must also maintain larger yarn-color inventories.

Solid-colored fabrics are ordinarily produced by *piece dyeing*, a process that tends to be more economical than either yarn or fiber dyeing (Figure 3–11). Manufacturers do not need to maintain a large stock of dyed fabrics because they can color them as ordered. Piece-dyed fabrics are usually of one color, but when a fabric is a blend of several different fibers, the different absorption rates of the fibers can produce a pattern. If a fabric is made of different fibers and a uniform color is desired, the fabric must be dyed separately with the type of dye appropriate for each fiber present. This is necessary because the various fibers have an affinity for different types of dye and will become colored only when the appropriate type is used. This same fiber characteristic, however, makes possible *cross-dyeing*, in which fabrics of two or more fibers are dyed so that each fiber accepts a different dyestuff and takes on a different color. Checks, plaids, stripes, muted colors, or other designs can be achieved in this way.

Design

Fabric design is important to the consumer primarily because of its aesthetic value. Design should be selected because it improves the appearance of the fabric, is appropriate

FIGURE 3-9 *The front and back of a typical hangtag on a garment of fabric with a permanent-press finish.* (Courtesy of Eastman Chemical Products, Inc.)

FIGURE 3-10 *This stain-resistant finish may be sprayed on textile products at home.* (Courtesy of Minnesota Mining & Manufacturing Company)

FIGURE 3-11 *An apparently endless length of fabric on its way through processing to be piece-dyed.* (Courtesy of American Textile Manufacturers Association)

FIGURE 3-12 *Examples of structural design.* (The University of Mississippi)

Antique satin has a very uneven surface because of the random slubs in the filling yarns.

The ribs that characterize rep are made by using very heavy filling yarns.

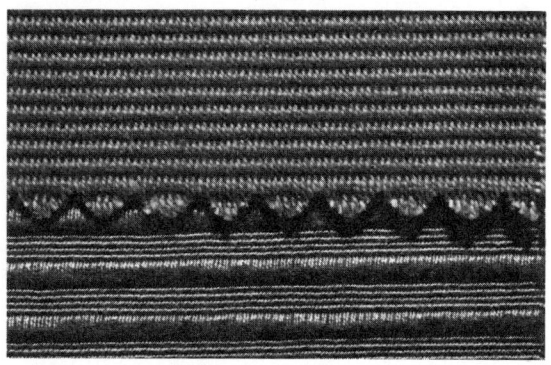

Variations of rep, showing different surface patterns.

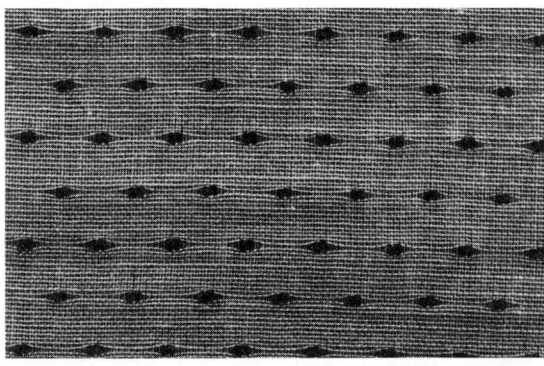

Additional filling yarns form the dots in dotted Swiss.

Here the design is created by using yarns in different thicknesses and different colors.

Coarse yarn used in the filling creates a design in casement cloth.

The check design of gingham is formed by use of white and dyed yarns in both warp and filling.

A fabric design is achieved by alternating the twill weave from right to left, making a checked effect on the surface of the fabric.

In seersucker, the stripes are formed by using white and dyed yarns alternately in the warp. The crinkle is caused by slack tension in the white yarns.

a

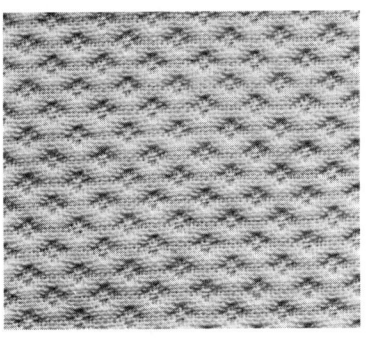

b

c

Three examples of structural design in piqué: (a) ribbed or striped; (b) waffle; (c) petit point.

for its intended use, and reflects or suits the personality of the owner. In addition, the design should be of a quality that will be durable for the lifetime of the product, and the design should also be cleanable in the same way that the basic fabric can be cleaned. The two broad categories that cover fabric design are *structural* and *applied* design.

STRUCTURAL DESIGN

These types of designs result from the various techniques used to manipulate simple or novelty-type yarns of different colors and textures during the weaving, knitting, or other fabric-making process.

The photographs in Figure 3-12 show fabrics that are examples of structural designs. Heavy cords used in the filling direction during weaving produce the crosswise rib effect found in faille fabric, for example. Gingham stripe, check, or plaid fabric is recognized by the alternated groups of colored yarns in the warp and filling. The elaborate woven designs created on the Jacquard loom are found in brocade and damask fabrics (Figure 3-13). Extra yarns may be used to weave cut-pile designs such as corduroy and velveteen, or to make uncut looped pile fabrics like terry cloth. The herringbone design of special twill-woven fabrics gives a zigzag look. The mottled colored surface of chambray is due to the use of colored warp yarns plain-woven with white filling yarns. Bouclé fabrics get their name from the use of novelty bouclé yarns, which give a loop appearance on the surface. The crinkled stripes of seersucker result from weaving the fabric with alternating tight and slack warp yarns. Tapestry fabric acquires its pattern by the use of colored threads in the filling. Structural designs are usually as durable as the dyes in the yarns and the fabric itself.

APPLIED DESIGN

Many different techniques are used to apply decorative design to the surface of the fabric by means of colors or chemicals. Because it is added to fabric after it has been made, applied design is really a fabric finish. Fabric may be first dyed and then have the design printed on by use of rollers, stencils, screens, or chemicals that resist dye. *Roller printing* makes possible the great and unlimited variety of printed goods available in every price range (Figure 3–14). *Stencil printing* is a more complicated process than roller printing, because a separate stencil is used for each color

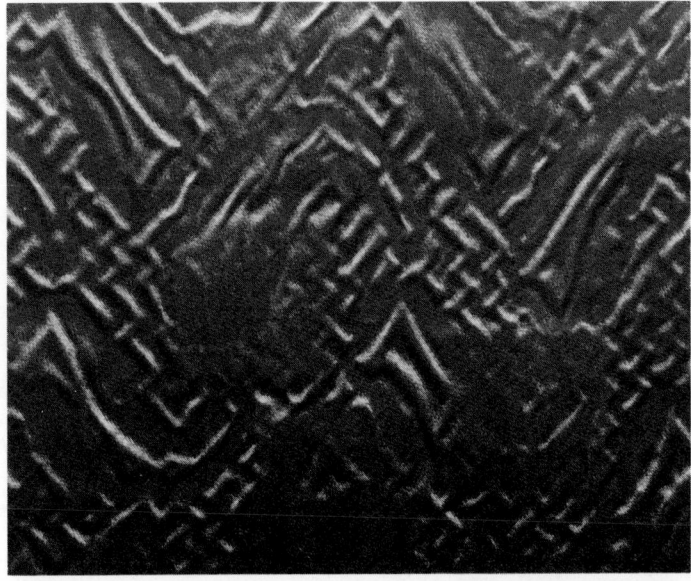

FIGURE 3-13 *Two types of matelassé, woven on a Jacquard loom. This fabric is characterized by the puffs on the right side.* (The University of Mississippi)

3 / Finishes

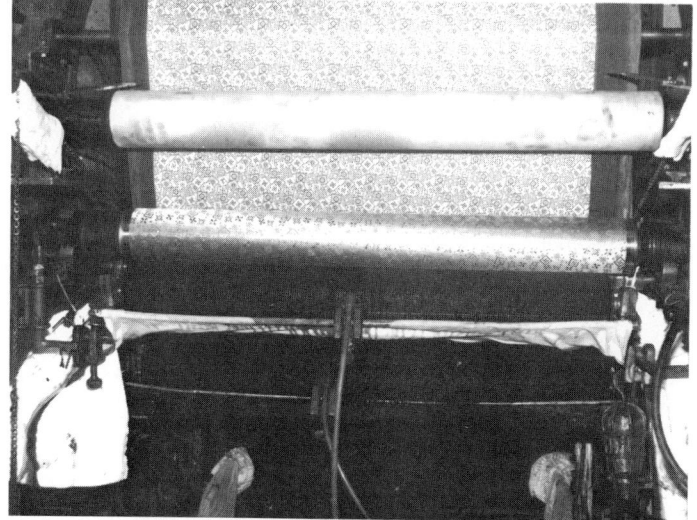

FIGURE 3-14 *A roller-printing machine, with the roller in the center of the illustration.* (Courtesy of Cranston Print Works Co.)

FIGURE 3-15 *Printing a large floral design. Notice that each screen (foreground) has a different part of the pattern.* (Courtesy of Cranston Print Works Co.)

and the stencils must fit together properly to make a perfect print. *Silk-screen printing* is an outgrowth of stencil printing that is well adapted to producing fabrics with large designs. Originally it was a hand process, but recently automatic screen-printing machinery has been developed, often with a rotary screen (Figures 3-15 to 3-17). Expensive, large-patterned fabrics may still be produced by hand, using silk or nylon screens that are moved from section to section of the fabric.

FIGURE 3-16 *Details of a design are being touched up on the screen.* (Courtesy of American Textile Manufacturers Institute)

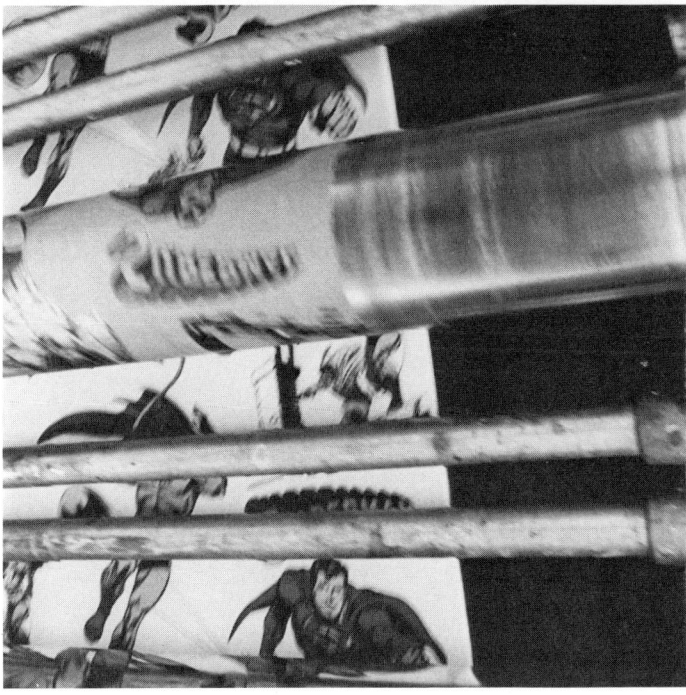

FIGURE 3-17 *A close-up of a rotary screen, taken while the machine was running.* (Courtesy of American Textile Manufacturers Institute)

FIGURE 3-18 *Examples of applied design.* (The University of Mississippi)

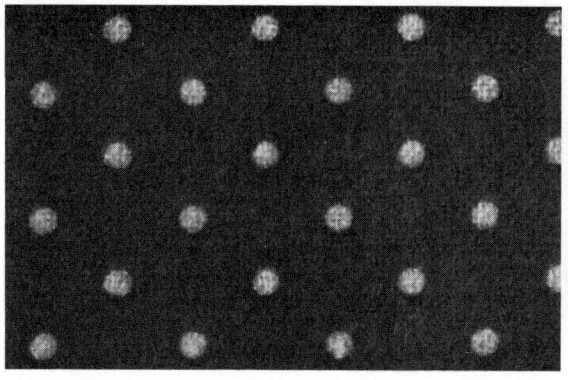 

A simple printed design. Note the distinct difference between the right side of the fabric (to the left) and the wrong side (to the right).

A small, printed floral design.

A larger printed design.

 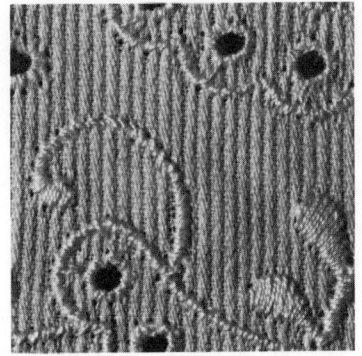 

Three examples of embroidered fabric. Various effects are created by the different fabric weaves and by different colors of embroidery thread.

A design created by flocking.

A design created by embossing.

3 / Finishes

In other methods the design is applied to the fabric through techniques which create areas that will resist the dyes. The fabric is painted with a certain type of paste; when the area that forms the design is stripped of its protective covering, it is left pale; the fabric is then piece-dyed and pale areas are colored. In *tie-and-dye*, parts of the fabric are tied off so that the dye does not penetrate to the fabric; the design is created by the contrasts between the dyed and undyed areas. *Batik* is another resist method that uses wax as a resist substance. Melted wax is poured or painted on the fabric in the desired pattern. When the fabric is dyed, the waxed area remains undyed. The wax is then removed with a solvent.

Fabric may also be decorated by application of yarn, thread, or fibers, either by machine or by hand. Embroidery adds both design and color. Quilted designs are produced by stitching through two layers with padding in between. Tiny fibers may be applied to the surface of a fabric with adhesive, in a process known as *flocking*. Fabrics may be embossed with a three-dimensional design, through the use of heat.

Figure 3–18 illustrates the various types of applied design.

Fabrics with applied designs present a particular problem. The design must follow the true grain of the fabric, so that the design will appear properly on the end product for which the fabric is used. This alignment of design with grain is especially important for geometric designs such as stripes and checks: if the design is not exactly on the grain, the stripes or checks cannot be matched correctly when the fabric is cut. When the design is not aligned with the grain, the fabric is said to be "printed off-grain."

Glossary of Color and Design Terms

BATIK   One of the oldest forms of dyeing known, in which portions of fabric are coated with wax, so that only unwaxed areas take up the dye.

COLORFAST   Describes fabrics that should retain their original color for the life of the fabric.

CROCKING   The tendency of excess dye to rub off during wear or use.

CROSS-DYEING   Different color effects obtained in one dye-bath, by using fabric made of fibers having different affinities for the dye.

DOPE DYEING   Addition of pigment or color to a manufactured fiber solution before the filaments are formed; also known as solution dyeing.

DYEING   Applying color to fibers, yarn, or fabric. See also BATIK, CROSS-DYEING, PIECE DYEING, RESIST, SOLUTION or DOPE DYEING, and YARN DYEING.

FABRIC   Also called cloth, material, goods, or stuff; the product formed by weaving or otherwise combining fibers or yarns; may also be a film.

FILLING   An individual yarn that interlaces with the warp yarn at right angles in woven fabric; crosswise yarns of fabric.

GRAIN   A line following either the lengthwise or crosswise yarns. Usually applies only to woven fabrics.

JACQUARD   A method of weaving or knitting fabrics in simple or elaborate designs.

PIECE DYEING   Fabric is dyed in the cut, bolt, or piece form; provides a single color for fabric.

PRINTING   Producing patterns, designs, or motifs of one or more colors on fabrics. See also ROLLER PRINTING, SILK-SCREEN, and STENCIL PRINTING.

RESIST   Treating yarn or fabric so that parts resist or do not take dyes.

ROLLER PRINTING   Patterns or designs are printed on the fabric by use of rollers.

SILK-SCREEN   Flat or rotary; a screen or cylinder is used for each color to be applied to the fabric, and color is forced through the screen to form the pattern.

SOLUTION DYEING   See DOPE DYEING.

STENCIL PRINTING   A stencil for each color is used to develop the pattern; all stencils used on a given fabric must fit together closely.

WARP   An individual yarn that interlaces with the filling yarn at right angles in woven fabric; lengthwise yarns of fabric.

YARN DYEING   The yarn is dyed before the fabric is made.

Study Questions

1. Name ten functional finishes that are applied to fabrics and explain the purpose of each.
2. Name the various stages during the manufacturing of fabric at which color can be applied.
3. What are the two broad categories of fabric design? Give two examples of each.
4. What is meant by the expression "fabric printed off-grain"?
5. How can you look for fabric that is printed off-grain?
6. What are the basic principles used in applying design by batik, silk-screen, tie-and-dye, and stencil printing?

Suggested Activities

1. Experiment with making a flame-retardant finish and apply it to swatches of several different fabrics. Then test its effectiveness by burning the swatches.
2. Visit a supermarket and list all of the products on sale that are finishes for fabrics. Read the labels for information relating to their use.
3. Using scraps of unbleached muslin fabric, experiment with design techniques such as: tie-and-dye, batik, stencil, silk-screen, block printing, etc. Why should you use unbleached muslin, instead of a fabric with a wash-and-wear finish or one made of hydrophobic fibers such as polyester or nylon?

Part Two
Care

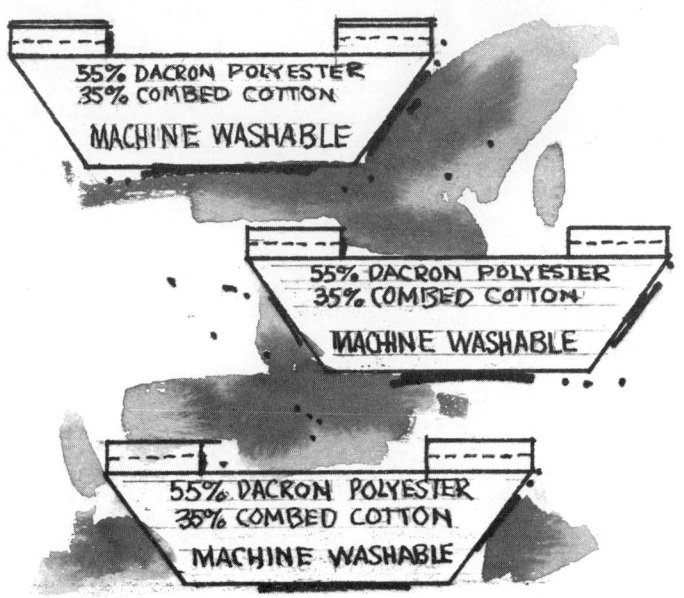

Chapter 4

Care Characteristics

KNOWLEDGE AND PRACTICE of appropriate laundry and dry-cleaning procedures can contribute to the serviceability of textile products and to the consumer's overall satisfaction. The kind of care that products should be given is determined by their textile elements. As we saw in earlier chapters, these elements include the characteristics of the fiber and yarn, fabric construction, and fabric finishes.

Fiber Properties and Yarn Structure

Individual fibers have unique characteristics, which should be considered in caring for products. Table 4-1 identifies some of these characteristics and suggests precautions to be taken in order to prolong the life and usefulness of the products.

Yarn structure may influence the care required by textile products in several ways. Filament yarns are relatively smooth, require little or no twist for cohesion, and have no short fibers. In many respects, these types of yarns are more easily

TABLE 4-1 *Fiber Care Characteristics*

Fiber	Characteristics	Precautions
Natural fibers		
Cotton	Durable and can withstand frequent hard laundering; easily ironed at high temperatures	Protect stored items against dampness to prevent mildew
Flax (linen)	Natural luster durable through frequent hard launderings; does not shed lint; wrinkles easily unless treated to resist wrinkling	Avoid pressing in sharp creases; protect stored items against dampness to prevent mildew; iron at high temperature for smooth appearance
Silk	Has natural luster and strength; moderate resilience to wrinkles and readily returns to shape; selected items may be hand laundered with extreme care, otherwise dry cleaning is recommended	Protect against prolonged exposure to sunlight, moths, and carpet beetles; do not bleach in chlorine; use fairly cool iron setting
Wool	Springs back into shape and requires little pressing	Dry cleaning recommended; may hand wash selected items in cold or warm water with little or no agitation; do not use chlorine bleach; protect against moths and carpet beetles; press with steam iron on wrong side, using press cloth
Manufactured fibers		
Acetate	Dries quickly; stronger dry than when wet; has poor abrasion resistance; subject to fume fading; heat-sensitive	Iron or press at *very low* temperature; avoid exposure to gas fumes; avoid excessive agitation during laundering; press on wrong side while still damp; may water spot if redampened
Acrylic	Resists wrinkling and effects of sunlight; heat-sensitive; oily stains difficult to remove	Remove oily stains before washing; use low temperatures for ironing, washing, and drying; fabric softener helpful; do not use steam iron
Anidex	High degree of stretch and recovery; retains resiliency through many washings and dry cleanings; can be chlorine-bleached; heat-sensitive	Use low temperatures for washing and drying; iron only if needed

Fiber	Characteristics	Precautions
Glass	Extremely strong; will not burn; heavy, wrinkle-resistant; and non-absorbent; resists sunlight, insects, rot, and mildew; will not shrink or stretch; fabrics are brittle and tend to split along fold lines	Hand wash only unless labeled machine-washable; wash separately; use mild detergent in lukewarm water; drip dry over towel-padded shower rod or clothesline; never use bleach
Modacrylic	Wrinkle- and chemical-resistant; nonflammable; highly heat-sensitive	Wash, dry, and iron at extremely low temperatures; fabric softener helpful; protect with press cloth
Nylon	Has excellent strength, elasticity, and shape retention; easily washed but tends to attract dirt; white articles attract other colors; heat-sensitive	Remove oily stains before washing; maintain whiteness by using commercial nylon whitener; use low temperatures; avoid chlorine bleach; fabric softener helpful
Olefin	Does not absorb water; very heat-sensitive	Wipe off spills; use low temperatures; fabric softener helpful
Polyester	Retains sharp pleats and creases; may resist pilling; exceptional wrinkle resistance; easily washed; heat-sensitive	Remove oily stains before washing; wash, dry, and press at low temperatures; fabric softener helpful; steam iron may be needed
Rayon	Moderately durable; lacks resilience; wrinkles easily; brushed or napped fabrics may be flammable	Launder in warm water and with care; dry cleaning may be recommended; iron while damp but sprinkling after dry may damage fabric
Rubber	High degree of stretch and recovery; damaged by oils and light; heat-sensitive	Wash frequently with mild soap or detergent; avoid heat; avoid constant overstretching
Saran	Resists soiling, staining, and weathering; flame-resistant but heat-sensitive	Blot stains to remove; rinse with clear water; avoid contact with hot temperatures
Spandex	High degree of stretch recovery; resists abrasion and body oils; discolored by chlorine	Machine launder in warm water; dry at lowest temperature and on very short cycle; do not bleach in chlorine; hand washing preferred
Triacetate	Similar to acetate but less sensitive to heat; mothproof and wrinkle- and mildew-resistant; generates static electricity; weaker when wet than when dry	Dry clean unless label suggests laundering; hand wash in lukewarm water and mild suds and drip dry; handle with care

cared for than spun yarns, which have more twist and tend to be fuzzy. Smooth yarns resist soiling and are more easily cleaned of any accumulated dirt than rough yarns that are spun or textured. Spun yarns frequently lose short fibers through abrasion, and unsightly pills may form on the surface of some wool garments. However, tough filament yarns such as polyester may become brittle, so that the fibers splinter off, forming pills which may be even more difficult to remove.

Complex yarns with protruding formations like loops, nubs, or coils are more easily snagged than are simple yarns. Damage may also occur from abrasion by equipment or other fabrics during cleaning processes. For this reason, terry cloth towels should not be laundered with garments that have zipper pulls or hooks, which could snag and distort the loop formations. Also, these types of yarn attract and retain soil readily and may make soil removal more difficult.

Yarns blended from fibers that require different care techniques should be given the type of care recommended for the fiber that is more easily damaged (see Figure 4-1). For example, a silk/cotton blend yarn probably would require dry cleaning, since this is the preferred method for cleaning silk. However, the percentage of each blended fiber must also be considered; as a general rule, the fiber present in the largest percentage determines the kind of care which is best for the fabric. A fabric of 85 percent wool and 15 percent polyester probably should be dry cleaned, although one made of 85 percent polyester and 15 percent wool may be safely laundered by hand, or, with care, even by machine.

Blending also may result in easier care for both fibers of a blend. A blend of polyester with cotton produces a yarn that is as easily laundered as cotton but which may dry more quickly and at a lower temperature than an all-cotton fabric (Figure 4-2). If laundry equipment can be operated as effectively at a lower temperature, this conserves energy and reduces the cost of maintenance.

The amount of yarn twist is also important. Woolen yarns, which have lower twist than worsted, do not retain creases as well. A pair of tweed pants may need to have the creases pressed more often than pants made of worsted yarns such as gabardine or serge. Also, high-twist yarns tend to resist wrinkling more than do those of a lower twist, although high-twist yarns may relax during washing and stretch. For this reason, some crepe fabrics should be dried flat rather than in a hanging position, because the pull of gravity could result in a permanently stretched garment. A rayon crepe

FIGURE 4-1 *A hangtag typical of those found on women's foundation garments. The back of the tag, at bottom, clearly provides care instructions for the different fibers used in the garment.* (Courtesy of Eastman Chemical Products, Inc.)

FIGURE 4-2 *This shirt of a polyester/cotton blend fabric would probably dry more rapidly after laundering than a shirt of 100 percent cotton. (Courtesy of the Manhattan Shirt Company)*

blouse, on the other hand, may appear to shrink during washing, but if it is pressed with a warm iron while damp it probably will return to its original shape and size.

Fabric Construction

The method used in constructing the fabric is a clue to the type of cleaning treatment it should receive. Fabric firmly woven in a simple weave is usually easily laundered unless fiber or finish prevents it. Fabrics woven with long floating yarns such as satins can be snagged during cleaning operations, resulting in an unattractive surface and a weakening of fabric strength. Garments of a satin-weave fabric should not be washed or dried with anything that might catch on the long float yarns.

Knitted fabrics usually resist wrinkling during both wear and cleaning, which is one reason for their continued popularity. However, the loop formation can be distorted in cleaning unless proper care is given. Most wool knit skirts and sweaters require blocking after they are cleaned, preferably by dry cleaning, although some are now machine-washable (see Figure 4–3). Knit fabrics of manufactured fibers can usually be machine washed and dried, but most care instructions suggest the use of warm water and a minimum of agitation to prevent shrinkage. Additionally, they should not be hung on hangers to dry, for the weight of the damp clothing may result in permanent elongation of the loop structure.

Lightweight and sheer fabrics, made in a loose or open weave, can suffer yarn slippage unless great care is taken during laundering (Figure 4–4). Leno-weave fabrics (such as marquisette) are less likely to undergo yarn slippage than plain-weave ones, because the interlocking of the warp yarns holds the filling yarns in place. These fabrics are often used for making glass curtains, to give an airy feeling to a room. As a rule, they retain their shape well even after many launderings, but the open spaces make leno-weave fabrics easily caught and torn, so it is better to wash them separately.

Nonwoven fabrics, such as felts, are not strongly constructed and may be permanently damaged if improperly cleaned. True felts are made of wool fibers, which will shrink when washed, and these should be dry cleaned only. Some nonwoven fabrics used as interfacings in garments may not be as strong as the garment fabrics. Those held together by adhe-

FIGURE 4-3 *Two wool sweaters that are certified for machine washability.* (Courtesy of The Wool Bureau, Inc.)

FIGURE 4-4 *This lightweight dress of French cotton lawn would require careful hand laundering, drying, and ironing.* (Courtesy of Cotton Incorporated)

sive substances may disintegrate if the cleaning treatment given the fabric dissolves the adhesive. Nonwovens, including felts, are easily torn or punctured and should be kept away from any sharp objects that might cause permanent damage.

Fragile fabrics such as laces usually require special handling unless they are made of strong, durable fibers. Most all-lace garments do better if dry cleaned or washed by hand, since the intricate design structures may be damaged by agitation during machine laundering and drying. Before purchasing lace-trimmed products it is wise to make sure that the trim can be cleaned in the same way as the article itself (Figure 4–5).

Fabrics of pile construction may need to be brushed to remove lint that collected on the surface during cleaning. When corduroy or velveteen garments are washed, they should be separated from other items of clothing to avoid lint accumulation. Also, when such fabrics are laundered, they usually look better if they are tumbled dry, since the

FIGURE 4-5 *This dress of 100 percent cotton plissé would launder easily. The fiber content of the lace trimming would have to be checked, to be sure the trimming would launder as easily.* (Courtesy of Cotton Incorporated)

dryer action tends to raise the pile and fluff the fabric. This may eliminate the need for pressing, which can crush the pile. If pile fabrics do need pressing, a needle board or a press cloth of a similar fabric will help keep the pile raised.

Fabrics of tufted construction usually can be laundered and tumbled dry provided the fiber content permits this type of care. Many blankets on the market today, especially those of manufactured fibers, are easily washed, if care instructions are followed.

Fabric Finishes

Finishes are applied to fabrics to increase consumer appeal and satisfaction. Quality is required in the finish itself, but proper care of the fabric is needed to ensure maximum performance. For example, even a fabric labeled "colorfast" may lose considerable color if it is subjected to chlorine bleach or exposed to intense sunlight for long periods of time. Colored clothing that is line-dried in hot sun for long

FIGURE 4-6 *Hangtag, front and back, showing fiber content and care instructions for a permanent-press-finished fabric. (Courtesy of Avondale Mills)*

FIGURE 4-7 *A hangtag on a durable-press-finished, double-knit garment. The buyer is told, on the back of this label, that any decoration is not of the same polyester/cotton blend. (Courtesy of Eastman Chemical Products, Inc.)*

periods of time usually becomes faded after a few washings. Fabrics of manufactured fibers such as polyester do not absorb water. Therefore, designs are often painted or printed on such fabrics. These designs are likely to rub off during wear, and vigorous agitation during laundering may cause even more color loss. It may be better to hand wash such clothing items unless the washing machine can be adjusted to a gentle agitation.

FIGURE 4-8 *The front and back of a typical hangtag for a garment made of polyester double knit. Note the instruction on the back for use of nylon bleach only.* (Courtesy of Avondale Mills)

Some resin finishes (permanent or durable press) used to give minimum-care properties to fabrics become less effective if washed and dried at very hot temperatures (Figures 4–6 and 4–7). These types of finish can actually be destroyed by extreme heat and the fabric then no longer has the minimum-care properties. Such textile products should be laundered and dried at warm rather than hot temperatures. Resin finishes may also be discolored by the use of chlorine bleaches (Figure 4–8). A white shirt with a minimum-care finish can turn yellow if bleached in chlorine, unless the label states that chlorine may be used.

Designs in otherwise plain fabrics may be raised or embossed to add interest. Usually these are heat-set and are permanent unless the fabric is subjected to hot temperatures comparable to those at which the design was originally set. If pressing is needed, the article may be placed right side down on a folded terry cloth towel and pressed lightly on the wrong side. The towel provides a protective cushioning for the design and keeps it from being pressed flat.

Some water-repellent finishes are not permanent and must be reapplied after several washings. Rainwear with such finishes may be safely laundered at home, unless the label states that the garment should be dry cleaned. Reputable dry-cleaning firms can renew most finishes at a minimal cost.

The consumer should consider the following questions when evaluating a special finish given to a textile product.

(1) Will the finish provide the desired effect? For example, if a stain-resistant finish is desired, it should resist both water- and oil-borne stains. (2) What special care will the finish require in cleaning? (3) Will the finish last through some cleaning method or will it require periodic renewal? (4) Will the finish become ineffective in either water or dry-cleaning solvent? (5) Is the finish permanent or will it wear out before the product does?

Care Awareness Shopping

The consumer naturally cannot keep all the details given in this chapter in mind when shopping for a textile product, but remembering basic facts can lead to a wiser selection.

Before making an actual purchase, the consumer should consider the kind of care the product will require. If an article does not have the right kind of cleaning care, it may lose its usefulness long before the owner has received satisfactory monetary value. Therefore, if the correct care cannot be given, some other article should perhaps be selected, to avoid frustration, dissatisfaction, and waste of money. It is worth taking time to consider this factor when buying expensive items such as upholstered furniture, carpets, or winter coats.

Home laundry equipment is expensive to buy and operate, and too many garments that require individual or special wash groups will increase operating costs even more. Some garments that should be tumbled dry do not look as well if they are dried in some other way. If one does not have a machine dryer, such garments may not be a wise buy unless a commercial laundromat is located conveniently—long drives are costly, too.

Maintenance of articles that require dry cleaning can also be costly unless do-it-yourself dry-cleaning services are nearby. Even then, the pressing that heavier garments need after self-service dry cleaning is a further consideration, since this work requires both equipment and some expertise.

The care instruction label on the article should provide helpful information. The next chapter will explain these labels and what they are required by law to show.

Study Questions

1. Give an example of how all these elements—fiber properties, yarn structure, method of fabric construction, and finishes applied—help determine the kind of care textile products need.

2. Which of these garments would pack well for travel and be ready to wear when unpacked, with no ironing required: rayon blouse, nylon dress, cotton skirt, polyester knit pants?
3. Which items would probably dry overnight after hand laundering: rayon slip, wool sweater, nylon blouse, cotton gown?
4. Which of the following should not be bleached with chlorine to restore whiteness: white wool sweater, white linen suit, white nylon dress, white cotton blouse?
5. What might happen to a cotton tablecloth if it is stored folded while still damp?
6. Which of the following should be ironed at about the same temperatures: rayon blouse, cotton shirt, linen pants, polyester dress, nylon top?
7. Explain what is meant by "care awareness shopping."

Suggested Activities

1. Look through textile items that have been used or worn for a long time and observe evidences of wear that relate to fiber properties, yarn structure, fabric construction, or finishes, for example, runs in stockings, pillings on sweaters, color loss from a printed design, or a dingy white wash-and-wear shirt. Suggest what you might do to avoid this in the future.
2. Plan a wardrobe of clothing suitable for a trip to include activities such as: shopping, hiking, lounging, and formal dining. Suggest items that would require a minimum amount of care.
3. Select swatches from several different fabrics suitable for draperies and/or upholstered furniture. Place them in direct sunlight for several days, then compare them with the original pieces. Which fabrics were faded the most? Which ones more nearly retained the original color? Which fabrics would you recommend for draperies or furniture that would be subjected to direct sunlight for long periods during the day?
4. Collect several different pieces of carpet large enough to be stepped on. These might include carpets made of wool, acrylic, nylon, or olefin fibers. Walk on each piece several times and observe which ones show footprints and which ones spring back after being crushed.
5. Cut swatches of several pieces of wash-and-wear fabric and launder them with your clothing several times. Observe which swatches retain their original appearance and those that change. Explain what you observed.

Chapter 5

Consumer Protection

IN THE PERIOD between the two world wars, there was increasing concern over consumers' lack of information about the fiber content of the many textile products on the market. In some cases, this allowed products to be misrepresented; in other cases, consumers were unable to determine how to care for goods purchased. Because of this unsatisfactory situation, legislation was passed, designed to protect and inform consumers.

Labeling

WOOL PRODUCTS

The Wool Products Labeling Act became effective July 15, 1941, and was last amended in 1965. The purpose of this act is to protect the consumer from misbranding of wool and wool products, including the addition of some or all of the specialty fibers (Figures 5–1 and 5–2). Its provisions require labeling of manufactured apparel, wool fabrics to be used for clothing, and other wool products that are composed of 5 percent or more wool, exclusive of ornamentation.

FIGURE 5-1 *These two marks appear on merchandise made from wool, new wool, or virgin wool. Left: the Woolmark label, your assurance of quality-tested products made of the world's best—Pure Wool. Right: the Woolblend Mark label, your assurance of quality-tested products made predominantly of wool. Generally, these marks are found on quality merchandise, not on items made of poor fabrics.* (Courtesy of The Wool Bureau, Inc.)

The Federal Trade Commission[1] requires use of the following terms for wool used in textile products:

1. "Wool," "new wool," or "virgin wool" describes a wool fiber that has been through manufacturing processes only once.
2. "Reprocessed wool" refers to wool fiber that has been reclaimed from woven or felted wool products that have not been in any end-product usage by consumers.
3. "Reused wool" identifies wool fibers reclaimed from products previously used by consumers.
4. "Wool product" means any product or part of a product that contains or is in any way represented to contain wool, reprocessed wool, or reused wool.

This act does not require any information to be given about the quality of the wool fabric, and the consumer must learn to identify quality through familiarity with feel and texture.

FIGURE 5-2 *The official Harris tweed label, found only in garments made of this fabric.* (Courtesy of The Harris Tweed Association)

FUR PRODUCTS

The Fur Products Labeling Act was approved August 9, 1951, and was amended in 1967 and 1969 (Figure 5-3). Under this law, labels, invoices, and advertising must state the true English name of the animal from which the fur comes and give the country of origin. The purchaser must be informed if the fur product is composed of used, damaged, or scrap fur, or of fur that has been previously dyed or bleached. The Federal Trade Commission prohibits use of fictitious prices

FIGURE 5-3 *This mark and wording appear on fur garments made in the United States.* (Courtesy of The American Fur Industry)

---

1. Although the Federal Trade Commission does not enact legislation, it does establish and seek to enforce trade practice standards for consumer protection.

in labels and advertising. The Fur Products Labeling Act includes these definitions:

1. "Fur" means any animal skin or part that has hair, fleece, or fur fibers attached, in either its raw or processed state. It does not include such skins as are later converted into leather or those which are to have the hair, fleece, or fur fiber completely removed in processing.
2. "Used fur" means any form of fur that has been used or worn by a consumer.
3. "Fur product" means any article of wearing apparel completely or partly made of fur or used fur, unless it is an item exempt by the Commission either because of the minute amount of fur used or because the value is small.
4. "Waste fur" refers to the ears, throats, or scrap pieces severed from the animal pelt.

FIBER CONTENT

With the increased production of manufactured fibers, a system was developed for the generic grouping and naming of fibers chemically similar. To date, twenty-one generic names have been approved by the Federal Trade Commission, and others are under consideration.[2] In 1958 the Textile Fiber Products Identification Act was passed, to become effective March 1, 1960, which required fiber content labeling of all textile products, including all fibers, yarns, and fabrics. Under this law, every textile product must have a label, conspicuously affixed to it in a secure manner and durable enough to remain intact through distribution, handling, and sale to the ultimate consumer, on which the following information appears (Figures 5-4 through 5-6):

1. The generic name and percentage by weight of each fiber present in the item in amounts by weight of 5 percent or more
2. The registered trade name or trademark used by the fiber manufacturer in conjunction with the generic name
3. The fiber generic names listed in order of predominance when more than one fiber is present in the product
4. If the item is imported, the name of the country where it was manufactured.

Also, the manufacturer must state if stuffing used in upholstered products has previously been used in another such product.

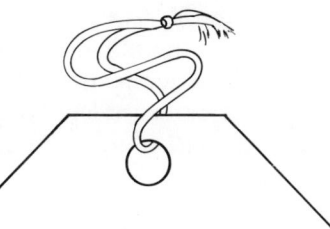

LABELS & HANGTAGS MUST SHOW

1. Fiber CONTENT by:
   ...generic name
   ...trademark

2. Percentage by weight of:
   ...each fiber over 5%

3. Manufacturer's name or number

4. Country where manufactured or processed

5. Recommended care instructions

FIGURE 5-4 *The information that must be provided on labels and hangtags for products purchased in the United States. If the product is not manufactured or processed in the United States, the fourth piece of information must be used. In 1971 care instructions became a requirement.*

---

2. See Chapter 1 for these names.

In advertising textile fiber products, the use of label information requires full disclosure of fiber content and manufacturer. When remnants of fabrics of the same fiber content are displayed for retail sale, a conspicuous sign may be used stating the fiber content information, instead of individual labeling.

PERMANENT CARE

While the laws requiring textile fiber product identification provided much valuable information, there appeared to be a need for additional information about the care which textile products should receive in order to increase customer satisfaction. In 1971 the Federal Trade Commission ruled that all textile products must bear information regarding proper care to be given the product (Figures 5–7 and 5–8).

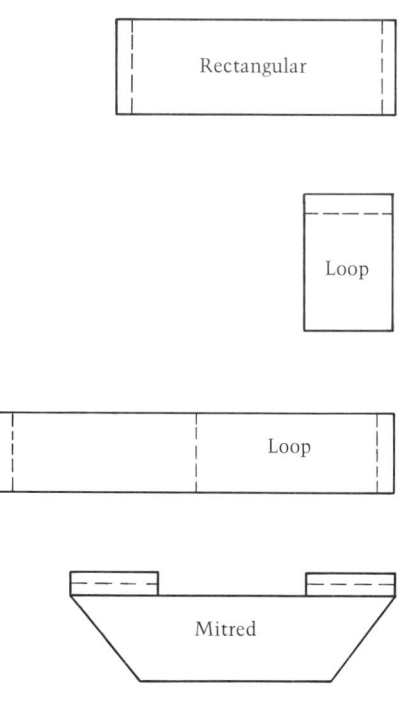

FIGURE 5-5 *The range of shapes for labels sewn in garments.*

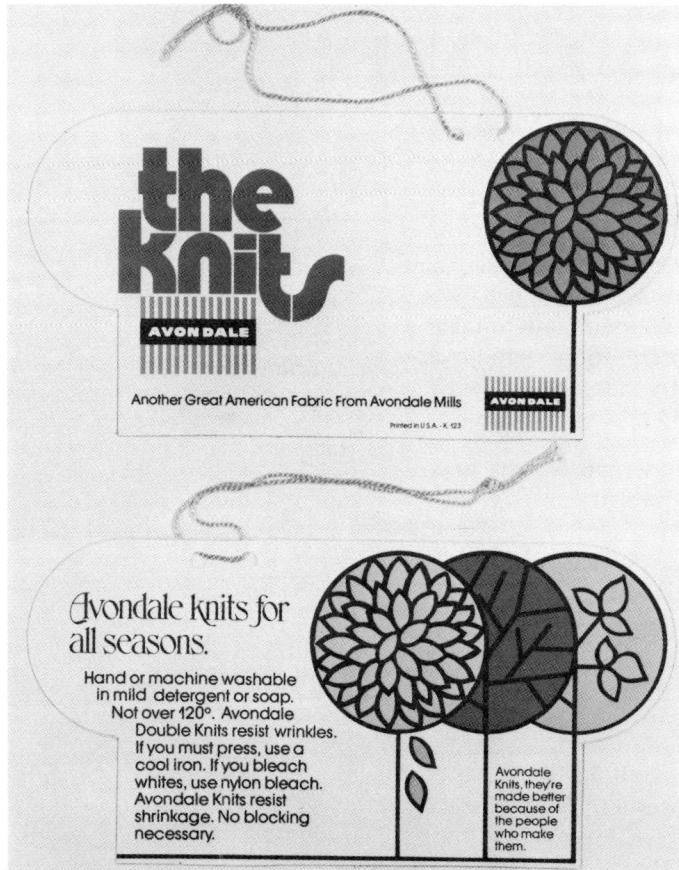

FIGURE 5-6 *This hangtag gives care instructions only. Fiber content would have to be provided on another tag or label.* (Courtesy of Avondale Mills)

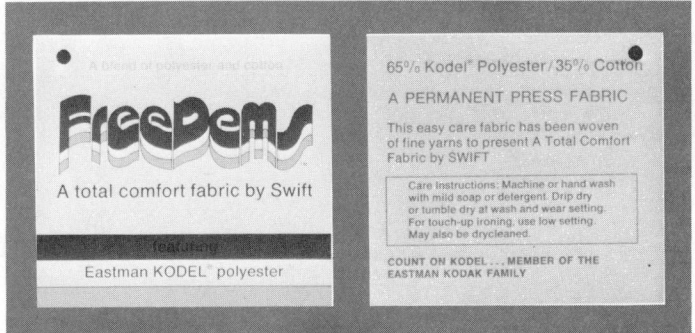

FIGURE 5-7 *The front and back of a hangtag found on a garment made of a polyester/cotton blend, with care instructions stated on the back (right). (Courtesy of Eastman Chemical Products, Inc.)*

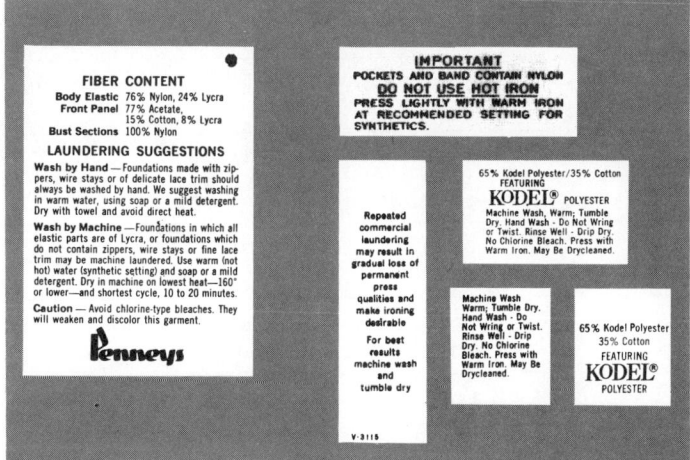

FIGURE 5-8 *Some typical care labels found stitched into garment seams. Note particularly the one at upper right, which warns against use of a hot iron because of nylon content. (Courtesy of Eastman Chemical Products, Inc.)*

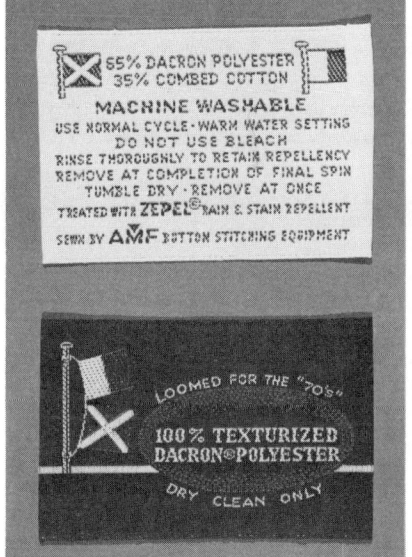

APPAREL   Effective July 3, 1971, the rule applies to all finished articles of textile wearing apparel. Each article must have a permanently attached tag or label which clearly states instructions for its care and maintenance. These instructions must be legible for the reasonable life of the article. When a positive statement such as "hand wash" is used, the negative, "do not machine wash," need not be used. If the article can be ironed or dry cleaned by any normal procedure, it is unnecessary to state this information unless there are restrictions, in which case explanations such as "do not iron," "use cool iron," or "do not bleach" must be included (Figure 5-9). Table 5-1 shows the wording for labels developed by the American Apparel Manufacturers Association for use on items produced in this country.

PIECE GOODS   The 1971 rule also applies to piece goods; when sold, they must be accompanied by a label which

FIGURE 5-9 *Labels stitched into outerwear produced by one American manufacturer. All needed information is provided, including a warning against use of bleach. (The University of Mississippi, courtesy of Misty Harbor Ltd.)*

TABLE 5-1 *Consumer Care Guide for Apparel (Made in the United States)*

	When Label Reads:	It Means:
Machine Washable	Machine wash	Wash, bleach, dry, and press by any customary method including commercial laundering and dry cleaning
	Home launder only	Same as above but do not use commercial laundering
	No chlorine bleach	Do not use chlorine bleach. Oxygen bleach may be used
	No bleach	Do not use any type of bleach
	Cold wash / Cold rinse	Use cold water from tap or cold washing machine setting
	Warm wash / Warm rinse	Use warm water or warm washing machine setting
	Hot wash	Use hot water or hot washing machine setting
	No spin	Remove wash load before final machine spin cycle
	Delicate cycle / Gentle cycle	Use appropriate machine setting; otherwise wash by hand
	Durable press cycle / Permanent press cycle	Use appropriate machine setting; otherwise use warm wash, cold rinse, and short spin cycle
	Wash separately	Wash alone or with like colors
Nonmachine Washing	Hand wash	Launder only by hand in lukewarm (hand comfortable) water. May be bleached. May be drycleaned
	Hand wash only	Same as above, but do not dryclean
	Hand wash separately	Hand wash alone or with like colors
	No bleach	Do not use bleach
	Damp wipe	Surface clean with damp cloth or sponge
Home Drying	Tumble dry	Dry in tumble dryer at specified setting—high, medium, low or no heat
	Tumble dry, remove promptly	Same as above, but in absence of cool-down cycle remove at once when tumbling stops
	Drip dry	Hang wet and allow to dry with hand shaping only
	Line dry	Hang damp and allow to dry
	No wring / No twist	Hang dry, drip dry, or dry flat only. Handle to prevent wrinkles and distortion
	Dry flat	Lay garment on flat surface
	Block to dry	Maintain original size and shape while drying

Part Two / Care

	When Label Reads:	It Means:
Ironing or Pressing	Cool iron	Set iron at lowest setting
	Warm iron	Set iron at medium setting
	Hot iron	Set iron at hot setting
	Do not iron	Do not iron or press with heat
	Steam iron	Iron or press with steam
	Iron damp	Dampen garment before ironing
Miscellaneous	Dry clean only	Garment should be dry cleaned only, including self-service
	Professionally dry clean only	Do not use self-service dry cleaning
	No dry clean	Use recommended care instructions. No dry-cleaning materials to be used

This Care Guide was produced by the Consumer Affairs Committee, American Apparel Manufacturers Association, and is based on the Voluntary Guide of the Textile Industry Advisory Committee for Consumer Interests. *The American Apparel Manufacturers Association, Inc.*

clearly explains care and maintenance instructions for normal household methods. The mechanics for distributing labels to purchasers of piece goods are a problem for each seller to resolve, but the rule requires that each consumer be given a care instruction label for each length of fabric purchased.

Most bolts of fabric now carry a number (usually red within a red triangle) that is a code number for the corresponding care label to be given to the customer. The care label should be sewn into the completed garment, for later reference. The wording used on these labels is shown in Figure 5–10. For typical instructions on yarn, see Figure 5–11.

UPHOLSTERY FABRICS In 1969, the furniture industry adopted a standard coding system to indicate the correct cleaning method for various types of upholstery fabrics. Many manufacturers provide this information with each piece of upholstered furniture, and the consumer should remember to check all labels and tags for these instructions. The hangtags or pamphlets that give these details should be kept and consulted before cleaning is done. At present, some manufacturers use the cleanability code in Table 5–2.

Extensive work is being done by the National Association of Furniture Manufacturers in Washington toward industry-wide adoption of standards for fabric durability.

5 / *Consumer Protection*

The proposed plan, which presumably will work on a self-regulatory basis, is for a coding system in which specified letters would identify fabrics that were intended for heavy-duty use, for medium-duty use, for light use, or delicate use. It appears that the letters now used for the cleanability coding will be combined with the letters for the durability coding.

TABLE 5-2 *The Cleanability Coding Used by Some American Furniture Manufacturers*

CODE	METHOD
W	Use only the **foam** from a water-based cleaning agent, such as a mild dishwashing detergent. Put 2 tsp. of Ivory, Palmolive or a similar detergent in a blender with 1/2 cup of water or mix in a bowl with an egg beater to achieve maximum foam. Apply this dry foam with a sponge or soft bristle brush over a larger area than that which has been soiled to avoid leaving rings.
S	Use a mild, water-free solvent dry cleaning product such as Energine, Carbona or Renuzit. Follow the instructions carefully. Keep the room well ventilated. Clean as large an area as possible around the soiled section to avoid leaving rings. Do not use any products containing Carbon Tetrachloride as it is highly toxic.
WS	Either of the above cleaning methods can be used.
X	Neither of the above cleaning methods should be used. A fabric coded X should only be vacuumed or brushed lightly to remove soil.

Source: Courtesy of Kroehler Manufacturing Co.

Flammability

After an increasing number of deaths and personal injuries resulting from flammable textile products had focused national concern on product safety, on June 30, 1952, Congress passed the Flammable Fabrics Act, which outlawed the manufacture or sale of wearing apparel that was so highly flammable as to be dangerous when worn. This law was inadequate because the standards it set forth eliminated from the market only those articles of clothing that were explosively flammable, while it exempted other fabrics that were dangerously flammable when ignited, even though they might not support spontaneous combustion. In 1967, amendments to the original act provided for new and more effective flammability standards for clothing and other household fabric items. Flammability standards for carpets were enacted in 1971.

Studies conducted by the Department of Health, Education and Welfare and released in 1971 estimated that annually there were still 3,000 to 5,000 deaths and 150,000 to

FIGURE 5-10 *The Triangle Care Labeling Plan developed for use on fabrics.* (Developed by Textile Distributors Association Inc. and The National Retail Merchants Association)

FIGURE 5-11 *Laundering instructions similar to those shown here appear on the inside of wrappers on yarns sold for hand-knitting and other handwork. (Reproduced by courtesy of the Educational Bureau, Coats & Clark Inc.)*

LAUNDERING INSTRUCTIONS

This article made of 100% DuPont Orlon® Acrylic Bicomponent Fiber is ideally suited for automatic laundering. A made up article actually stretches when wet to allow for better washing action and then automatically blocks itself when completely dry.

1. MACHINE WASHING AND DRYING

Machine wash on "gentle" or Synthetic setting using warm water and any detergent which does NOT contain bleaching agents. A small amount of fabric softener added to the final rinse will help keep your articles soft and static-free. Machine dry at regular setting. ALWAYS MACHINE DRY AFTER MACHINE WASHING.

2. HAND WASHING AND DRYING

Wash gently in warm water using any detergent which does NOT contain bleaching agents. Always support the article during washing and rinsing and when removing it from cold rinse, bunch together and lift out in both hands. Squeeze out excess water, roll inside a towel, twist and squeeze again while in the towel. Spread to dry on a flat surface, bunch into shape and allow to dry thoroughly before moving article. NEVER DRY ARTICLE IN DIRECT SUNLIGHT AND NEVER HANG ARTICLE TO DRY.

3. PLEASE NOTE:

Orlon® must be absolutely dry to insure automatic blocking. If stretched during wear or washing, wet thoroughly, squeeze and tumble dry thoroughly in home or coin operated dryer to reshape.

250,000 injuries from burns associated with flammable fabrics in the United States. The clothing items most frequently involved in fabric burns were underwear, nightclothes, shirts, blouses, and trousers, with bedding, upholstery, and rugs chiefly responsible among household items.[3]

---

3. U.S. Department of Health, Education and Welfare, *Studies of Deaths, Injuries and Economic Losses Resulting from Accidental Burning of Products, Fabrics or Related Materials through June 1970*, U.S. Government Printing Office, Washington, D.C., 1971, pp. 2–3.

Testing specifications have been developed for each textile product, and products which do not meet the legal standards must so state on the label. These standards state that fabrics either must contain fibers that are inherently fire-retardant or must be made chemically flame-retardant. Fibers differ in their degree of combustibility and may be divided into four groups, ranging from highly combustible to noncombustible fibers:

1. Highly combustible fibers include cotton, rayon, acetate, and acrylic.
2. Fibers that ignite slowly, melt, and drip include nylon, polyester, and olefin.
3. Fire-retardant fibers are wool, modacrylic, and saran.
4. Noncombustible fibers include asbestos, glass, metal, graphite, and carbon.

Cotton and rayon fibers are the most widely used fibers for clothing and household items and therefore are most often involved in fires. However, they are the easiest to treat with a durable flame-retardant finish. A temporary finish can be made at home and applied by the consumer from a solution of 30 percent boric acid and 70 percent borax (as described in Chapter 3).

Research conducted at the U.S. Department of Agriculture, Southern Regional Research Laboratories led to the discovery of tetrakis (hydroxymethyl) phosphonium chloride (THPC), which was perfected for use as an effective flame-retardant finish for cotton fabrics. Fabrics treated with THPC, when held in a flame, form a tough, black char, which keeps the fiber structure and retains some strength. This char is crucial in that it not only protects but also insulates the body, thus reducing the possibility of skin damage from burns and intense heat.[4]

Recent amendments to the Flammable Fabrics Act extend its provisions to include home furnishings and fabric, and to amend provisions on wearing apparel. They also prohibit introduction or movement in interstate commerce of such items of wearing apparel and fabrics that are so highly flammable as to be dangerous if worn by individuals or used for other purposes. The act also requires the establishment of

(1) "PROPERLY CONSTRUCTED FABRICS OF SEF® MODACRYLIC FIBER WILL EXTINGUISH THEMSELVES WHEN THE SOURCE OF IGNITION IS REMOVED."

(2) "GUARANTEED FOR ONE FULL YEAR'S NORMAL WEAR, REFUND OR REPLACEMENT WHEN RETURNED WITH TAG AND SALES SLIP TO MONSANTO."

FIGURE 5-12 *The hangtag used by one fiber manufacturer to inform consumers that the garment meets flammability standards. The manufacturer stipulates that statements (1) and (2), shown here under the tag, must be used.* (Courtesy of Monsanto Textiles Company. ® Registered Trademarks of Monsanto Company)

---

4. George L. Drake, Jr., and Leon H. Chance, "Flame-Retardant Fabrics Safeguard Your Life," *Science for Better Living*. The Yearbook of Agriculture 1968, U.S. Department of Agriculture, U.S. Government Printing Office, Washington, D.C., pp. 279–282.

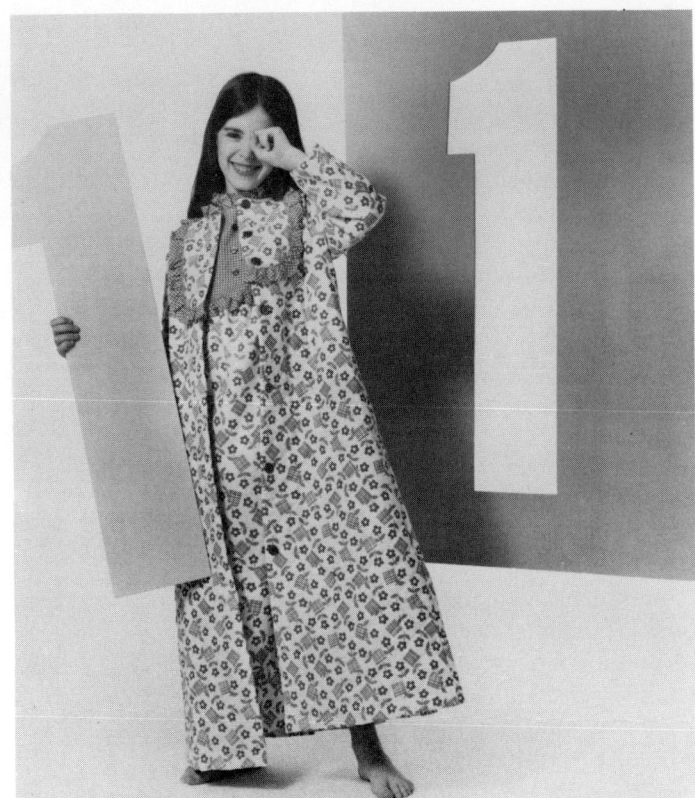

FIGURE 5–13 *This cotton flannelette robe and pajama set has a FIRE STOP flame-retardant finish, for safety, as required by law.* (Courtesy of Cotton Incorporated)

appropriate flammability standards that products must meet.[5] (See Figure 5–12.)

Flame-retardancy standards for children's sleepwear now require that all pajamas, nightgowns, robes, and fabric intended for use by infants and small children pass a flame test developed at the National Bureau of Standards (Figure 5–13). Garments that do not meet these standards are not to be manufactured. The tests require that the garment must retain its fire-retardant character through at least fifty test washings. All sleepwear for children (sizes 0–14) is covered.

Other similar regulations apply to home furnishings. All small carpets and rugs under twenty-four square feet must either meet the requirements or carry a warning label. Car-

---

5. U.S., Congress, House, Committee on Interstate and Foreign Commerce, and U.S., Congress, Senate, Committee on Labor and Public Welfare, *Compilation of Selected Public Health Laws*, U.S. Government Printing Office, Washington, D.C., 1973, p. 237.

pets larger than twenty-four square feet must meet flammability requirements. A proposed flammability standard is being considered by the Consumer Product Safety Commission. Some states have passed laws requiring use of flame-retardant fabrics in motels, hotels, and institutional residences.

Currently, the Consumer Product Safety Commission is considering a broad new flammability standard that would cover all sizes of dresses, shirts, pants, nightgowns, robes, and pajamas. The question has been raised whether the additional cost of the clothing to the consumer would be offset by the additional safety the flame-retardant materials would provide. Consumers' freedom of choice also must be considered, since they might have to pay at least 25 percent more for this flammability protection.[6]

CARE INSTRUCTIONS

Care instructions on flame-resistant textiles must be followed strictly, or the products may become highly flammable. Since the effect of flame-retardant finishes is counteracted by soap and hard-water mineral deposits on the fabric, often such products are labeled with a caution: "Do not use soap. Launder with phosphate detergent." This may present a problem for the consumer, which is discussed in the next chapter.

Study Questions

1. What are the major provisions of each of these acts or requirements: Textile Fiber Products Identification, Permanent Care Labeling, Flammable Fabrics, Wool Products Labeling, and Fur Products Labeling?
2. How do permanent care labeling requirements differ for ready-made clothing and yard goods?
3. Does the passage of such acts infringe on the rights of individuals? Explain.
4. What is the Federal Trade Commission and what does it do?
5. Can you think of other types of legislation related to labeling that should be passed to help consumers in their buying and use of textile products?
6. How would you go about getting new laws passed that relate to textile product labeling?

---

6. See Man-Made Fiber Producers Association, Inc., *Focus on Man-Made Fibers*, no. 1 (Fall 1974), for additional information.

Suggested Activities

1. Make a trip to fabric and department stores. Look for labels on textile products and observe the information included on each.
2. Write a news story for the local or college paper explaining the provisions of one or more of the textile laws.
3. Take a group of high school girls (such as a 4-H Club group) on a trip to a fabric store. Show them how to read and interpret labels.
4. Prepare a radio or television program for a local station on one or more of the textile laws as they relate to consumer protection.
5. Make a survey of customers in some type of textile product store (such as furniture, clothing, or fabric) to determine how many are aware of textile laws and how they can be of benefit to consumers.
6. Make a survey of merchants in your area to see whether they comply with labeling requirements.

Chapter 6

Laundering and Stain Removal

INFORMATION for fabric care appears on labels permanently attached to garments and other textile products. Care labels are provided by retailers to accompany yard goods, and these labels should be sewn into the finished garment. Directions for care must be followed as closely as possible, in all instances. In many cases, using different wash cycles in machines or different ironing temperatures will damage the garment permanently (Figures 6–2 and 6–3).

In addition to the specific instructions on the labels, some general hints may be helpful to consumers. Fabrics labeled machine-washable are also hand-washable. Chlorine bleach is not safe to use on all fabrics. White fabrics may become yellow when fabric softener is used. Fabrics with special finishes are more resistant to soiling than other fabrics, but when a stain does penetrate the finish, it is more difficult to remove.

Examine all articles of clothing for stains before washing, and loosen oil and grease stains. This is done by rubbing detergent solution into the soiled areas and letting the garment stand about fifteen minutes before it is washed.

 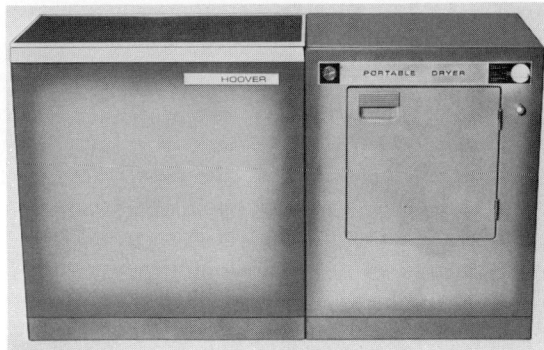

FIGURE 6-1 *Home laundering is not what it used to be. Left: a 1914 arrangement for washing; clothes were line-dried. Right: a 1975 washer and dryer.* (Left, J. C. Allen & Son; right, courtesy of the Hoover Company)

Sort laundry according to any special treatment the various items should receive. Two general groups might be those to be machine washed and those to be washed by hand. Items for the machine might be sorted into smaller piles: white and colored; heavy and light soil; delicate and regular agitation; hot and warm water.

Several wash groups may be dried together, so long as the drying temperature is appropriate for all items included in the load. As an economy measure, all items that can be safely washed and dried together should be so done.

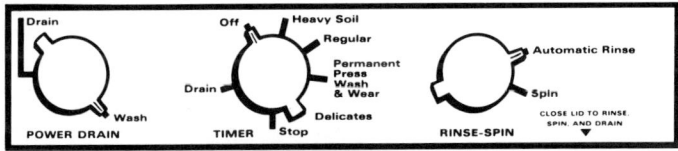

FIGURE 6-2 *The dial settings on a portable spin-dryer washing machine, in the correct position before starting. Note the timer choices, for different types of clothing.* (Courtesy of the Hoover Company)

FIGURE 6-3 *The different settings available on a modern electric clothes dryer.* (Courtesy of the Hoover Company)

6 / Laundering and Stain Removal

Laundry Products

SOAPS AND DETERGENTS

Soaps and detergents make water penetrate soiled fabric more easily, loosen dirt from the fabrics, and then suspend the dirt so that it will not be redeposited on fabrics. Detergents are specially built to be used in hard water; soaps may react with minerals in hard water to form an insoluble film, which causes clothing to look dingy gray or dull. For most home laundering, all-purpose detergents may be used for the regular family wash and usually may be used on all washable fabrics (Figures 6–4 to 6–6). Light-duty detergents are suitable only for delicate and lightly soiled fabrics.

The amount of detergent or soap needed depends on the hardness of the water, the amount of soil in the clothing, the load size, water volume, and water temperature. Recommended appropriate amounts are usually given on the box; they should be measured with a standard measuring cup.

Sometimes all-purpose detergents are classified by their sudsing action. Normal-sudsing detergents provide lasting suds on the surface of the water when a sufficient amount is used and they can be used in all kinds of top-loading washers. Intermediate-sudsing detergents provide a lower level of suds, can be used in all top-loading machines, and are especially appropriate for use in washers that are sensitive to suds. Low-sudsing detergents are designed specifically for use in front-loading tumbler-type automatic washers, but can also be used in all top-loaders. When used in the correct amounts, most all-purpose detergents will work satisfactorily in all water temperatures, but all detergents, including cold-water types, give better cleaning results in warm water than in cold.

PRETREATMENTS

Some garments with stains and soiled areas may need treatment before being laundered with an all-purpose detergent. This is more likely to be the case with garments that have minimum-care or permanent-press finishes containing resin, if oily or greasy stains are involved. Items such as men's work clothes and children's play clothes should be inspected for such stains and treated with one of the various stain removers available. Information on the box or can should be checked, since the suitability of these products generally depends on the type of stain involved. Instructions for use should be followed carefully for best results (Figure 6–7).

FIGURE 6–4 *A heavy-duty liquid detergent, for home laundry use.* (Courtesy of Lever Brothers Company)

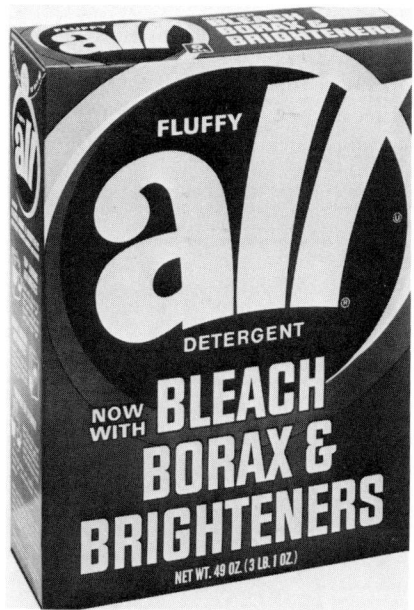

FIGURE 6–5 *This detergent for home laundry use contains bleach, borax, and brighteners.* (Courtesy of Lever Brothers Company)

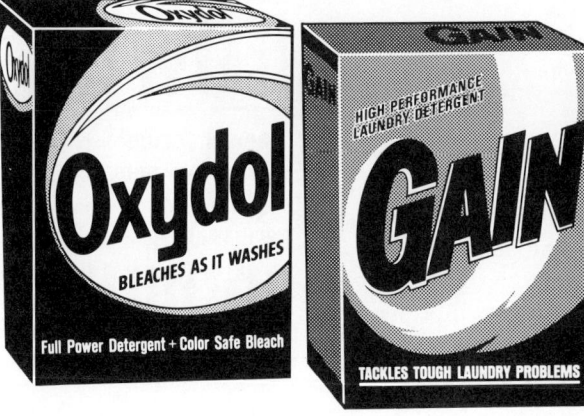

FIGURE 6-6 *These two detergents serve particular purposes. Oxydol contains an oxygen bleach; Gain contains enzymes.* (Courtesy of the Procter & Gamble Company)

Enzyme products are used as a presoak because they can break down certain oils and stains, making removal easier during washing. They do not take the place of detergents, but should be used with them; some detergents contain enzymes. These products are intended primarily for soaking fabrics with heavy soils or stubborn stains, before washing. Enzyme products help remove body soil around collars and cuff lines, and they are effective in removing protein stains like blood, egg, baby formula, and other food stains. They are especially good at removing fresh fruit and grass stains and work well on many stains that have been previously "set." They are also effective in removing the yellowish or dingy gray tinge some white fabrics develop. Enzymes are safe for all washable fabrics, including all fibers and colors. However, while the enzyme itself is safe for colored fabrics, the prolonged exposure to water may cause sensitive dyes to "bleed."

BLEACHES

Two basic types of bleach are available for home use. Chlorine, which is available in both liquid and dry forms, whitens, removes stains, disinfects, and deodorizes. It is the least expensive type but cannot be used on all washable fibers or colors. It may safely be used on washable white and bleach-fast colored cottons, linens, nylon, polyester, durable-press finishes, and acrylics. It should not be used on silks, wool, mohair, and spandex, or on garments with a permanent-press finish. Oxygen-type bleach, although usually less effective than chlorine, satisfactorily handles light-duty bleaching jobs (Figure 6–8). It may be used on all washable fibers and

FIGURE 6-7 *A pretreatment stain remover, for use before laundering with an all-purpose detergent.* (Courtesy of Texize Chemical Company)

most washable colors and works best in hot water or in a long soak. When using bleaches of either type the consumer should always read package directions thoroughly and measure the recommended amount accurately.

STARCH

Starch helps to restore the original body or crispness to fabrics, gives a fresh, smooth appearance, and aids in soil removal. Aerosol starch, available in a container with a spray device (Figure 6–9), may be sprayed onto fabrics while the garment is being ironed and is ideal for touch-up jobs like collars and cuffs. It is the most convenient and most expensive of the starches.

Liquid starch is a precooked, concentrated starch solution that is mixed with water before being used. It is more convenient than the kind of dry starches that come as precooked flakes to be mixed with cold water and that require no cooking before use. And liquid starch gives a more flexible finish than regular dry starch, which is uncooked and available in lump, cube, or powdered form. While regular dry starch is the most economical, it is the least convenient form of starch, since it must be mixed with hot water or cooked before using.

All starches should be used according to the directions on the container. Starching may be done in a large container or in the washer. Washer starching ensures an even distribution of starch but it is practical only for a large quantity of clothes that require about the same amount of stiffness.

FABRIC FINISH

Fabric finish may also be purchased in a spray container ready for use while ironing. It is especially good for restoring body and freshness. It has a lower solids content than aerosol starches and is less apt to stick to the iron or to scorch. It gives a finish that is slightly less stiff and more flexible than starches.

Temperatures

WATER

The water temperature used for laundering fabrics is important because it affects the cleaning, wrinkling, dye stability, and durability of fabric finishes. Frequently hot, warm, or cold

FIGURE 6–8 *A bleach for home use that is advertised as safe for permanent-press fabrics.* (Courtesy of Gold Seal Company)

FIGURE 6–9 *A spray-type starch, for use while ironing garments.* (Courtesy of Boyle-Midway)

temperatures are recommended for various fabrics. Hot water, usually registering 140°F. or above, is recommended for use on sturdy whites, colorfast items, diapers, and heavily soiled durable-press and wash-and-wear finishes. Hot water gives the quickest and best cleaning for fabrics and it is the best sanitizer, but it is not suitable for use on all kinds of fabrics.

Warm water around 100°F. is recommended for colored fabrics that are not colorfast, silks, wools, durable-press and wash-and-wear finishes, nylon, acrylic, polyester, and other manufactured fiber fabrics. It reduces fading, preserves the durable-press finish, tends to reduce wrinkling of fabrics containing nylon and polyester, and minimizes shrinkage of knits and wools. It is the temperature most often used for handwashing.

Cold water, 80°F. or cooler, is good for washing extra-sensitive colors and very lightly soiled items and for rinsing durable-press and other easy-care fabrics. Special detergents may be needed (Figure 6–10). While cold water does not give the same cleaning results as hot or warm water, it minimizes wrinkling and fading of colors and saves the cost of hot water.

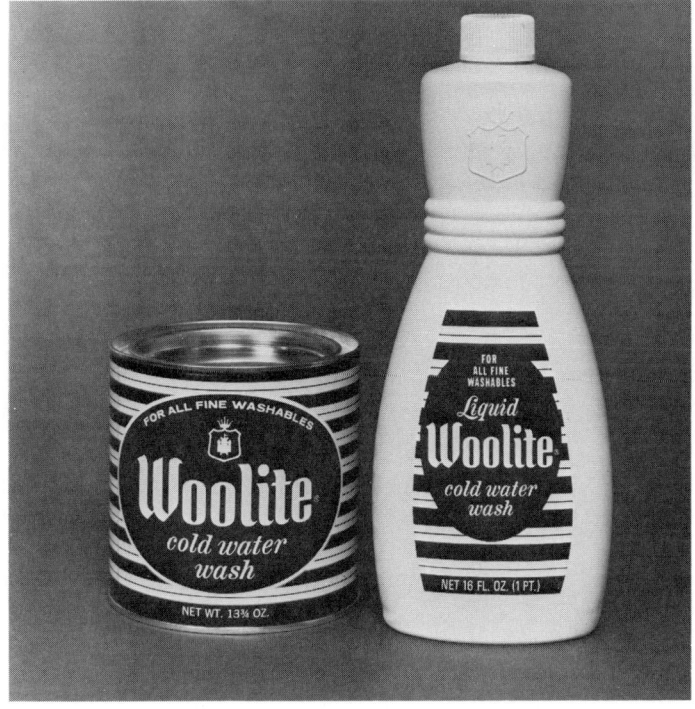

FIGURE 6-10 *A product that is used by many people for hand washing wool or other delicate fibers in cold water.* (Courtesy of Boyle-Midway)

DRYING

Clothing may be dried in an automatic dryer, hung on a line either outside or indoors, or spread out flat. Tumble drying implies the purchase of the equipment and space for placing it, and thus increases the cost of care of textile products. However, it saves time and effort, makes items soft, smoothes them out, and is not dependent upon the weather.

Outdoor line drying is dependent upon the weather and often results in products that are stiffer and sometimes even dirtier, in industrial areas, but line-dried clothing usually smells fresh. Indoor line drying usually takes longer and without adequate space it is an inconvenient method. Because of the lack of air movement, textile products tend to be stiff when dried indoors.

While flat drying may be a more appropriate way to dry certain items, such as wool sweaters, items dry slowly and require more space.

Stain and Spot Removal

Stain and spot removal is likely to be more effective if the proper treatment is given promptly, before the stain dries. Test the fabric for colorfastness in the seam or other inconspicuous section before applying the remover to the affected area. If a garment needs overall cleaning, it is better not to treat isolated stains, since the clean area may show up conspicuously by contrast.

If the origin of the stain is unknown, a little cool water and cleaning fluid may be tried. First sponge with cool water, let dry, then apply cleaning fluid. Always work from the underside of the stain to avoid forcing the stain through the fabric. Stains may be identified by observing their appearance, odor, location, or feel.

Some general stains may be removed by using commercially prepared removers, such as Energine (manufactured by d-Con Co.) and Renuzit (manufactured by Renuzit), or hydrogen peroxide. Oil and grease may be removed by Carbona (manufactured by Carbona), and light greasy stains with perchloroethylene and trichloroethylene. Glycerine can be used on ink, soft drink, and alcoholic beverage stains. Acetone removes nail polish effectively but should *not* be used on acetate fabrics. Methods of removing other types of stain are given in Table 6-1. The directions in the table apply to stain removal from white and colorfast cotton, linen, nylon, rayon, acrylic, and modacrylic, or blends of these with cotton and linen. Never use a chlorine or chlorine-type bleach on silk, wool, or acetate. When bleaching rayons, be sure the article is 100 percent rayon.

TABLE 6-1 *Stain Removal*

Type of stain	Method of removal
Any unknown stain	Sponge with cold or lukewarm water on washable fabrics or use a commercial spot remover
Adhesive tape	Sponge with a commercial spot remover
Alcoholic beverages	Soak fresh stain in cool water, then launder; soak old stain in bleach, then launder
Blood and meat juices	Soak in cold salt solution, rinse; if stain remains, soak in bleach, then launder
Butter and margarine	Dust both sides of stained fabric with talcum powder; leave overnight, then launder in warm suds; if stain remains after drying, sponge with cleaning fluid or spot remover and launder
Candle wax	Rub stain with ice and gently scrape with dull knife; then place fabric between clean white blotters or several layers of facial tissue and press with warm iron
Candy	Sponge with clear cool water, then launder; if stain remains, soak in bleach and rinse thoroughly
Carbon paper, pencil marks	Rub detergent into dampened stain and rinse well; if stain is not removed, put a few drops of ammonia on stain and repeat detergent treatment; rinse well
Chewing gum	Harden gum with ice, then remove excess by scraping with dull knife; sponge with cleaning fluid and launder
Chocolate or cocoa	Soak in cleaning fluid, then launder; if stain remains, soak in bleach and rinse thoroughly
Coffee, tea	If mixed with cream, sponge with cleaning fluid, pour hot water over stain, then launder; if stain remains, soak in bleach, rinse thoroughly
	If beverage only, pour hot water over stain; if stain remains, soak in bleach, then launder
Duplicating fluid (Ditto), indelible pencil marks	Sponge stain with alcohol; if stain remains, rub detergent into dampened stain, wash, and rinse well; if needed, use a bleach

TABLE 6-1 (*cont.*)

Type of stain	Method of removal
Dye stain (light dye transfer, as in mixed wash)	Launder; if not completely removed, soak in bleach and rinse thoroughly; if dye stain is heavy, bleach may not remove it. *On white fabrics only*, use a packaged color remover
Egg	Remove excess with dull knife; sponge with cleaning fluid; launder in warm water (hot water makes stain difficult to remove)
Fingernail polish	Sponge stain with acetone or nail polish remover and launder; if stain persists, sponge with rubbing alcohol to which a few drops of ammonia have been added; launder in hot water and detergent; *do not use acetone on acetate fabrics*
Fruit juice	Rinse fresh stain with cold water; soak in bleach and rinse thoroughly; for old stain, pour boiling water through stain; if stain remains, soak in bleach and rinse thoroughly
Grass	Sponge with cleaning fluid; rub liquid detergent or a paste of soap or detergent into fabric, launder; if stain remains, soak in bleach, rinse thoroughly
Grease, tar	Remove excess with dull knife, sponge with cleaning fluid; launder in hot water; if stain remains, soak in bleach and rinse thoroughly (alcohol may remove some stains)
Indelible pencil	Soak in alcohol and launder; if stain remains, soak in bleach, rinse thoroughly
Ink	For water-soluble ink, soak in warm water, launder; for permanent ink, sponge with cleaning fluid; if stain remains, soak in bleach and launder; if permanent ink has iron base, a yellow spot will be left; remove spot by sponging with oxalic acid solution; rinse thoroughly
Ink (ball-point pen)	Pour denatured alcohol through stain; rub in petroleum jelly, sponge with nonflammable dry-cleaning solvent; soak in detergent solution, launder with detergent and bleach with product safe for fabric; or saturate with hair spray, then wash in detergent

TABLE 6-1 (*cont.*)

Type of stain	Method of removal
Iodine	Sponge with diluted ammonia and launder
Lipstick, rouge	Work petroleum jelly or lard into stain, sponge with cleaning fluid, launder; if stain remains, soak in bleach, rinse thoroughly
Mercurochrome	Soak in bleach, launder; or soak in alcohol, then in vinegar solution, repeat alcohol soak, and launder
Mildew	Launder; soak in bleach, rinse thoroughly (deeply grown mildew is almost impossible to remove)
Milk, cream, ice cream	Soak in warm water, launder; if spot remains after drying, remove grease with cleaning fluid
Mustard	Launder; if stain remains, soak in bleach, rinse thoroughly
Paint	Soak in paint remover, rub out as much as possible, launder; rubbing in petroleum jelly or lard may soften paint
Perspiration	Launder; if stain remains, soak in bleach and rinse thoroughly
Rust	Sponge with oxalic acid solution, launder; or add 4 teaspoons cream of tartar to 1 pint of water, heat to just below boiling, immerse stain in solution until removed and rinse thoroughly; for small rust spots, place stained portion of fabric over pan of boiling water, squeeze lemon juice directly on stain, and rinse thoroughly; *do not use chlorine bleach*
Salad dressing	Apply paste of baking soda to stained area, launder in cool water; if stain remains after fabric is dry, sponge with cleaning fluid and launder again
Scorch marks	If fabric has not been damaged, light scorch may wash out; on heavier scorching, cover stain with cloth that has been dampened with hydrogen peroxide and rinse well
Shoe polish	Apply detergent directly to dampened stain, rub in well until outline of stain is gone, then rinse well; if needed, use bleach and rinse well
Soot	Brush spot; work dry starch over stained area, brush off; sponge with liquid detergent and launder

TABLE 6-1 (cont.)

Type of stain	Method of removal
Tobacco	Sponge stain promptly with cold water or soak in cold water for 30 minutes, or longer if necessary; rub detergent into any remaining stain, rinse; if stain persists, use bleach, launder with detergent and hot water; if color of fabric has been changed, sponge with ammonia or vinegar and rinse well
Water spots	Soak in vinegar solution, rinse, and launder
Yellowing from chlorine bleach	Rinse fabric thoroughly with water and use commercial color remover according to directions

Concentration of Solutions

Stain-removal agents mentioned in this table should be used in the following concentrations:

Alcohol	1 part denatured alcohol or rubbing alcohol to 2 parts water
Ammonia	2 tablespoons household ammonia per gallon water
Bleach	Use at stain-removal strength recommended on container
Cleaning fluid	Any accepted brand of commercial cleaner used at full strength
Oxalic acid	(May be purchased at drugstore) 1 tablespoon per cup of water
Salt solution	2 tablespoons per cup of water
Vinegar solution	$\frac{1}{4}$ cup per quart of water

An Environmental Concern

No chapter dealing with laundering and laundry products would be complete without consideration of the problems that have arisen in connection with certain detergent products. The rate and extent of pollution of the nation's waters have become matters of concern to many individuals. The problem has developed because cities and industries dispose of untreated or inadequately treated wastes into the available rivers and streams, impairing the quality of the water. Such practices have resulted in an obvious and continuing deterioration of the nation's lakes and other bodies of water, to the point of drastically reducing their usefulness to humans as sources of fish and water. This situation has accelerated since 1940, when phosphate-built detergents were introduced. Phosphates in the water promote growth of algae and other aquatic plants, which eventually decay and create additional pollution in the water.

Waste-water treatment plants are of three types. Primary treatment plants remove very little phosphate and other substances from the water; secondary plants remove more, but not all. Tertiary plants, which completely remove hazardous substances of all types, are extremely expensive to build and require considerable construction time. Development of plans for and construction of tertiary plants adequate for the country, or even sections of it, would involve millions of dollars and many years. Further, while phosphates do account for a certain amount of water pollution, chemical fertilizers and animal wastes also contribute to it. Thus, construction of tertiary treatment plants would make a significant improvement in water quality but could not provide a full solution.

A subcommittee was appointed to study the problem, and the conclusion presented to the House Committee on Government Operations was that elimination of phosphates from detergents would bring about some significant reduction in the phosphorus pollution of water. The results of the committee report led to the recommendations by the House Committee for the immediate reduction and eventual elimination of phosphates in detergents, the education of consumers to choose washing products with the least amount of polluting ingredients, and a prompt issuing of regulations by the Federal Trade Commission requiring detergent package labels to include a list of ingredients with information about the use of detergents in soft and hard water. An additional recommendation was for the implementation of testing on nitrilotriacetate (NTA), to prove that this product would be an environmentally promising substitute for phosphates in detergents.[1]

After the hearings on phosphate detergents and water pollution, the Environmental Protection Agency established nationwide standards for quality water management, which included four major provisions: defining the uses to be made of the interstate water supply; developing criteria to protect those uses; implementing protection plans; and enforcing

---

1. U.S., Congress, House, Committee on Government Operations, *Phosphates in Detergents and the Eutrophication of America's Waters: Hearings before a Subcommittee*, 91st Cong., December 15-16, 1969. U.S. Government Printing Office, Washington, D.C., 1970.

these plans. The standards also contained an antidegradation statement to protect existing high-quality waters.[2]

Experiments were then begun to develop a satisfactory detergent product that was free of phosphates. Many of the test products possessed a high degree of alkalinity, which would be undesirable for reasons of safety, and the high carbonate content of many products caused stiffening and/or roughening of fabrics (due to the deposits of insoluble calcium and magnesium carbonates which accumulated after several washings). Sodium carbonate had relatively no effect in improving the performance of the detergents and NTA use had to be discontinued because it was potentially harmful to humans. The products that did prove satisfactory were sodium acetate, sodium citrate, and sodium gluconate. It was concluded that phosphate-free detergents could be developed and made available for general consumer use.[3] While no national laws were passed regarding the continued use of phosphates in the manufacturing of detergents, many states passed laws banning their sale.

One important consideration which has evolved from the unresolved problem of phosphate-containing detergents concerns textile products with flame-resistant finishes. The effect of these finishes can be counteracted by use of soap in laundering, and by hard-water mineral deposits which may result from use of soap. Therefore, many products with flame-resistant finishes are labeled with a caution: "Do not use soap. Launder with phosphate detergent." Use of phosphates is essential, to allow the finish to remain effective. For households in areas that have banned the sale of phosphate detergents in order to lessen water pollution problems, the dilemma is not resolved at present.[4]

The American Home Economics Association is concerned about both types of safety needs to ensure optimum health and welfare of consumers. In 1973, the association passed a

---

2. U.S., Environmental Protection Agency, *Water Quality Standards Criteria Digest, A Compilation of Federal/State Criteria on Phosphates*, Environmental Protection Agency, Washington, D.C., 1972.

3. U.S., Environmental Protection Agency, *Technical Evaluation of Phosphate-free Home Laundry Detergents*, Water Pollution Control Research Series 16080 DVF, U.S. Government Printing Office, Washington, D.C. (February 1972), 54.

4. William L. Mauldin and Marianne S. Beeson, "Reading the Labels on Apparel and Household Textiles," in *Handbook for the Home*, Yearbook of Agriculture 1973, U.S. Department of Agriculture, U.S. Government Printing Office, Washington, D.C., 1973, pp. 311–315; *Journal of Home Economics* (September 1973), 47.

resolution stating that "national, state and local associations support the principle of the right of consumer choice in purchasing cleaning products and further support the purposes of the Clean Water Act and encourage efforts toward removal of all algae growth producing nutrients through improved waste treatment facilities."[5]

Study Questions

1. Explain the reasons for using detergents, enzyme products, and bleaches.
2. On what basis should clothing be sorted into loads for washing?
3. If clothing becomes dingy gray or dull in appearance after several washings, what might be the cause? What could be done to prevent this from happening in the future?
4. What determines the amount of detergent that should be used in washing a load of clothing?
5. What is the difference between high-sudsing and low-sudsing detergents? When should each be used?
6. What are the two basic types of bleach available for home use? Give an example of how each one may safely be used.
7. How does water temperature affect laundering of garments?
8. What guidelines may one use to identify stains in clothing?
9. Name seven different agents that may be used to remove stains.
10. Why do garments with flame-retardant finishes sometimes have instructions to avoid the use of soap and to use phosphate detergents?

Suggested Activities

1. Select and cut swatches from five or six different pieces of fabric. Stain each with several substances such as ketchup, mayonnaise, ink, lipstick, fruit juice. Test the various removal recommendations for each to see which stains are removed most easily from each fabric swatch.
2. Prepare a basic stain-removal kit (that would be ready for use in case of an emergency).

---

5. *Journal of Home Economics* (September 1973), 47.

3. Experiment with the effect of both oxygen and chlorine bleaches on fabrics made from various fibers such as nylon, spandex, wool, polyester, and cotton.
4. Cut swatches of white fabric such as nylon, unbleached muslin, polyester, and wash-and-wear cotton. Soak them in a diluted solution of chlorine for about an hour, then rinse. Repeat five or six times. Observe any color changes that take place.
5. Cut swatches of cotton, polyester, and cotton/polyester blend fabric. Press each on a low temperature setting, then a medium setting, then a high temperature setting. Observe each swatch as the temperature increases.
6. Make a file identifying the type of care appropriate for your clothing. Prepare an index card for each item, noting laundering instructions, drying temperatures, and pressing tips.

Part Three
Selection

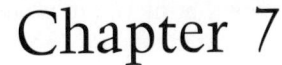

Textile Consumption

THE SOCIAL, ECONOMIC, and political conditions of a country and the resulting changes in its society are reflected in its industries, and, overall, all four factors interact. Thus, in the early days of the United States, people lived comparatively simply and the major efforts of most citizens were devoted to making a living. Industry as we know it today did not exist; instead, there were skilled craftsmen who produced furniture and other household commodities, metalworkers, and other artisans. The majority of households grew their own foodstuffs and were self-sufficient for most of their other needs.

Because people were involved primarily in matters relating to their households or to simple social events, their need for clothing was small. Many households, particularly in the colder climates, raised their own sheep. Spinning and weaving wool were skills expected of the homemaker. Sheep were brought to the New World by Columbus, and, by the latter part of the eighteenth century, wool of high quality was being produced from merino sheep imported from Spain.

Flax was grown primarily to produce a fiber for home use. Since raising flax involves a great deal of hand labor, the crop was limited. Flax and wool were used to make a cloth blended of wool and linen, called linsey-woolsey, which was sturdy and quite adaptable to the requirements of the day.

Cotton rapidly became a popular textile fiber crop, in areas where the climate allowed production, because it was acceptable for domestic uses. Although initially the amount grown was limited to that which could be hand cultivated and harvested, cotton became an important fiber, especially after development of machinery that was specially designed to handle the fiber.

Developments of the Twentieth Century

During this century, the American economic system has changed from an agricultural to an industrial basis, thereby creating a society that is one of consumption rather than production of goods and services. Agriculture has become a specialized operation, rather than a family business. Industry now involves extensive use of machinery in every type of business endeavor. Young people who grow up in country areas seek employment in cities, thereby generating a migration from farm to nonfarm occupations and from rural to urban residence. At the same time, urban dwellers have moved to suburban sections in search of a less complex mode of living. Families are smaller in size and tend to live as single-family units. People enjoy a more informal life style and a maximum number of modern conveniences.[1] Workweeks are shorter and families have more time for leisure and recreation. For many families, vacation means travel, although inflation may affect their plans.

In general, salaries and wages are at a higher level now than at any previous time in history. An increased number of women work for pay outside the home, enabling some families to have more than one paycheck. Easy forms of credit allow consumers to enjoy goods and services while they pay for them. For example, an individual can drive to the airport in a rental car paid for with a credit card, board a "fly now pay later" flight to Mexico, pay for living costs

---

1. More information is available in U.S. Department of Agriculture, *A Place to Live*, The Yearbook of Agriculture 1963, U.S. Government Printing Office, Washington, D.C.; and *Power to Produce*, The Yearbook of Agriculture 1960, same source.

there with a bank loan, and wear clothing purchased on a time-payment charge account. However, one must question whether a "credit-card" life style is economically sound.

The early popularity of cotton has continued and it accounts for the major share of the textile market, although per capita consumption in the United States has gradually declined about 12 percent since 1964.[2] It is still a major fiber because blends with manufactured fibers improve some of its less desirable features. Newer finishes have been developed to cut care and thereby increase acceptability. New fabrication methods have made cotton fabric wearable during the whole year and the use of the fiber in home furnishings has increased.

Flax is still grown in the United States, but the quantity has steadily declined. Because of high production costs, the depleting effects on the soil, and manufacturing expense, most linen fabrics used today are imported.

The sharpest decline in natural fiber consumption has been in the woolen and worsted industry—a drop of about 66 percent in the last decade.[3] Wool prices tend to be unstable and there has been a decline in the production of men's suits, topcoats, and overcoats made from wool fabrics. The general trend today is toward lighter-weight clothing produced from certain manufactured fibers that can be given woollike properties.

With the development in 1910 of rayon, the first manufactured fiber produced in the United States, a new concept in textile products was introduced. Through the decades since then, a noticeable change has taken place in textile fiber consumption within the United States. With the steady improvements in these manufactured fibers, people seemed increasingly to prefer their lightweight and easy-care qualities. They provided some of the luxurious qualities of silk and soon became an acceptable substitute for this very expensive fiber, which had always been produced overseas and which was eliminated from the wardrobe before World War II. Although it reappeared in 1946, when French designers introduced the bouffant silhouette created in pure silk, today comparatively little silk is worn by Americans because of its high cost. Qiana nylon is predicted to become an acceptable imitator of silk in fashion designing. Thus, since 1964, the largest increase in fiber consumption has been in the area

---

2. *Textile Organon* (December 1973), 192.

3. *Ibid.*

U.S. TRADE ROUTES

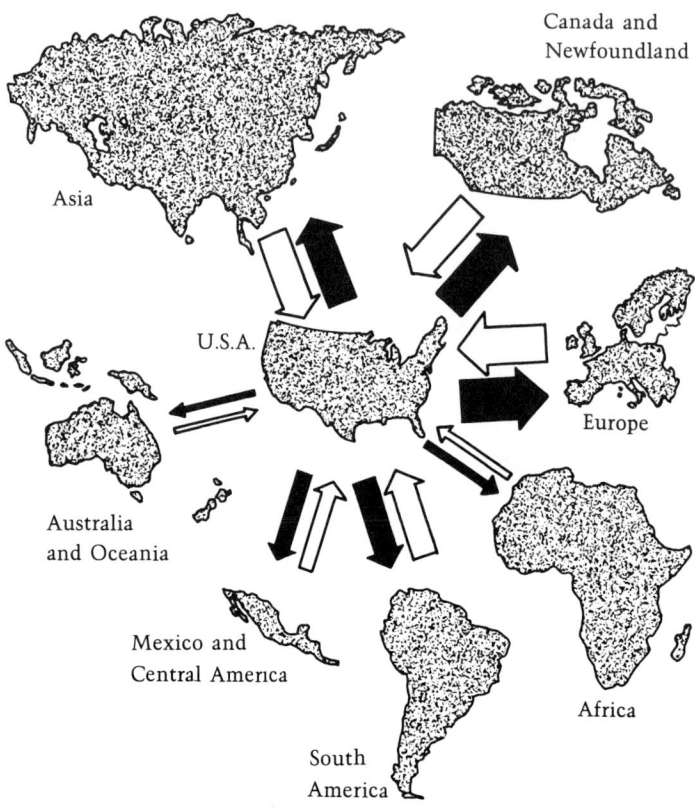

FIGURE 7-1 *The main trade routes of the United States.* (Reprinted, by permission, from Marilyn J. Horn, *The Second Skin*, Houghton Mifflin, Boston, 1968, p. 378.)

of manufactured fibers, with an astonishing jump of 180 percent, constituting the major part of the increase for all fibers (67 percent).[4]

TEXTILE TECHNOLOGY

The American textile industry has experienced many changes in recent years. Continuous automatic machines are replacing older machinery in yarn production and processing, with a resulting higher level of efficiency. Efforts to improve textile properties and to overcome certain less desirable qualities in thermoplastic fibers have led to texturing techniques, which give filament yarns the attributes

---

4. *Ibid.*

of spun yarns. Fiber and fabric blending is increasing, particularly of manufactured and natural fibers. Blending improves aesthetic qualities and gives certain functional or service characteristics not inherent in the fiber. It also improves easy-care and durability properties and extends the usefulness of fabrics.

New and improved fabrication methods, such as bonding, knit-sewing, tufting, and stitchless quilting, result in lower production costs, in both time and money. The knitting process of making fabric is considerably faster than weaving, and usually less expensive. Some knitted garments do not require cutting and sewing processes, so additional time and money are saved in their manufacture.

New processes developed for dyeing manufactured fibers have made available a much wider choice of colors, in deeper hues and more interesting designs, in these once hard-to-dye fabrics. Functional finishes provide certain added qualities that may be desired in a particular fabric and minimize the undesirable qualities. The recently developed finishes include antiseptic, chlorine-resistant, insulating, soil-release, and wrinkle-resistant qualities.

Efforts to standardize and regulate fabric and textile product quality are directed toward consumer protection. Legislative acts have been passed since 1939 to regulate trade practices, establish minimum standards, identify textile fibers, improve safety in fabrics, and make recommendations for care of textile products through permanent labeling procedures.

INTERNATIONAL TRADE

With the development of more rapid and efficient transportation systems, international trade has steadily increased in the past few decades, resulting in the availability of a much wider selection of products on the market (Fig. 7–1). During the twentieth century, American imports of textile products have increased so rapidly that one of the provisions of the Textile Fiber Products Identification Act is specification of the country of origin of all imported products (Figure 7–2). Between 1960 and 1972 the imports of manufactured fibers alone increased 529 percent and imports of all textile products containing manufactured fibers increased 1,248 percent.[5] Five major international trade organizations or

---

5. Man-Made Fiber Producers Association, Inc., *Man-Made Fiber Fact Book*, Man-Made Fiber Producers Association, Inc., Washington, D.C., 1974, p. 30.

FIGURE 7-2 *A Hebrides Islander weaving Harris tweed in his own house, using a domestic loom.* (Courtesy of The Harris Tweed Association)

countries now compete in textile exports and imports: the *European Economic Community* (EEC, or Common Market), consisting of Belgium, Denmark, Ireland, France, Italy, Luxembourg, the Netherlands, the United Kingdom, and West Germany; *European Free Trade Association* (EFTA), including Austria, Norway, Portugal, Sweden, Switzerland, and Finland (associate); *Western Europe outside EEC and EFTA*, specifically Greece, Spain, and Turkey; *Japan*; and the *United States*. Other countries engage in textile fiber production but they participate in international trade primarily as importers.[6] Statistical trends indicate that the foreign competitors of the United States have an increasingly favorable balance of trade in relation to the United States in manufactured fabrics. Mexico, a much closer neighbor to the south, is beginning to make substantial gains in the textile industry since its major textile operation began in 1954.[7]

Although imports have increased the variety of textile items on the American market, they have presented competition on the domestic front in the areas of labor and retailing. European and Asian labor is less expensive than American, so products can be manufactured at lower cost in those geographic areas (Figures 7-3 and 7-4). Even after paying

FIGURE 7-3 *This tag from a knit shirt made in Central America gives very little information. Inclusion of the words "We recommend Woolite for washing" allows the buyer to infer that the shirt is indeed washable. A care label is stitched into the garment.*

---

6. Ibid., p. 32.
7. Harvey S. Turner, "Miracle in Mexico," *American Fabrics and Fashions* (Winter 1973), 31.

Part Three / Selection

import duties and tariffs, American merchants often can retail imported textile products at a lower price and with a higher profit than would be possible for comparable domestic goods (Figure 7-5).

In the early 1970s, the United States imposed an import tax on textile products that would make their selling price comparable to that of domestic products. However, the act threatened to impair international relations, especially with the Far Eastern countries, specifically Japan, and the tariff was repealed.

Foreign and domestic products compare quite favorably in quality of style and design, and consumer acceptance of imports is high. For many years it has been common practice to combine various European and American styles in all areas of home furnishings. Similarly, a smartly dressed American woman may wear a French-designed suit

FIGURE 7-4 *This tag is typical of those found on some garments that are improperly labeled. No care instructions are given: the customer must know how to care for the garment. No care label is stitched into the garment.*

FIGURE 7-5 *The inside of a modern garment plant in the United States. (Courtesy of International Ladies' Garment Workers' Union)*

fashioned of English woolen fabric, a silk blouse from Hong Kong, a Swiss-made scarf, and leather shoes and gloves made in Italy.

Trade competition has encouraged manufacturers in the various countries to develop special products, available only as export items and not for sale within the country. American tourists traveling in Europe have found that the beautiful Swiss-made scarves found in London were not available in Switzerland, and the stylish Italian knit suits worn by so many Americans could not be found in Italy. The only explanation is that both items were manufactured for export only.

Current Trends in Fiber and Fabric Consumption

Obviously, Americans have changed their preferences for fibers through the years and several factors have probably brought about these changes.

1. As people enjoy higher incomes, they have become more fashion-oriented and have tended to replace rather than wear out textile products.
2. The current trend is toward lightweight apparel. This is due to the use of fewer yards of fabric per garment, the popularity of the new lighter-weight fibers, and year-round controlled indoor temperatures.
3. Modern home laundering facilities and the new washable fabrics decrease the need for an abundance of garments of any one type.
4. With a change in the nature of work today, there is a need for more tailored or sporty, business-type clothes and less heavy-duty work clothing.
5. Shorter workweeks, higher incomes, and the trend toward outdoor living have increased the use of casual clothing.
6. The general life style has become more casual and there is less need for formal clothing, even for entertaining.
7. Increased travel means that wrinkle-resistant clothing is now a necessity instead of just a convenience.
8. With the population distribution shifting to the young, fiber preferences for apparel and furnishings have changed from the traditionally acceptable to those with less cultural association. For example, fewer brides of today wear the traditional wedding gown, of satin and lace.
9. Home furnishings now include carpets for kitchens and bathrooms as well as for patios and other outdoor areas.
10. Space exploration has placed different requirements on fibers, fabrics, finishes, design, yardage, construction

techniques, and serviceability properties of textile products (for example, the emphasis on lightweight and streamlined products).

In general, people today prefer looking well groomed in aesthetically pleasing fabrics which can be cared for with a minimum of effort. Cotton is considered the most versatile fiber for both summer and winter and it is becoming more acceptable for formal and special occasion wear. Wool is still unequaled for its tailoring properties. Manufactured fibers provide lightweight, minimum-care clothing in colors and designs suitable for any occasion.

The American public is enthusiastic about fashion trends but is equally interested in getting its money's worth. Consumer interests in product quality and price controls are reflected in the various consumer movements, which have been successful in communicating to the fashion industry the wants and desires of the public. To a large degree, the buying power of the consumer has a realistic influence. If the fashion industry is able to sell only what the consumer wants and will buy, then the industry will be successful to the extent that it is attuned to the demands of consumers.

The use of textile products in home decorating offers the consumer more opportunity for creativity and self-expression as the selection of fabrics and materials for such purposes has expanded. Textile products for the home are decorative, functional, and safe as a result of modern technology. They add a charm, an individuality, and a beauty to the homes of today.

Changes in Use of Textiles

Despite all that appears favorable in the textile industry, some trends are developing that may present real problems in the future. In the recent past, the rise and decline trends in fiber consumption have made textiles both cause and effect in the future. In the recent past, the up-and-down trends in textile fiber shortage.

WOOL FIBER

Over the past few decades the demand for wool fiber has declined steadily; today it makes up only about 1 percent of fiber consumption in the United States.[8] Since wool-producing

---

8. *Man-Made Fiber Fact Book*, 1974, p. 27.

FIGURE 7-6 *Sheep being sheared. Notice the thick, heavy mass of wool grown by each animal.* (Courtesy of American Sheep Producers Council, Inc.)

animals (Figure 7-6) have not been the most popular ones for food consumption, the raising of such animals has not increased appreciably either. Much of the land required for animal grazing has been used for other, more profitable agricultural purposes or for urban expansion. However, various government price support programs have provided some incentive to sheep growers. The American Wool Council has recently been trying to bring about a greater demand for wool fiber and the sheep growers' associations have been promoting a lowered fat content in lamb as a means of encouraging more consumption of wool-producing animals. Their efforts may help to increase the popularity of wool fiber in clothing, especially as research continues to improve its wear and care qualities. To some extent, blending wool with other fibers has overcome some of its less desirable features and made it more acceptable for year-round wear. All-wool and wool-blend fabrics are being used more widely for men's suits and women's coats,[9] but it is not clear whether this is the beginning of a trend toward increased demand for and use of wool. Many Americans have become accustomed to new standards of cleanliness introduced by the easy-care fabrics, and a return to clothing that is cleaned less frequently, as is typical of wool clothing, may be difficult. Another factor to be considered is the lack of a stable world supply of wool fiber at prices that do not fluctuate greatly.

---

9. Virginia Britton, "Clothing and Textiles: Supplies, Prices, and Outlook for 1975," *Family Economics Review*, U.S. Department of Agriculture, Washington, D.C., ARS-NE-36 (Winter 1975), 15.

FIGURE 7-7 *A vast field of cotton in the American South, ready for picking.* (Courtesy of the National Cotton Council)

COTTON FIBER

The overall demand for cotton has declined also, although not to the extent experienced by wool. Cotton has continued to be a profitable agricultural crop, especially in the southern United States (Figures 7-7 and 7-8). Although agriculture has many ups and downs (due to unpredictable elements of nature), farmers, including those who produce cotton fiber, have received certain benefits in the form of government aid. Parity provides a form of government price support during economic stress periods, so that the farmer is guaranteed a reasonable level of income, comparable to a time when agriculture was at its peak. Additionally, the government makes relief payments to needy farmers when floods have destroyed a year's crop. The government implements programs to increase the demand for farm products or reduce the cost of production. The educational efforts of the Cooperative Extension Service are one way farmers can learn how to improve and increase acreage yield in a more efficient manner.

Cotton is one of the crops included in the limitation programs, which are aimed at cutting down on the supply to maintain a high price. Both acreage allotments and crop quotas have been aids to cotton farmers. Surplus produce is frequently purchased by the government and stored for sale or use at a later time in an effort to balance supply and demand.[10]

FIGURE 7-8 *A mark like those used for wool and fur, to indicate textile products made of 100 percent cotton.* (Courtesy of Cotton Incorporated)

---

10. Edwin Mansfield, *Micro-Economics*, W. W. Norton & Company, New York, 1970; Paul A. Samuelson, *Economics, An Introductory Analysis*, 7th ed., McGraw-Hill Company, New York, 1967.

Gradually, the demand for cotton fiber exceeded the current supply and the recent increased volume of cotton exports to Japan and other Asian countries depleted the reserves. Consequently, cotton, once an inexpensive, readily available fiber, became not so plentiful—and therefore expensive. Cotton farmers who committed their crops when the price was lower negotiated for a more profitable selling price. Some farmers who were attempting to break their earlier commitments held out for some benefit from the booming prices. Additionally, a shortage of fertilizer used in growing cotton developed, and this further tended to decrease the cotton crops.

MANUFACTURED FIBERS

The overwhelming popularity of manufactured fibers has resulted in increased consumption of around 200 percent since the early 1960s, while demand for natural fibers has been curtailed accordingly. However, the manufactured fibers are very much a part of the national energy problem because they are all made from petroleum products (Figure 7-9). During the oil embargo of 1974, some producers, both in the United States and abroad, sharply reduced their out-

FIGURE 7-9 *The national energy problem is complicated by the fact that oil must be transported over great distances in vessels like the* Universe Kuwait. *(Courtesy of Gulf Oil Company)*

put.[11] Thus, until the petroleum problem is stabilized in one way or another, the manufactured fiber section of the textile industry may be subject to fluctuations in supply of basic raw material and in the cost of its products. Such fluctuations would, of course, have an effect upon the availability and cost of end products to the consumer.

CONSIDERATIONS FOR THE CONSUMER

One solution to the textile problem, at least for the moment, may involve some basic rethinking about our life style. Because of the toughness of the fibers used in today's fabrics, long-wearing qualities are "built into" garments. Since this is so, should not the garments be worn for a longer period of time? If the original owners cannot continue to use them, might they not be passed on to others who can?

Another point for possible consideration is the built-in obsolescence in clothing in the form of frequent fashion changes. In recent years, styles have remained fairly constant. Is this a desirable trend? Should rapid fashion switches be discouraged?

The idea of recycling textile products is not a new one, but it should perhaps be taken seriously and become more widely practiced. For many years, Americans have possessed more garments at any one time and have discarded more wearable items than people in other parts of the world. Should they begin to change their life style and wear out rather than throw out their clothing?

There are already signs of such a development. Used-clothing shops that cater to people of all income levels are increasing in number. In some cities, there are even shops that handle the castoffs of wealthy persons. Middle-income people shop at second-hand stores, then use their ingenuity and creative skills to turn their bargains into fashionable, attractive outfits. Garage and yard sales, once rare, are now widely held in many areas, and all kinds of textile products, including clothing and household items, find ready buyers.

CLOTHING RECYCLING

In addition to the questions raised above, the personal economic factor in recycling clothing can be a major factor in deciding to renovate a particular garment. Often, the fabric in a garment is still very good, but the styling has become

---

11. Britton, p. 15.

FIGURE 7-10 *Five recycling projects.* (The University of Mississippi)

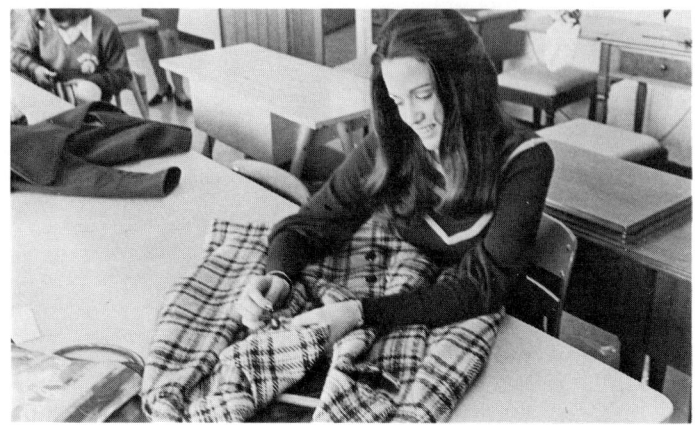

A full-length coat, left over from high-school days, has been shortened and darted front and back to make a current-style pants coat.

A full-length evening skirt is being converted into a nightgown.

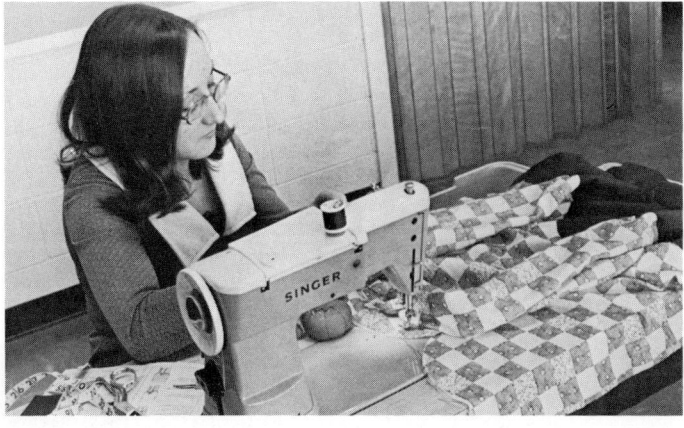

Left-over scraps of fabric have been combined into "whole cloth" from which a Western-style shirt will be cut.

For this skirt, the legs were cut from an old pair of jeans and the seams were opened. Two long triangular sections were cut from the bottom of the legs and inserted to add a little fullness for ease in walking.

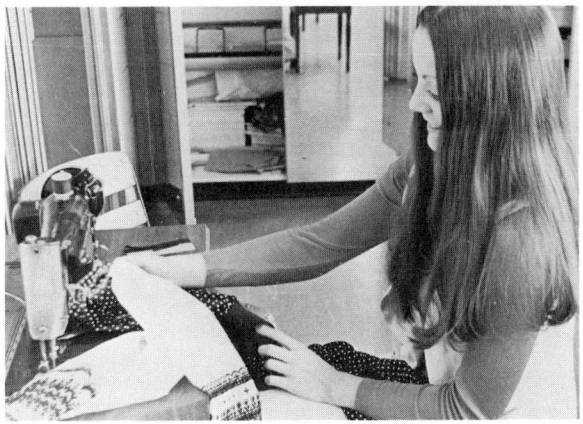

A too-short polka dot dress has been improved by the addition of embroidered sleeves from another old dress and a band of solid black at the waistline.

7 / *Textile Consumption*

outdated. In some cases, restyling is possible; in others, the fabric can be used for another type of garment. In general, recycling can be accomplished by restyling, renovation, and patchwork techniques (Figure 7–10).

RESTYLING   Garments may be restyled by changing portions of the particular item. Dress sleeves may be shortened, and cuffs or bands added. Collars may be replaced by neckline ties, or by reshaping. Pants can be changed into skirts by ripping out the leg seams and inserting matching or contrasting fabric to fill the gap. Loose-fitting long coats may be shortened, then darted or seamed to make pants coats. Simple dresses can be made into jumpers or tops for pants. Dresses may be lengthened by adding a band of fabric at the waistline or at the hem, in such a way as to make the addition appear part of the design. Trims or bands of contrasting fabric may alter the look of different parts of a garment.

RENOVATING   Garments can be renovated by making them into "new" garments. Adult-size coats, dresses, pants, or skirts can be taken apart and the larger pieces used to cut pieces for children's garments. Dresses that have wide, full, or long skirts can be made into a child's dress or suit, depending upon the fabric. Pleated or gathered skirts may be recut into gored or flared skirts. A long skirt may be made into a child's dress, or into a sleeveless vest or jacket. Sleeveless shortie nightgowns may be made from short or long dresses of suitable fabrics. The possibilities are endless and depend on the amount, shape, and type of fabric involved.

PATCHWORK   Patchwork techniques may be used to decorate or make garments. Jeans decorations have made patches fashionable, and bright-colored fabric scraps may be applied by zigzag stitching to pants or children's garments, whether they have actual holes or not. Skirts or pants may be lengthened by adding pieces of fabric that contrast or coordinate in color or design. Western-style shirts may be made by using different fabric for yoke, collar, and cuffs. Attractive long skirts or hostess dresses can be made by sewing together patches or blocks left over from other clothing construction, for a total patchwork look.

Whatever the technique used, a few basic principles should be followed.

1. The garment or fabric to be used should be inspected carefully to make certain that sufficient wear is left to warrant the time and effort involved.

2. A definite plan should be made before the job is started, to avoid disappointment. The darts in a fitted garment, for example, should be checked to see whether they are slashed, since the slashes will mean holes in the fabric when the garment is taken apart.
3. When two or more fabrics are to be combined in any manner, all should be cleanable in the same way, at the same temperature.
4. When new fabric is to be combined with that from a used garment, the difference should not be obvious. New fabrics with grayed color tones may blend in better than those with strikingly bright tones.
5. New fabric, either knit or woven, should be preshrunk thoroughly before it is combined with old fabric.
6. Stitching-line marks must be removed from ripped-out garment pieces before the pieces are recut. Sometimes this may be done by damp pressing the markings with a cloth dipped in a solution of equal parts of white vinegar and water. (Fabric must first be tested for colorfastness, since the vinegar may cause color changes in some fabrics.)
7. If the ripped-out garment pieces have tears or holes, they should be marked with pins or circled with chalk, to make them conspicuous during recutting of pattern pieces.
8. Garment pieces recut from used fabric must be planned for correct alignment on the fabric grain, to ensure proper fit and hang.
9. When new sleeves or collars are to be added to old garments, they must be cut so they will fit properly into the armholes or neckline involved. Sleeve caps should measure about 1 to $1\frac{1}{2}$ inches larger than the circumference of the armhole, and collar neck edges should have the same measurement and shape as the neckline.

As in all clothing construction work, it is best to start with a fairly simple recycling project, to avoid disappointment and waste. A little practice in thinking over possibilities, plus the expertise gained in carrying through a few projects, can lead to continued service from clothing already in the closet and to a definite reduction of clothing costs.

Study Questions

1. What are the major factors influencing textile consumption today? Discuss each briefly.
2. Name five major trade organizations or countries that now compete in textile exports and imports.

3. Explain how increased imports of textile items affect the markets for similar or compatible products made domestically.
4. Discuss ten factors influencing current trends in fiber consumption.
5. Explain the role of textiles in the energy crisis.
6. What can consumers do to help conserve textile fibers and products?
7. How is the economy of the country related to textile fiber consumption?
8. How is the economic principle of supply and demand reflected in the current textile product situation?

Suggested Activities

1. Make a trip to a local textile products store and list the names of the countries where the various products were made. What percentage was made in the United States? What percentage was made in each of the other countries? Compare the quality and price of equivalent textile products, both domestic and foreign. What conclusions do you draw?
2. Make a display depicting the current trends in textile fiber consumption.
3. Interview other college students and/or noncollegiate consumers to find out their views on textile product trade.
4. Study the fabrics in a local store to determine the fiber(s) most in abundance. Talk with a salesperson about the current availability of specific fibers in fabric, such as cotton, wool, flax, silk. Which types of fabrics can the store personnel most easily obtain? How have prices changed within the past year or two? Why?
5. Inspect your wardrobe for a recycling possibility. Make a plan for the project and carry it out. Write a brief paragraph or two setting forth the problems encountered and your solutions.

Chapter 8

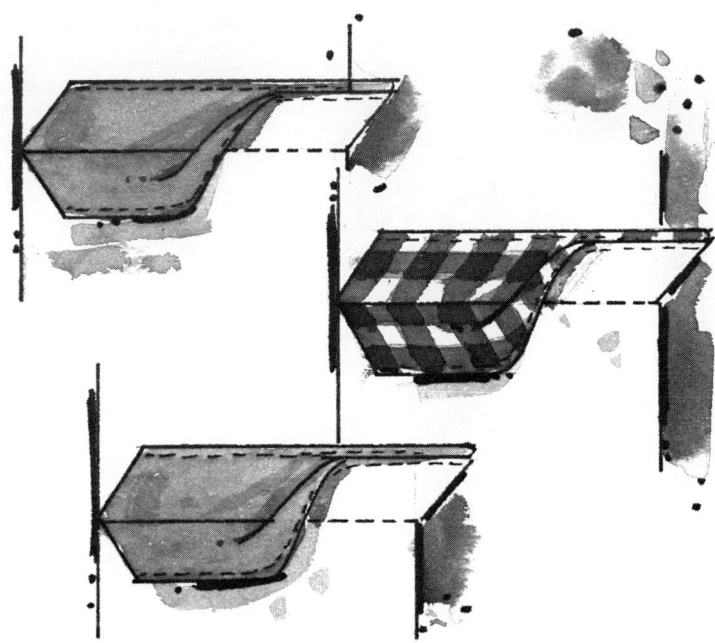

Consumer Satisfaction

INFORMED SELECTION of a suitable product may determine whether a given textile will be satisfactory for a particular purpose. Knowledge of all the manufacturing processes—yarn making, fabric construction, and finishes—and how they affect the fibers allows the consumer to make the best choice from the many available items. The aspects involved are beauty, hand, serviceability, comfort, and care.

Beauty

Appearance is probably the first characteristic of fabric that the consumer notices; pleasing colors, unusual designs, and interesting textures influence reactions (Figure 8-1). Beauty is a subjective evaluation that depends on individual personal taste and preference and is based on the person's response to the fabric's appearance. However, this response is determined by all the processes involved in manufacture.

FIBER PROPERTIES

Fabric's beauty often is found in its color. To have bright, clear, and long-lasting color, the cloth must be made of fibers that can be dyed or colored in some way. Absorbent fibers, like the natural ones, usually are more easily dyed with brighter, longer-lasting shades, while manufactured fibers are generally more difficult to dye and often do not hold colors as well. Wool is considered the most easily dyed fiber and it is available in beautiful and varied hues. Glass is more difficult to dye and fabrics made from this fiber are limited in color and design.

Luster gives a touch of elegance to fabrics. Silk fiber is lustrous in its natural state, after the gum or serum has been removed. Pima cotton has some luster because of the longer length of its fiber, as compared with other fibers. Too much luster, however, may detract from the beauty of a fiber. Unless a delustering substance is added to the solution used to make the fiber, rayon may be too shiny.

Some fabrics tend to pill or form surface balls, which may break off in wear. Strong fibers, such as polyester and nylon, hold these balls on the surface of the fabric, so they pick up lint from other fabrics. The result is an unattractive appearance long before the fabric wears out, unless the pills are removed mechanically by singeing.

YARN PROCESSES

Interesting fabric texture often results from use of novelty or unusual yarns (Figure 8–2). Rough, textured yarns used in tweed fabrics may result from uneven spinning operations. Bouclé fabrics derive their name from the characteristic loop formation of the bouclé yarn. Hand-spun yarns generally are more interesting and unusual than even, smooth, machine-spun yarns. Combed yarns are extra smooth, fine, and strong, and they represent only the best grades of the fibers. Some homespun and tweed knit fabrics have a heather look because the fiber is blended when the yarn is spun. Metallic yarns add beauty to fabrics that otherwise would be uninteresting.

FABRIC CONSTRUCTION METHODS

The intricate and elaborate designs found in fabrics such as brocade, brocatelle, damask, and tapestry (Figures 8–3 and 8–4) are produced by a special Jacquard loom. Varia-

FIGURE 8-1 *A woven wool tweed, showing how the contrast of light and dark yarns adds to the attractiveness of the fabric.* (The University of Mississippi)

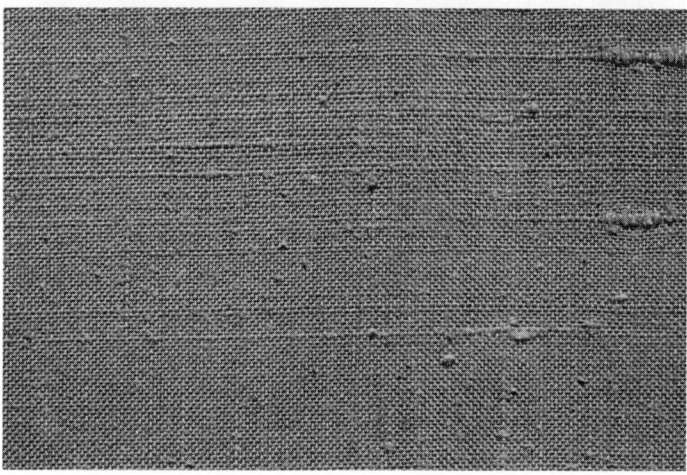

FIGURE 8-2 *Silk shantung, showing the uneven surface of the fabric, created by use of slubbed yarns in the filling direction.* (The University of Mississippi)

FIGURE 8-3 *Three example of fabric woven on the Jacquard loom: (a) brocade; (b) brocatelle; (c) tapestry.* (The University of Mississippi)

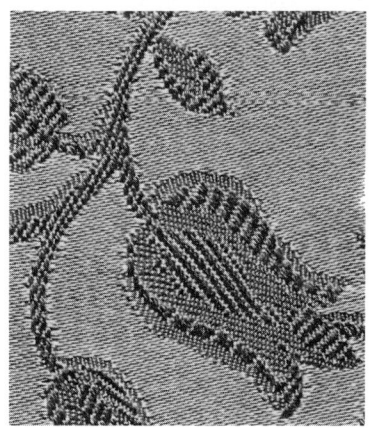  

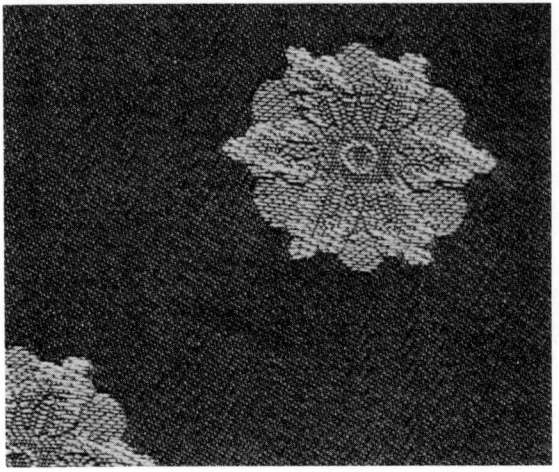 

FIGURE 8-4 *Both sides of a double-woven fabric, damask, which has a reversible design.* (The University of Mississippi)

tions of the plain weave, such as the basket weave found in monk's cloth or the rib weave characteristic of faille, make otherwise plain fabrics more attractive. The satin and twill weaves both create attractive designs, and the long float threads characteristic of the satin weave add luster. Beautiful laces and delicate nettings are available because of developments in construction methods. Knitting processes make possible fabrics that compare with and often surpass woven fabrics in color, design, and texture appeal. The wide selection of single- and double-knit fabrics available today indicates the extent to which this is true. Marquisette curtains, made by the leno-weave method, add charm and grace to many homes. Elegant fabrics with rich-looking colors are characteristic of pile-constructed fabrics such as corduroy and velveteen.

FINISHES

Color may be added to piece goods after construction by all-over dyeing methods or by techniques such as roller and silk-screen printing, batik, and tie-and-dye, which add color and design to otherwise plain fabric. Both texture and color are added by flocking, and embossing gives a three-dimensional raised effect. Moiré pressing uses light to enhance the watermarked design characteristic of some taffeta (Figure 8–5). Tension mercerization finishing gives luster to some fabrics that would be dull-looking if not so treated.

FIGURE 8-5 *The moiré finish applied to taffeta gives the characteristic watery pattern.* (The University of Mississippi)

Hand

Hand is the way a fabric feels to the touch, and the way it hangs or falls into folds. Fabric may feel soft or crisp, smooth or rough, light or heavy; it may be springy or limp when crushed. The various textile properties of the fiber and fabric are responsible for this characteristic.

FIBER PROPERTIES

The fiber shape, diameter, length, and the presence or absence of crimp all influence hand. These properties are largely uncontrollable in natural fibers but may be selected and built into manufactured fibers during fabrication. Silk fibers, naturally very long, smooth, and of small diameter, make fabrics with a soft, smooth hand and easy draping ability (Figure 8-6). The very short length and larger diameter of cotton fiber make fabrics with more body and a rougher feel. The natural crimp of wool fiber (Figure 8-7) makes it feel springy, and wool fabrics have resiliency or "bounce" when crushed. These properties can be controlled in the production of manufactured fibers by manipulating fiber length and diameter. If crimp is desired, it can be added mechanically. Thus, nylon, for example, may feel springy in a blanket, stiff in a taffeta umbrella, soft in pajamas, and very silky and supple in Qiana dress fabric (Figure 8-8).

YARN PROCESSES

During yarn spinning, short natural fibers can be made to feel and behave more like manufactured fibers, while manufactured filaments can be given characteristics that

FIGURE 8-6 *Silk chiffon, a very light, sheer fabric, makes a dress that "floats" in a beautiful way when the wearer moves.* (Hakim Raquib)

make them respond more like natural fibers. Combing straightens and lengthens cotton fibers before they are spun, so that percale sheets, which are usually made of combed cotton, feel smoother and silkier than muslin sheets, made from uncombed cotton yarns. Twist makes yarns shorter, more compact, rougher, and less pliable. High-twist worsted wool yarns, such as found in wool crepe (Figure 8–9), are rougher in touch and have a firmer hand than lower-twist yarns. Manufactured yarns can be given a hand more like that of natural yarns by cutting the filaments into short staple fibers and spinning them like natural fibers. Acrylic yarn, for example, strongly resembles wool and can be made into fabrics very similar in hand. Additionally, the thermoplastic (heat-sensitive) properties of acrylic make it possible to add crimp to the yarn.

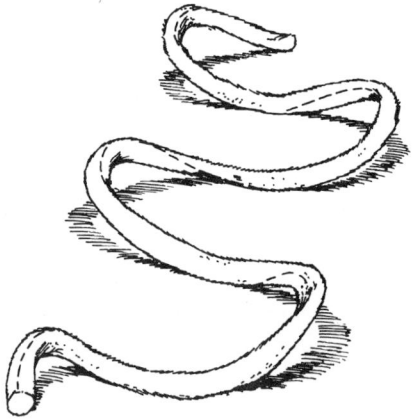

FIGURE 8-7 *Wool fiber has a natural crimp, which makes the fiber feel springy.* (Reprinted, by permission, from Marilyn J. Horn, *The Second Skin*, 2nd ed., Houghton Mifflin, Boston, 1975, p. 307)

FABRIC CONSTRUCTION METHODS

Hand is influenced by the number of yarns used, the closeness of the yarns to each other, use of extra or filler yarns, and the way in which these yarns are held together to form fabric. The thread count gives the number of yarns used in a square inch of fabric and this indicates the closeness of the weave. Closely woven fabrics of a plain weave have a firmer hand than loosely woven fabrics in which the yarns are held apart (Figure 8–10). Consider, for example, the difference in the feel of bed sheets and marquisette curtains. Corduroy, made with extra yarns, has a heavier hand and is less pliable than cotton percale. The same comparison can be made between tricot-knit and double-knit fabrics (Figure 8–11). Knit fabrics have more bounce than woven fabrics of comparable weight and fiber. Compare the feel of a knitted cotton T-shirt and that of a woven cotton shirt. The long float yarns of satin-woven fabrics feel smoother than plain-woven fabric, which lacks the long floats.

FIGURE 8-8 *A length of Qiana nylon knit, showing hand and drape.* (The University of Mississippi)

FINISHES

Finishes applied to fabrics affect the hand in different ways. Some improve it, others impart less desirable features, and a few leave the fabric unchanged to the touch. Mercerization softens cotton fabrics; embossing leaves a rougher feel because of its raised design; napping makes fabrics feel softer; and glazed fabrics usually feel stiffer than they were before the finish was applied. Some finishes give wrinkle-resistance and minimum-care properties; if these have a resin base, the finished fabrics feel stiffer, are less pliable, and do not drape as well. Some wool fabrics are presensitized, so that later they can be made into permanently pleated

FIGURE 8-9 *The highly twisted yarns used to make crepe give the fabric its typical rough surface.* (The University of Mississippi)

garments. This process usually decreases the springiness and softness characteristic of wool fabric, making it somewhat stiffer and less resilient.

Serviceability

Consumers consider the purpose for which they plan to use fabric when they purchase it, and the fabric in textile products is evaluated in the same way. Serviceability is judged by the extent to which the fabric or textile product will be useful for its intended purpose. It should retain its original shape and size, be safe to use, be not easily destroyed by insects or biological organisms, and have a reasonable life expectancy (Figure 8–12). Fabric serviceability, like other aspects, may be improved, impaired, or unaffected by the various textile processes given it.

FIGURE 8-10 *Woven wool fabric hangs in fairly stiff folds. Compare these with the soft folds in Figure 8-8.* (The University of Mississippi)

FIBER PROPERTIES

By nature, some fibers are easily shrunk or stretched out of their original size and shape, while others are dimensionally stable. Natural fibers change shape more easily than do manufactured ones, and wool is the most susceptible to change. After an initial shrinkage, cotton, silk, and flax shrink very little, but wool may continue to shrink because of its ability to felt, or mat together. Manufactured fibers

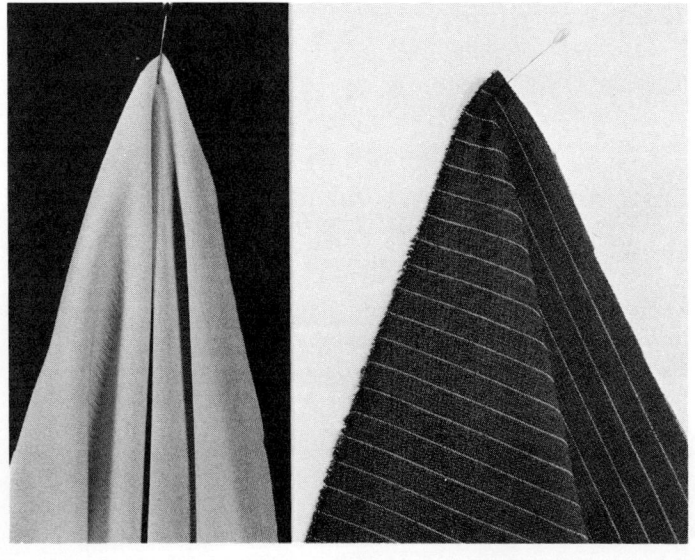

FIGURE 8-11 *Single knit (left), a comparatively light fabric, drapes more softly than double knit (right).* (Reprinted, by permission, from Evelyn A. Mansfield and Ethel Lucas, *Clothing Construction*, 2nd ed., Houghton Mifflin, Boston, 1974, p. 91)

Part Three / Selection

tend to retain their original shape and size during normal use, unless they are improperly handled during wear or care.

Fibers vary in safety. Glass does not burn at all; wool will burn while held in the flame, then self-extinguish; and cotton ignites very easily and continues to burn after it is removed from the flame. Nylon is not safe to use near highly flammable substances because it may emit sparks from static electricity build-up. For this reason, nylon uniforms are not worn in hospital operating rooms. Cotton, which can be sterilized by boiling, is safe to use for medical purposes.

Fibers that are easily destroyed by insects or biological organisms reduce the usefulness of products unless they are properly protected. Cotton and flax may be damaged by mildew; wool is attacked by moths and carpet beetles. Ants have been known to damage nylon—when nylon stockings were very new on the market, women often were advised to keep them in tightly capped jars for protection from ants.

Textile products intended to last for a reasonable length of time must be durable. Resistance to rubbing or abrasion in part determines durability. Since glass is brittle and breaks easily, glass-fiber curtains may split where they fold, such as at the bottom of the hem, thus reducing their longevity. Polyester fiber pilling reduces serviceability, because it spoils the appearance of the fabric. Nylon and polyester are both very strong, and they are used in products requiring great strength, like automobile tires. Rayon is weak, and its use is limited to items not subjected to much strain and stress.

"GUARANTEED FOR ONE FULL YEAR'S NORMAL WEAR, REFUND OR REPLACEMENT WHEN RETURNED WITH TAG AND SALES SLIP TO MONSANTO."

FIGURE 8-12 *One producer of manufactured fibers specifies in detail the information to be used on the hangtag. Notice use of the registered trademarks. (Courtesy of Monsanto Textiles Company. ®Registered trademarks of Monsanto Company)*

YARN PROCESSES

High-strength fibers generally make yarns that also are strong, while weak yarns are likely to be made of weak fibers. Nylon is a strong fiber and a strong yarn, but wool is weak both as a fiber and as a yarn. Up to a point, twist increases yarn strength, so that high-twist yarns are often stronger than low-twist ones. The compactness of high-twist yarns may inhibit air flow and thus make them slower to burn, even when made of highly flammable fibers. Low-twist yarns of short fibers with protruding ends may catch fire easier than yarns of longer fibers and medium to high twist.

Simple yarns are less vulnerable to snags and to pulls than are complex yarns of loop construction. Yarns that are unevenly twisted, such as those with slubs, are likely to show wear sooner than yarns that are evenly twisted their full length. Low twist also may make yarns less durable, since yarns of medium and higher twist are more resistant to abrasion.

FABRIC CONSTRUCTION METHODS

Fabrics with high yarn or thread counts are considered to be strong. Tight, plain-woven fabrics and fabrics of double-knit construction are usually stronger than loosely woven or single-knit ones. Clinging fabrics of tight construction that make close-fitting garments, like some sleepwear, are considered safer to wear than those that are open in construction and less pliable. Because of the long float yarns, satin-weave fabrics are less durable than either plain- or twill-woven fabrics. Double knits tend to be more durable than single knits, which snag and run easily. Firmly made fabrics usually are more dimensionally stable than fabrics of loose construction. Double knits retain their shape better than do single knits, and tightly woven fabrics are apt to shrink less than those of open weave.

FINISHES

Fabrics that can be given flameproof or fire-retardant finishes are safer to wear than untreated fabrics. Cotton and wool fabrics that shrink considerably can be treated to reduce or minimize shrinkage. Wool fabric labeled "London-shrunk" has undergone a special process which substantially decreases the amount of relaxation shrinkage that will occur. Cotton fabric that has been Sanforized is guaranteed to shrink no more than 1 percent, whereas fabric that has been only preshrunk may shrink up to 5 percent. Mercerization increases fabric strength and makes it more durable.

Mothproofing finishes applied during regular cleaning protect wool fabrics against moth damage and thus increase fabric life. Sanitizing kills bacteria and makes fabric more hygienic. Colorfast processes make fabrics retain their color longer. Fabrics treated to resist water have extensive use in rainwear. Fabrics also can be treated to resist sunlight and rot damage.

Comfort

Comfort is related to personal sensitivity and is a highly individual matter. It involves direct contact of the body with the fabric when used for such purposes as temperature control, concealment, or adornment. Fabric qualities such as heat conductivity, air permeability, absorbency, weight, and stretch contribute to comfort and are affected by fiber properties, yarn processes, fabric construction, and finishes.

FIBER PROPERTIES

Fibers that conduct heat away from the body and permit air to circulate give a feeling of coolness, while fibers that hold heat close to the body and inhibit air circulation keep the body warm (Figure 8–13). Thus, cotton clothing feels cool in summer and wool feels warm in winter. Fibers that absorb body moisture are more comfortable than fibers that trap the moisture next to the body and give a clammy, sticky feeling. Many people find nylon and polyester fabrics uncomfortable for this reason.

Lightweight fibers generally produce lightweight, cool fabrics, but there are now available lightweight fabrics that also are warm enough for protection in cold weather, because of the development of new manufactured fibers such as acrylic. This has contributed to the comfort of cardiac patients, who may find heavy clothing not only uncomfortable but an extra burden on the heart. Some fibers, for example, wool and polyester, are irritating to the sensitive skin of certain individuals because of their scratchy physical properties. Fabrics that do not "give" with body movements are less comfortable than those that have some stretch. Wool fibers will stretch more than cotton or flax and thus make fabrics that are less constricting.

YARN PROCESSES

High-twist yarns are less absorbent and permit better circulation of heat and air than yarns of low twist. Some wool fabrics advertised as being cool enough for summer wear are made from high-twist worsted yarns. Bulky yarns (made from either low-twist natural fibers or manufactured fibers that have been crimped) are good insulators and often provide warmth with a minimum amount of yarn. Rough-textured yarns can make fabrics feel uncomfortably scratchy, while smooth-surfaced yarns are less irritating. Yarns that stretch, such as anidex and spandex, can be made into fabrics that also stretch and give with body movements. Lightweight fibers can be made into lightweight yarns and fabrics that weigh less.

FABRIC CONSTRUCTION METHODS

Tightly constructed fabrics inhibit air circulation and are not as cool to wear as fabrics that are loosely woven or knitted. Felted fabrics and those that are bonded or laminated also reduce air circulation and add to body warmth.

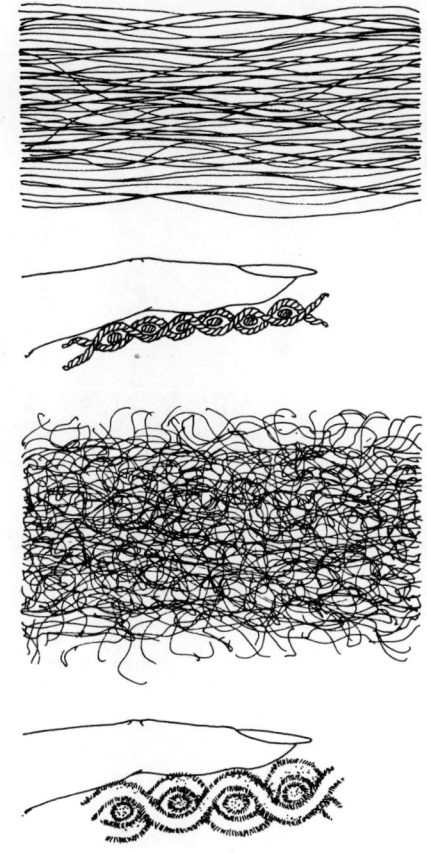

FIGURE 8–13 *The type of yarn and the way it is woven affect the insulating quality of the fabric. Top: a tightly twisted yarn, woven into a tight fabric, which would hold more heat close to the body. Bottom: a thick, loosely twisted yarn, which makes a fabric with many air spaces. This fabric would allow a good deal of heat to pass through, thus cooling the body. (Reproduced, by permission, from Marilyn J. Horn, The Second Skin, 2nd ed., Houghton Mifflin, Boston, 1975, p. 306)*

FIGURE 8-14 *This pure cotton velveteen suit would be warmer than a suit made of lightweight cotton denim. The additional yarns in the velveteen provide more insulation than the finer yarns in denim.* (Courtesy of Cotton Incorporated)

Construction techniques that use additional yarns produce warmer materials, such as velveteen, corduroy, and intricately patterned double knits (Figure 8–14). These often weigh more than simply constructed fabrics and garments may feel heavier. Knitted fabrics are comfortable because the loops formed during construction enable the fabric to stretch with body movements.

FINISHES

Finishes which make fabrics feel soft add to comfort in wearing, while those that stiffen them may be less comfortable. The resin-type finishes used to give minimum-care properties often make the fabric feel stiff and less pliable. They also tend to reduce or eliminate the amount of stretch the fabric might otherwise have, thereby making them more constricting when worn. Fabrics with resin finishes are less porous and therefore warmer. Similarly, permanent-press finishes increase fabric weight, so clothing of such fabrics may feel a little heavier, and they also reduce the fabric's absorption and increase its warmth. Cotton fabrics that might be too cool to wear in cold weather may be quite comfortable if they have a resin-type finish.

Care

The kind of care a given fabric will require is of concern to the consumer. Care factors are related to soil and stain removal, maintenance of a fresh appearance, and storage during off-seasons. Fabrics that retain soil and stains on the surface are more easily cleaned than those that permit penetration. The extent to which fabrics resist wrinkling during wear and respond to minimum touch-up pressing contributes to a fresh appearance. Storage needs relate to the way in which fabric responds to being folded or hung for long periods of time and possible damage from attack by biological organisms or insects. All these are related to and influenced by fiber properties, yarn processes, construction methods, and finishes of fabric.

FIBER PROPERTIES

Absorbent fibers let soil and stains penetrate them, while nonabsorbent fibers tend to hold them on the surface. For this reason, manufactured fibers generally are more easily cleaned than natural fibers. However, wool resists soiling more than the other natural fibers and wool fabrics can be kept fresh-looking and relatively clean longer by brushing and spot cleaning. Resilient fibers such as wool and polyester recover from wrinkling easily and make fabrics that look better longer (Figure 8–15). Most fabrics made from resilient fibers require little or no touch-up pressings between wearings.

Heat-sensitive fibers can be deformed if subjected to high temperatures. Fabrics made of these fibers can be wrinkled permanently during laundry processes, or even while garments are being carried in a car trunk in very hot weather. Such wrinkles are difficult to remove and often require steam pressing.

Fibers that may be damaged by moths or mildew during storage need special protection when not in use. Wool fab-

FIGURE 8–15 *Wrinkle-resistant polyester knit twill makes a durable, easy-to-care-for jacket and jeans.* (Courtesy of Levi Strauss & Co.)

rics should be mothproofed, and cotton and linen should be stored in a dry condition in airtight wrappers. Because linen fibers break when bent, linen fabrics should be rolled for storage rather than folded.

YARN PROCESSES

High-twist yarns tend to resist wrinkling and are less absorbent, thus facilitating soil removal. However, the high-twist yarns in fabrics like crepe may shrink when laundered.

Pressing such fabrics while they are damp often restores them to their original size and shape. Complex yarns with loops, slubs, or uneven surfaces may be damaged by abrasion during laundry processes. These yarns also tend to snag more easily during wear and fabrics made of them may soon become unattractive.

Yarns blended of two or more different fibers should be cleaned in the manner appropriate for the most dominant fiber. A fabric of 65 percent cotton and 35 percent polyester, for instance, will probably require more touch-up pressing after laundering than a blend of 65 percent polyester and 35 percent cotton (Figure 8–16). An all-wool fabric usually requires dry cleaning (Figure 8–17), while wool and acrylic blended in the right proportions may be washed safely by hand.

FIGURE 8-16 *A hangtag provided for a knit garment made of a polyester/cotton blend. The care instructions on the back show that hand washing is the first recommendation; that chlorine bleach must not be used; and that the garment should not be treated roughly during laundering. Note that the garment may also be machine washed (at a low setting) or dry cleaned. The tag tells the consumer the possible alternatives and allows for choice.* (Courtesy of Eastman Chemical Products, Inc.)

FIGURE 8-17 *A woven blanket-cloth poncho and knit turtleneck and pants of pure wool. These three garments would be warm, because of wool's insulating quality, but all would require dry cleaning.* (Courtesy of Pendleton Woolen Mills)

FABRIC CONSTRUCTION METHODS

Generally, fabrics that are firm, smooth, and compact may be cared for by the methods appropriate for the fiber content. During leno-weave construction, for example, the warp yarns are interlocked, which prevents yarn slippage when the fabric is cleaned. However, yarn slippage may occur in loose, plain-woven fabrics. Nonwovens may lose their adhesive or be torn during cleaning. Fiber strength will determine whether sheer, fragile fabrics require special handling. Double knits tend to shrink less than single knits, which often must be blocked to maintain their original shape and size, but double knits of manufactured fibers will shrink if subjected to high temperatures during cleaning. All knits shed wrinkles easily during wear; this helps them maintain a fresh appearance longer than woven fabrics. Fabrics woven with float yarns or decorative designs may be more easily damaged by snagging during wear and cleaning. Pile fabrics attract lint and may require brushing between wearings.

FINISHES

Fabrics that ordinarily wrinkle easily can be finished to require little or no ironing after cleaning. Most fabrics on the market today bear minimum-care labels, but improper handling, especially during cleaning operations, can make the finishes ineffective. Cleaning instructions included on labels must be followed very carefully for satisfactory results.

Much of the fabric that will receive hard wear, such as that used for home furnishings, is treated for spot and stain resistance; such finishes are a useful protection for children's clothing also. Spot- and stain-resistant finishes may be applied by the consumer to both clothing and furnishings. Fabrics may be finished to make them resistant to damage from body perspiration, thus helping them maintain freshness longer. Some of the minimum-care finishes absorb dirt and stains, and fabrics so treated are more difficult to clean. However, additional soil-release finishes may be applied to resin-finished fabrics to make cleaning easier.

Study Questions

1. Name the five aspects of fabric that affect consumer satisfaction. Explain each.
2. Why is wool more easily dyed than glass?

3. What causes some fabrics to pill more readily than others?
4. What causes wool fabric to be resilient?
5. Why do percale sheets usually feel smoother and silkier than muslin ones?
6. Why do glass-fiber curtains sometimes split at the bottom of the hem?
7. Which might be expected to shrink less: a cotton fabric labeled "preshrunk" or one labeled "Sanforized"? Why?
8. Why do many people find nylon and polyester fabrics uncomfortable to wear?
9. Which type of fabric might be more easily cleaned: polyester or cotton? Why?
10. Why should a linen tablecloth be rolled for storage rather than folded?

Suggested Activities

1. Collect fabric samples to illustrate beauty, hand, serviceability, comfort, and care. Explain how the particular property is seen in each of the samples.
2. Survey a group of students or friends regarding their fabric likes and dislikes. Have with you several different samples of fabric and ask the people what they like and/or dislike about each piece of fabric. How many of the answers relate in some way to the properties of beauty, hand, serviceability, comfort, and care?
3. Talk with a salesperson in a store that sells textile products. Ask what type of fabric seems to be most popular with the customers and the reasons why.
4. Make a bulletin board illustrating the properties of beauty, hand, serviceability, comfort, and care in fabrics.

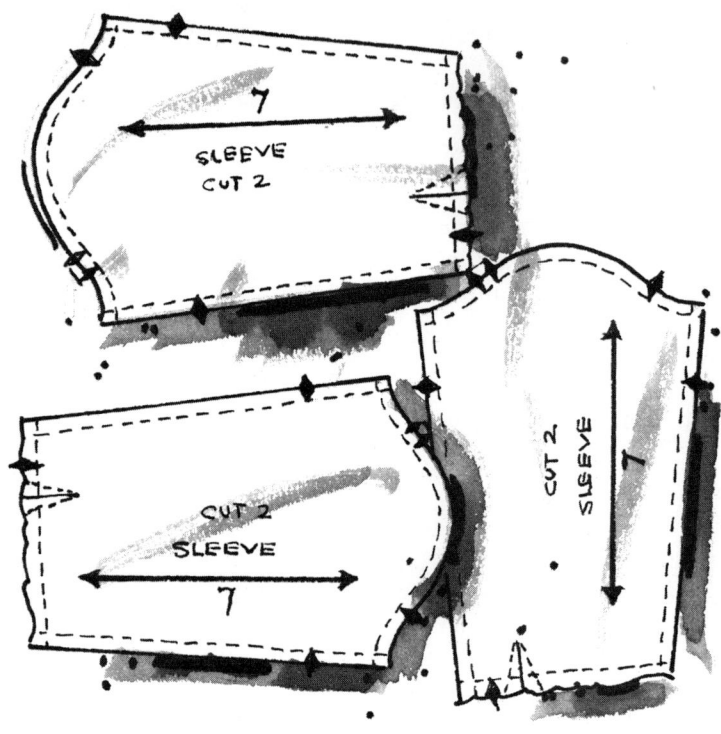

Chapter 9

Textile Properties in Home Sewing

INDIVIDUALS SEW for many reasons other than to save money, although this is important. Home sewing has increased in recent years. During a study in which one hundred rural and urban homemakers were personally interviewed about home sewing practices, 77 percent indicated they did sew at home. The reasons given showed that 59 percent sewed for a hobby, 67 percent to save money, 68 percent to have better-quality garments, 66 percent for better-fitting garments, and 69 percent to have more clothes.[1] It may well be, with the increasing inflation of today's economy, that their relative importance has altered, but these reasons for sewing are likely to have remained the same.

For whatever reasons individuals choose to sew, their knowledge and understanding of the textile properties that relate to fabric sewability largely determine the success of

---

1. Patsy Ruth Alexander, "Problems and Practices of Rural and Urban Homemakers in Clothing Construction and Buying, Bossier Parish, 1964," Master's thesis, Louisiana State University, Baton Rouge, 1965.

their projects. The significant textile properties, in this connection, are fiber content, fabric construction, and applied finishes. The techniques that usually present the most problems relate to fabric and pattern compatibility, fabric preparation, stitching operations, and pressing techniques.

Fabric and Pattern Compatibility

The first commercial dressmaking patterns were designed for use with fabrics woven of natural fibers, which were then about the only type of fabric available. Because of the limited stretch properties of these fabrics, pattern pieces allowed a certain amount of fabric above that needed for actual body measurements, to permit body movement and comfort. This allowance is known as "body ease" and is found in most patterns available today. This allowance for body ease is adjusted in pattern making and is manipulated through the use of seams, darts, gathers, and tucks, all of which shape the flat planar fabric around the curved human body.

An example of the problems encountered with patterns is setting in sleeves. Success depends on controlling the extra fabric allowed around the sleeve cap by easing it into the armhole, which is designed to be two to three inches smaller in circumference than the cap of the sleeve. Although the stretch of natural fiber fabrics is slight, it is enough to allow a sleeve to be sewn successfully into an armhole without puckers.

The development of manufactured fibers made a new type of fabric available, which presented problems when used with the commercial patterns. Woven fabric of manufactured fibers has even less stretch than that made of natural fibers, so that patterns designed for use with natural fiber fabrics included more body ease than could be handled. Manufacturers made pattern adjustments to accommodate the new fabrics, and home sewers found that one way to handle the matter was to discard their old patterns and purchase new ones.

The wide availability of knit fabrics presented a different challenge to home sewers. Because of the loop formations, knits have considerable stretch, compared with woven fabrics, and single knits tend to stretch even more than the double knits. Home sewers eager to construct knit garments soon found that the patterns they had used successfully to make well-fitting garments from woven fabrics resulted in clothing with very poor fit when used with the knits. In most cases, the knit garments seemed to be too large in certain places, if not all over. The problem was in the body ease allowance—necessary for woven fabrics, it was not needed for the new knits. Again, new designs and new patterns were the answer.

The person who sews should remember that large companies now offer three types of commercial pattern, each related to fabric type:

1. Conventional patterns are designed for fabrics that do not stretch and an allowance for body ease is included. In order to use these patterns on knit fabrics, one may

FIGURE 9-1 *This very simple shirt, McCall Pattern 4354, is suitable for men and women of all ages. Depending on the fabric selected, the garment could be worn all year or only in certain seasons, with "party pants" or with jeans.* (Courtesy of The McCall Pattern Company)

have to alter the pattern, take larger seams, or purchase the pattern in a size smaller than the body measurements indicate.
2. Some patterns are designed for use with woven fabric but are also suitable for knits because of their simple styles. Some of these patterns have two seam lines, one indicated for use with woven fabric and the other for knits.
3. Patterns designed for stretchable knits only should not be used with woven fabric; they will result in garments that are too small.

Patterns may or may not be marked, to indicate what type of fabric may be used. If there is no phrase on the envelope saying, for instance, "For Knits Only," it is wise to check the list of recommended fabrics on the back of the envelope. The McCall pattern (number 4354) shown in Figure 9-1 suggests:

Cotton broadcloth	Chino	Cotton blends
Poplin	Velour	Lightweight corduroy
Woollike blends	Chambray	Wool or synthetic
Lightweight wool		double knits

From this list, it is obvious that both woven and knit fabrics may be used for this pattern—and to be specific, only double knits are suitable.

Resin-type finishes applied to woven fabric to give minimum-care properties are the ones that present problems for the home sewer. These finishes reduce the stretch of the natural fibers and cause the fabric to take on characteristics more like those of manufactured fiber fabrics. Conventional patterns used on fabrics with such finishes may need slight alterations, particularly in the sleeve cap.

Fabric Preparation

Adequate preparation of fabric is important for a satisfactory product. Particular attention must be given to shrinkage control and grainline maintenance.

Under certain conditions, both natural and manufactured fibers shrink, and appropriate precautions should be taken to prevent this. Wool fabric probably presents the most shrinkage problems. Unless the label guarantees that the maximum amount of shrinkage to be expected will not affect the fit of the garment, fabric should be preshrunk. As a general rule, fabrics of silk or manufactured fibers do not require preshrinking.

FIGURE 9-2 *Photograph showing the selvage (left edge) and lengthwise fabric grain, running in the same direction as the selvage. The crosswise grain runs from left to right of the fabric. The true bias is shown at the lower left corner, by a 45-degree fold.* (Reproduced by courtesy of the Educational Bureau, Coats & Clark Inc.)

Firmly woven fabric usually will shrink less than loosely woven fabric, which often has had sizing added to make it look fuller. Fabric can be checked for sizing by rubbing a part of it between the hands. If a chalky substance falls away and the fabric appears to have a more open weave, it probably has been sized and can be expected to shrink considerably. Because of tension on warp yarns during weaving, woven fabric usually shrinks more in the length than in the width.

Much of the fabric on the market today is treated in such a way that shrinkage is greatly reduced. However, the home sewer should not assume this to be the case without reasonable evidence. Sanforization guarantees the maximum shrinkage of cotton and linen not to exceed 1 percent, and fabrics so labeled may be safely used without additional shrinking. However, no other process guarantees this, and some fabric labeled "preshrunk" may shrink up to 3 or 5 percent.

Some of the resin finishes applied to cotton and linen fabrics also help to control shrinkage. Wool fabric may be finished to give shrinkage control if it is labeled Dylanized or Wurlan. Otherwise, it should be properly preshrunk before use in clothing items.

Maintaining the *grainline* in woven fabric is very important, since garment pieces that are cut off-grain do not hang correctly, fit properly, or look well. Fabric grainline refers to the direction of the lengthwise and crosswise yarns (Figure 9-2). Major pattern pieces usually are placed parallel to the lengthwise grain because most fabrics are stronger in this direction, and the garment will wear better. Any direction other than lengthwise or crosswise is considered to be off-grain and on the bias.

Unlike the grainline, the bias has considerable stretch. The true bias, formed by a line cutting across both grainlines at a 45-degree angle, stretches the most. Some pattern designs use pieces to be cut on the bias, for fullness or a draped effect. Such pieces must be handled with care, in laying out and in cutting.

Knit fabric does not have grain like woven fabric. However, the courses of the loop formation usually form the lengthwise direction of knit and may be treated as the lengthwise grain in pattern placement (Figure 9-3). It often is unnecessary to cut knit fabrics on the bias since they stretch enough to serve the same purpose as bias. Contrary to common belief, knit fabrics will shrink because of the loops in their construction, and they should be preshrunk by methods appropriate for the fiber content. Even nylon and polyester should be preshrunk, although woven fabric of the same fibers does not require preshrinking.

Printed fabric designs actually are applied finishes and must be printed on the grain. Designs with definite pattern directions should be parallel to the appropriate grainline. If fabric is printed off-grain (Figure 9-4), the design cannot be straightened, and one must choose to follow either the fabric or design grain in cutting pattern pieces. Such fabric is best left in the store.

Fabrics with resin finishes may be difficult to straighten if they were finished in an off-grain position. Sometimes shrinking the fabric will straighten the grain. If the fabric cannot be straightened, the home sewer can cope with the problem by cutting each pattern piece on a single layer of fabric, one at a time.

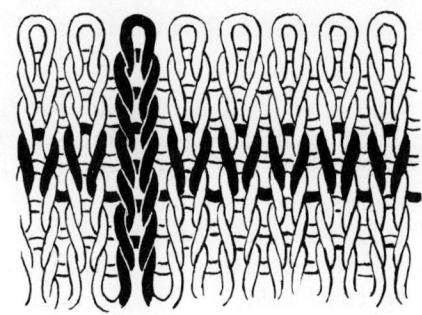

FIGURE 9-3 *Diagram of the crosswise and lengthwise loops (dark threads) in a knit fabric.* (Reproduced by courtesy of the Educational Bureau, Coats & Clark Inc.)

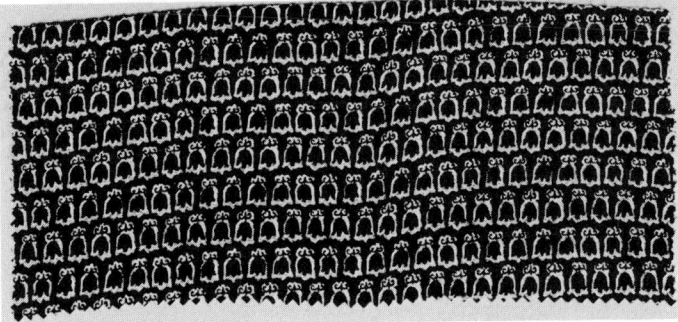

FIGURE 9-4 *A fabric that has been printed off-grain.* (Reprinted, by permission, from Evelyn Mansfield and Ethel Lucas, *Clothing Construction*, 2nd ed., Houghton Mifflin, Boston, 1974, p. 114)

Stitching Operations

In sewing modern fabrics, concern arises about machine adjustments, suitable needles and thread, tension and stitch length regulation, seam finishes, zipper applications, seam tapes, and appropriate support fabrics for interfacings, linings, and underlinings. In each case, these choices are made with respect to the fabric properties.

Heat sensitivity and shrinkage properties of fibers must be considered in choosing thread compatible with fabric. Mercerized cotton thread can be used satisfactorily for almost any type of fabric, although it may shrink and cause seam puckers in many minimum-care fabrics. Some of the threads that have been developed more recently—made of polyester, nylon, and cotton-covered polyester, for example—work better on fabrics of manufactured fibers (Figures 9-5 and 9-6). However, only the cotton-covered thread is not heat-sensitive. When an unwrapped polyester or nylon thread is used, it may be necessary to operate the sewing machine at a low speed to keep the thread from fraying and melting.

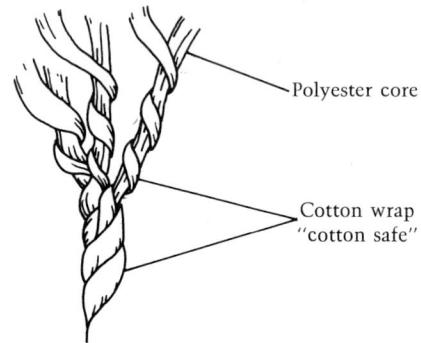

FIGURE 9-5 *How a cotton-covered polyester thread is constructed.* (Reproduced by courtesy of the Educational Bureau, Coats & Clark Inc.)

Fabric and thread type usually determine the amount of tension the machine requires to make a balanced stitch. Fabrics of manufactured fibers, and especially those with some stretch, may require a fairly loose upper and bobbin tension. This is also true for threads that stretch, such as cotton-covered polyester and spun polyester types.

Quality sewing used to include a neat inside appearance to the garment, especially the finishing of all raw seam edges. Fabric that ravels still must have seam finishes, and the type of seam finish should be appropriate for the fabric weight. Some examples of seam finishes are bound, overcast, pinked, and zigzagged seams. Properties that contribute to raveling are smooth-filament yarn structure and loosely woven construction. Knit construction, tight weaves, and resin finishes inhibit raveling.

Shrinkage is an important consideration in selecting all sewing notions or findings. The tape of most zippers is made of cotton fabric that has not been treated for shrinkage control; the package printing must be read (Figure 9-7). When used in garments made of natural fiber fabric, the tape usually shrinks in the same proportion as the fabric. However, when these same zippers are used in fabrics of manufactured fibers, they tend to shrink more than the fabric, and the seam puckers where the zipper is applied. To prevent this, zippers should be preshrunk if not so labeled. Some zippers have tape made of nylon or polyester and these do not

COATS & CLARK'S "O.N.T."
SILK TWIST

J. & P. COATS
"Dual-Duty Plus"

J. & P. COATS
"SUPERSHEEN"

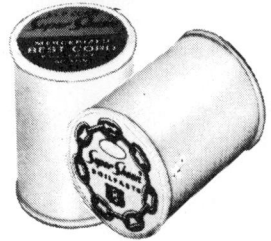

J. & P. COATS
"Dual-Duty Plus"
DRESSMAKER SPOOL

J. & P. COATS
"SUPERSHEEN"

J. & P. COATS
"Dual-Duty Plus"
EXTRA STRONG
BUTTON & CARPET

J. & P. COATS
"Dual-Duty Plus"
EXTRA FINE FOR
LIGHTWEIGHT FABRICS

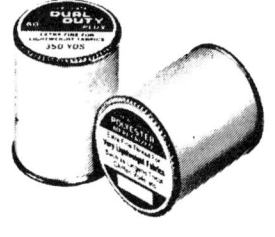

FIGURE 9-6 *Thread manufacturers usually produce a range of threads for different home sewing uses.* (Reproduced by courtesy of the Educational Bureau, Coats & Clark Inc.)

require preshrinking (Figure 9–8). All seam or hem tapes and other trimmings should be preshrunk unless the package label states that it is not necessary.

Support fabrics (those used for interfacings, linings, and underlinings) should be compatible in weight, stiffness, and care needs with the garment fabric in order to maintain the properties of the outer fabric. Woven fabric is best for all areas where support is needed because it has more flexibility than nonwoven fabric.

Most of the discussion thus far is appropriately applied to woven fabric, but the techniques that follow relate primarily to sewing on knits. A slightly longer stitch, about 10 to 12 per inch, is usually recommended for sewing on knit fabrics. Ball-point machine needles of size 9 or 11 give satisfactory results. The ball point pushes the threads aside instead of sewing through them, as regular needles do.

Cotton-covered polyester thread gives very good results, as does the spun polyester type. For either type, machine tension should be rather loose since these threads stretch slightly. This makes them ideal for knit construction, but a tight tension can eliminate the stretch.

Seam edges of knit fabric, especially double knit, do not require finishing, but they may be zigzagged if desired. Single-knit fabrics tend to roll on the edge and may require special techniques in handling.

As for use in woven fabric, zippers and tapes should be preshrunk if they are not so labeled as purchased. Bias or stretch tape should be used on knits (Figure 9–9), except when the purpose is to limit stretch in areas such as shoulder seams. Woven fabrics can be used satisfactorily for interfacings, linings, and underlinings. Cutting these pieces on the bias gives them stretch, so that they respond in a way more like knit fabric.

Adhesive-type fabrics are often sold for use as interfacings and many people like the crisp appearance they give, especially to collars and cuffs in garments made of knits. However, the adhesive backing often loosens after a few washings and the lining then is more like plain-woven fabric.

As was mentioned earlier, resin-type finishes present the most problems. Many of the same techniques recommended for sewing on fabrics of manufactured fibers apply to those with resin-type finishes. These include the use of slightly loosened tension; sharp needles (ball-point ones work very well here also); cotton-covered polyester thread; and preshrunk zippers, tapes, and support fabrics. The home sewer should be careful to avoid mistakes when machine stitching

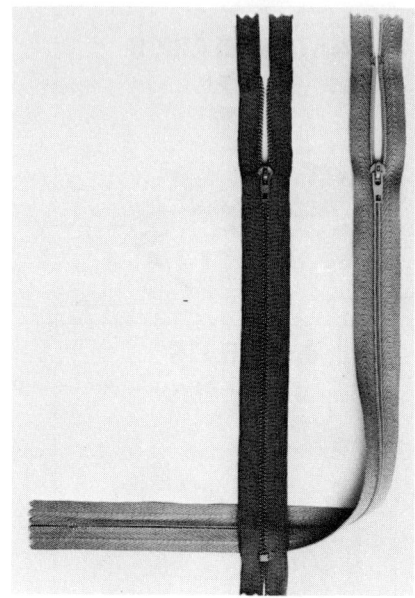

FIGURE 9-7 *Two types of zippers presently available. The one on the left uses metal teeth molded to the tape and painted with enamel. The zipper on the right uses a polyester coil and a permanent-press tape.* (Reproduced by courtesy of the Educational Bureau, Coats & Clark Inc.)

so that stitches do not have to be removed. It is often very difficult, if not impossible, to remove the needle marks from resin-finished fabrics.

Pressing Techniques

Resilient fibers, such as wool and many manufactured ones, require more pressure than less resilient fibers such as cotton, to make sharp creases and flat seams. In tailoring wool garments, pressing should be supplemented by weighting down pressed areas with clappers or a brick. Moisture in the form of steam helps to obtain the best results in pressing and, for some fibers, a steam iron is adequate. However, resilient fibers may require a damp cloth. Wool almost always presses best with a damp press cloth. Some fabrics take on a shine when the iron is placed next to them, so a press cloth, either damp or dry, should always be used when they are pressed on the right side.

Safe pressing temperatures are determined by the heat sensitivity of the fibers. Highly sensitive fibers such as polyester require lower temperatures than do cotton and other less heat-sensitive ones. The control guide on the automatic iron should be followed for appropriate temperatures.

Fabrics that are constructed to be resilient require more pressure and moisture in pressing construction details. Worsted wools and crepes, in particular, fall into this category. Cotton fabrics, usually among the easier to press, are more difficult to handle when constructed by methods that use two or more sets of yarns: velveteen and corduroy are examples. Both of these fabrics require special handling to avoid crushing the pile during pressing motions.

Resin finishes present some problems in pressing. They require adequate moisture for a flat appearance, but the finish often needs a pressing temperature lower than the normal one for pressing the fiber. A too-hot iron placed on a fabric finish may scorch the fabric. Care should be taken when pressing heat-set finishes such as embossed designs to keep temperature, moisture, and pressure at levels that will not destroy the raised effect.

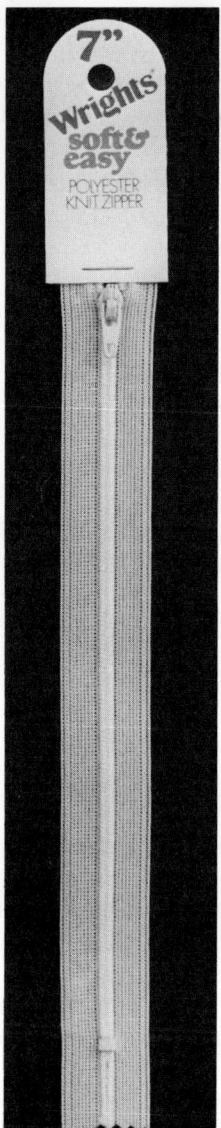

FIGURE 9-8 *A heat-resistant nylon coil zipper, made with 100 percent polyester knit tape.* (Courtesy of Wm. E. Wright Co.)

Study Questions

1. What is "body ease" that is found in today's patterns?
2. How does the kind of fabric selected for a garment determine the amount of body ease needed in a pattern?

3. What are the three types of commercial patterns offered by large companies? How is each designed for a particular type of fabric?
4. Which kind of fabric presents the most shrinkage problems?
5. What is fabric sizing? Why is it added to fabrics? How can the consumer test fabric for the presence of sizing?
6. Why does woven fabric usually shrink more in the length than in the width?
7. What is fabric grainline? What effect does cutting major pattern pieces "off-grain" have on the completed garment?
8. When sewing on knit fabric, what may be used as a cutting guide that is comparable to the grainline in woven fabric?
9. How can one tell whether fabric with a printed design is printed on-grain?
10. Why does some fabric ravel while other fabric does not?
11. Why should zippers be preshrunk before using them in fabrics of manufactured fibers?
12. What are the differences in pressing techniques suitable for wool and cotton fabrics? Explain the reasons for these differences.

Suggested Activities

1. Compare a knit garment with one in a similar style made of woven fabric. Both garments should be a good fit for you or a friend. Try them both on to check fit and comfort. Then remove and measure them. How do they compare?
2. Visit a garment store and make a check of garments for grainline. Make a notation of the ones that are cut off-grain.
3. Cut swatches of fabric about six inches square. Include several kinds of woven and knit fabric. Draw around each one on a piece of paper and label each paper. Then wash the swatches either in a washing machine or by hand. After they dry, match each swatch with its appropriate pattern. How do they compare? Which fabrics would need to be preshrunk?
4. Look through your clothing for "zipper puckering."
5. Cut swatches of fabric about six inches square. Include fabrics of several different types of fibers. Experiment with different pressing techniques: different temperatures; with a damp press cloth; with steam iron only; with a dry press cloth only. What are your conclusions?

FIGURE 9-9 *A seam-binding tape made of 100 percent nylon lace. This product has built-in stretch and thus is suitable for use on knits; it also may be used on woven fabrics. A replacement guarantee is printed on the outside of the label, on the back.* (Courtesy of Wm. E. Wright Co.)

Chapter 10

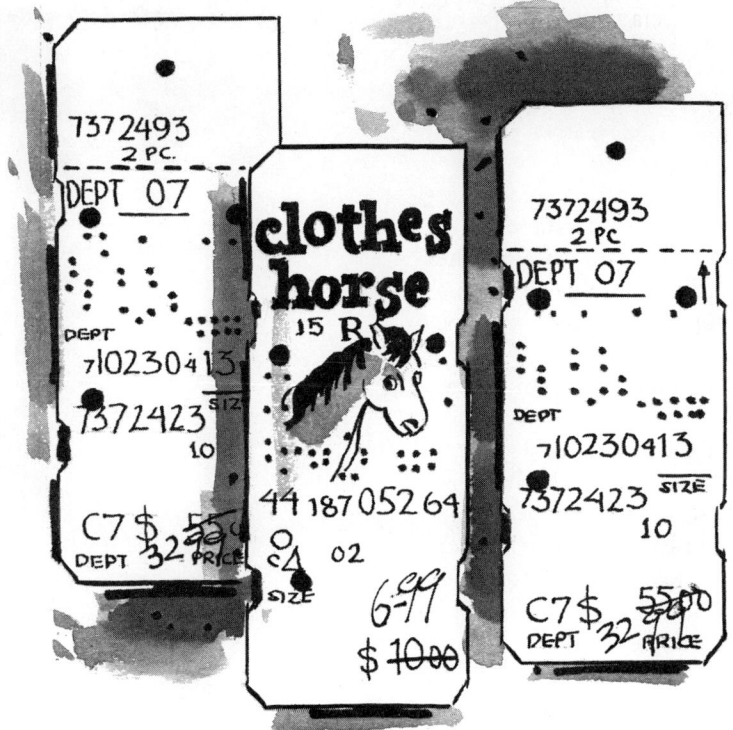

Stores, Sales, and Credit

MANY KINDS OF STORES exist today to serve consumers with varying tastes. Merchandising methods vary from store to store, and consumers need to consider several points carefully when deciding which stores may serve their purposes most satisfactorily.

Quality-conscious customers desire a fairly wide range of items at different prices from which to choose. They will look for a variety of styles, colors, and sizes as they make their selections.

For many people, store location is important, particularly as regards cost of travel, parking facilities, or accessibility to public transportation. Store services are an important consideration for customers who want or need special assistance from salespeople, delivery service, charge privileges, or special-order merchandise not in stock. Other conveniences sought include comfortable lounges, nurseries for children, and pet rest or wait centers.

Intelligent consumers are conscious of both price and value but do not equate the two. They look for stores with the reputation for giving value for money. Honest practices and fair business dealings are usually reflected in truthful advertising and labeling that is both accurate and adequate.

Types of Stores

Regardless of where people shop for clothing and other textile products, they need to have some understanding of the purposes and methods of the various retail outlets. The informed consumer who has some basic knowledge of textile products can become a skillful shopper in almost any type of store.

Even the most knowledgeable consumer sometimes has problems when shopping for clothing and other textile products. Some of these may relate to the type of store where purchases are made and the customer services that are offered. One group of homemakers studied a few years ago reported they mainly shopped for clothing items at higher and moderately priced department stores, chain and discount stores, and mail-order houses. Among their major problems in buying ready-made clothing were: selecting size and style, recognizing quality, finding time to shop, making needed alterations, and budgeting.[1] It is likely that the same pattern applies today.

Retail stores are businesses engaged in selling merchandise to consumers. Several different types of store now stock textile items: specialty or exclusive shops, department, chain, variety, and second-hand stores, mail-order houses, supermarkets, and discount stores.

SPECIALTY OR EXCLUSIVE SHOPS

These stores usually specialize in a limited type of clothing, such as men's wear, shoes, or children's clothing. The consumer can find a larger variety within the specialty area than may be available at other stores, and at varying prices. Salespeople are often well trained and will give valuable assistance.

DEPARTMENT STORES

Often these are large stores that stock a wide variety of different items that may include clothing for all members

---

1. Patsy Ruth Alexander, "Problems and Practices of Rural and Urban Homemakers in Clothing Construction and Buying, Bossier Parish, 1964," Master's thesis, Louisiana State University, Baton Rouge, 1965, pp. 63–65.

FIGURE 10-1 *An everyday scene in a large department store, typical of this kind of arrangement of goods.* (Ray Ellis, Photo Researchers, Inc.)

of the family (Figure 10-1). However, because of this very wide range of stock, selection within the individual category, such as men's shirts or ladies' shoes, may be more limited than in a store that specializes in particular items. Department stores vary in price range, also, both within the store and from one store to another. Some stores are owned independently, while others are part of a chain. Salespeople may or may not be well trained to give useful information to the consumer in making decisions about textile products purchases.

CHAIN STORES

These businesses belong to a network of stores that may be independently owned but affiliated with a group, or may be all owned by an individual or corporation and leased for local management. Volume buying usually enables such stores to make savings that may be passed on to the consumer in the form of lower prices. Generally, salespeople are not very helpful in supplying information about fabrics or anticipated performance and care.

VARIETY STORES

This type of store usually stocks many items other than textile goods. Prices generally are lower because of the high amount of self-service and open-counter displaying (Figure 10–2). Selection may be limited, but the customer can save time in shopping. Salespeople are not often available for assistance the customer needs to make an evaluation of textile products.

FIGURE 10-2 *A typical variety store, which carries a very mixed assortment of goods.* (Anna Kaufman Moon, Stock, Boston, Inc.)

SECOND-HAND STORES

These shops are becoming more numerous, and sometimes have good buys for the budget-minded shopper and the shopper who knows how to judge quality and condition. Some carry a miscellaneous assortment of goods, while others specialize in furniture or clothing. Items of clothing, however, may lack any kind of labeling, including size and care instructions, and this can create a real problem. Frequently, these stores are sponsored by civic groups to raise money, and they rely on volunteer help as sales staff. These salespeople usually have no training in assisting customers, other than in how to locate specific items.

MAIL-ORDER HOUSES

These businesses provide an opportunity for the consumer to save time and energy by not having to go to stores for goods. However, selection usually must be made by looking at catalog pictures rather than by seeing actual items. There is added inconvenience if items have to be returned because they do not fit or are unsuitable for the purpose intended. Delay in delivery of the merchandise can vary from a week or two to several months on the initial purchase. Delays on returned goods also vary.

SUPERMARKETS

In recent years food stores have increased their stock of textile items and some of the larger chain markets feature a fairly wide selection of items for the family and home. Such stores advertise the convenience of one-stop shopping for furnishings, food, and clothing and their business seems to be sizeable. Since supermarkets are organized for self-service, customers have little or no assistance available in the purchase of clothing. Items are usually prepackaged and the consumer must make decisions based on the information on the package and any past experience from such purchases. The reputation of the supermarket for selling high-quality food items may be a clue to reliability in other kinds of merchandise.

DISCOUNT STORES

These stores have increased in popularity within recent years as retailers of textile products. Volume buying, few customer services, cash-and-carry practices, and self-service

FIGURE 10-3 *A typical example of a seasonal sale from a long-established and respected store.* (Courtesy of Filene's, Boston)

displaying cut the cost of overhead expenses and the savings are passed on to the consumer in the form of somewhat lower prices. These stores sometimes carry "irregulars, seconds, and unknown brands." The consumer needs to examine such merchandise very carefully before buying. Irregulars may be sweaters or knit tops with sleeves not the same size or length, for example. Flaws in design or construction in fabric may be detected in garments, or the close observer may find garment pieces that differ in color owing to the use

Part Three / Selection

of fabric from different dye lots. These stores frequently market imported clothing, which can be retailed at a lower price than similar garments made in the United States.

How to Shop at Sales

Wise consumers can make considerable savings at the various sales offered by stores, if they have some knowledge of the kinds of sales and understand how to use them to financial advantage (Figure 10-3).

As a general rule, the first customers present when a sale begins gain the most, for the choice of merchandise decreases

FIGURE 10-4 *An advertisement for a sale of special-purchase merchandise from another well-known and highly reputable store.* (Courtesy of Jordan Marsh, Boston)

in both variety and value as the sale continues. Some stores notify "preferred customers" of forthcoming sales before the public announcement is made.

Sales featuring quality or well-known merchandise brands at drastically reduced prices should be regarded cautiously, for these are sometimes misleading gimmicks. It often happens that the supply of such items is so limited that they are available to only a very few customers who are at the store when it opens. After the supply of advertised merchandise is sold out, usually very early in the sale, substitute items may be offered in its place, which may be either of a lower quality or at a higher price than the original merchandise.

The consumer should be skeptical of sale advertising which claims that prices have been slashed in half, unless the store is well known and highly reputable (Figure 10-4). Some merchants mark up such items before the sale begins and the sale price actually corresponds very closely to the original price.

As a general policy, stores do not permit the return of sale merchandise, so the consumer must be very careful. Items should be examined closely for any damage such as tears or stains, and workmanship should be inspected. If the item will not provide good service, it is a poor buy. If the product is not something the consumer would usually select, it may end up as another "white elephant" purchase, stashed away out of sight.

During the year, most reputable stores feature several types of sale for specific purposes (Figure 10-5). The wise shopper can probably make some savings at all of them.

PRECLEARANCE SALES

A wide choice usually is offered at these sales, perhaps more than at later sales, but the savings generally are not significant. The consumer can wait until the merchandise is reduced further, later on, and realize a larger savings. However, there is always the risk that the item wanted will have been sold before the later sale.

CLEARANCE SALES

These sales are held at the end of a season, and savings may be very high, especially on regular stock merchandise. The shopper must be alert for any items added just for the sale, for these are unlikely to be as good a bargain as items

FIGURE 10-5 Typical headlines in newspaper advertisements for different sales that stores run at various times during the year.

actually marked down from regular stock. Regular stock items often can be identified by a mark through the price on the original tag.

PREINVENTORY CLEARANCE SALES

These sales help merchants reduce the stock left over at the end of a season, to avoid storage. While such sales may provide considerable savings, the buyer may have to store the items himself before they can be used, and certain fad clothing items purchased at the very end of a wearing season may be outdated before the next season for their use.

SPECIAL ITEM SALES

Held throughout the year, such sales feature specific merchandise such as shoes, linens, carpets, and so on. Most consumers are familiar with the semiannual "white sales," usually held in January and July. Savings can vary greatly with the items featured and may be up to as much as 50 percent on some national brands.

Credit

Purchase of goods at sales implies that the consumer has the money available to use in this way. This may or may not be the case, and today few people will pass a lifetime without making use of credit in some form. Consumer credit is both good and bad, depending on how it is used. It is a form of ready cash and makes it possible for individuals to enjoy goods and services while they are accumulating the money to pay for them. However, unless the consumer has some understanding of the various forms of credit, he can make mistakes that will cost him both money and reputation. An adequate discussion of all the aspects of consumer credit is beyond the scope of this book, so the points now presented are limited to those which pertain to the acquisition of textile products.

The main reason people use credit is to have immediate purchasing power, usually at the expense of money they will have available in the future. In no way does credit increase the total amount of purchasing power which an individual has, and the use of credit today will decrease the power to purchase in the future, at least until the indebtedness is paid. As a rule, the borrower is required to pay in some way for the use of credit, most often as interest which increases at a fixed rate until the money is repaid. Thus, the interest paid on the credit added to the price of the purchase increases the overall cost of the item to the consumer. The use of credit is not necessarily bad, but wise consumers will carefully consider the situation before obligating themselves to any form of credit. They should consider whether they actually need credit, become familiar with the different types available, and be knowledgeable about any kind of protection to expect during credit transactions.

DETERMINING THE NEED FOR CREDIT

The consumer needs to decide whether the purchase is justifiable and whether credit is needed for it. Consideration must be given to how payments will fit into the family budget and if other necessities must be sacrificed in order to meet the regular payments incurred by the debt. The period of usefulness of the purchase should be weighed against the time required to pay off the debt. No one likes to be paying for an item that has already been used up or worn out. The cost of the credit itself is important to consider. It might be more economical to use money deposited in a savings account, if the family has one, and pay cash. Some merchants offer thirty- to ninety-day payment plans without adding credit charges. If the purchase could be paid for within that length of time, the consumer would do well to make such an arrangement with the retailer, if possible, and save the cost of credit. One major problem with the use of credit is that consumers find it easy to obtain and run themselves so heavily into debt that credit becomes a liability instead of an asset as a means of acquiring goods and services.

TYPES OF CREDIT

The type of credit a consumer needs is largely determined by the amount of money he must obtain. Whatever amount is needed may be available from one or more of several sources.

CHARGE ACCOUNTS This kind of credit is probably the most commonly used and is economical for the consumer who knows how to use it wisely. Charge accounts are of the most financial benefit when the bills are paid before service charges are added. Some merchants allow from thirty to sixty days' credit before adding a service charge. Negligence in paying bills on time may cost the consumer an interest rate as high as 18 percent a year. Wise individuals will guard against charging more to their accounts than they can realistically and safely handle financially.

CREDIT CARDS These cards have become one of the most convenient forms of credit available within recent years. They enable the consumer to charge purchases at different stores, restaurants, and so on, throughout the month, with the added convenience of making one end-of-the-month payment to cover all. However, like regular charge accounts, they may be used unwisely in that the consumer may make more purchases than he can afford to pay for at the billing time. A service charge of 18 percent is added to the unpaid balance for most credit-card holders.

PERSONAL LOANS This type of loan is obtained from credit unions or banks if the amount of cash needed requires this type of approach. The interest rate usually runs around 10 to 12 percent annually. Most consumers find it relatively easy to make such loans with payment arranged in installments that fit into the budget.

CHECK-CREDIT PLAN This money is obtained in the form of a preapproved loan from the bank for a maximum amount of money. After the funds in the regular checking account are depleted, credit is extended to the consumer up to the previously arranged amount. Usually a 10 to 18 percent interest rate is applicable until the debt is paid.

Although several other forms of credit are available to the consumer, those mentioned above offer the most assistance in the purchase of textile products.

CONSUMER CREDIT PROTECTION

The passage of the Consumer Credit Protection Act (truth-in-lending law), which became effective July 1, 1969, has provided help to many consumers who might otherwise have experienced difficulty in their credit transactions. The law requires written disclosure of credit terms before the credit is extended. Although it does not limit finance charges, it requires disclosure of percentage rates and binding terms relating to finance charges, the total number of payments, and the amounts of each. Misleading advertising of a deceptive nature is prohibited and wage garnishment is limited by this law.

Since the Fair Credit Reporting Act was passed on April 24, 1971, the consumer has some protection against false information that is detrimental to his credit rating. A consumer must be notified in writing if a credit-reporting agency is investigating his credit rating and the agency is required to provide a copy of the report if so requested. An individual also has the right to see information in his credit files and be told the sources of the information, by requesting this in writing from the credit bureau. It is in the consumer's best interest to keep a good credit rating in case of future credit needs.

Shopping Tips

1. Determine your real need for an item and shop with this need in mind.
2. Buy the best quality that your budget will permit.
3. Select the right time to make purchases. Certain sales, such as end-of-season sales, often provide valuable buys.
4. Compare values among the various stores as well as within each store itself. Basement departments in larger stores often provide opportunities to make real savings on quality merchandise.
5. Consider the conveniences offered by the store and their cost. Don't overpay for conveniences such as delivery service and gift wrapping if you don't use them.
6. Check the store's private brands when possible. They often give more value for the money than do the nationally advertised brands.
7. Check the middle-price items. These usually have quality comparable to higher-priced merchandise but lack decorative touches that tend to increase the price.
8. Read all labels and consider the facts they provide. Take time to think about the fiber content and the care instructions.
9. Whenever possible, avoid buying on credit. The added expense of finance charges ultimately increases the cost of the merchandise.
10. Select basic styles and avoid extremes that may last for a limited period of time, in both clothing and furnishings.
11. Remember that occasionally it may be more economical to buy in quantity ("three pairs for $4.50"), if the extra items can be used within a reasonable time.

Study Questions

1. Name eight different types of stores where textile products are sold.
2. Describe briefly the characteristics of each type of store that handles textile products.
3. Explain briefly the meaning of these types of sale: preclearance, clearance, preinventory clearance, and special item.
4. What is meant by each of the following: charge account, credit card, personal loan, check-credit? Discuss some advantages and disadvantages of using each form of credit.
5. What is the Consumer Credit Protection Act? How can it benefit consumers?
6. What is the Fair Credit Reporting Act? When was it passed? How can it benefit consumers?
7. State five tips to follow when shopping at sales.

Suggested Activities

1. Go to three or four different stores where textile products are sold. Compare the selection of products available in each store as to: quality, styles, prices, services offered, and so on.
2. Watch the newspaper and other forms of local store advertisements for announced sales. Identify the types of sales being featured and the listed prices for the sale items. Which ones would make the best buys? Why?
3. Visit a store, bank, and/or loan company. Find out the procedure used by each to provide credit to consumers.
4. Survey customers shopping in a textile product store and ask them if they ever use credit to make purchases and the type they prefer to use.

Chapter 11

Guidelines for Purchasing

A BASIC INFORMATION need of today's consumer is an understanding of the forces, such as values and needs, that influence his or her personal decisions and choices. These forces consciously or unconsciously influence the decisions each person makes.

Decision Making

The consumer has to make decisions based on information from many different sources (Figure 11-1). All forms of advertisement supply information, but often for the sole purpose of convincing the individual of the need to purchase a specific brand of product. Before the consumer purchases the advertised product, he or she should first determine whether the decision is based on an actual need for the product, as determined by personally identified values and goals.

Decision making is a process that includes these steps: defining the problem, seeking alternative solutions, evaluating them, and deciding from among the alternatives. Consumer education begins with decision making, values, and goals,

FIGURE 11-1 *Consumers carefully inspecting merchandise in a clothing store.* (Ellis Herwig, Stock, Boston, Inc.)

and it includes many other concepts that are directly or indirectly related. When individuals and consumers as a whole become better managers of their resources, including money, they receive greater satisfaction from the goods and services obtained with their resources. Oftentimes this satisfaction results from an increase in knowledge and understanding that causes the consumer to make changes in buying habits.

Changes also occur as a result of family resource management that is based upon values. These values are determined by wants, needs, attitudes, customs, habits, exposure, and education, and they lead to the formulation of goals. Action results from goal identification and requires decision making about consumption of goods and services. Style, standards, and status, when considered in relation to environment, identify the family's standard of living, socioeconomic status, and life style. These become interpreted as the family level of living, which is measured in terms of satisfaction, and achieves family welfare.[1]

---

1. Ann Smith Rice, "Where Are We in Consumer Education?" *What's New in Home Economics* (January 1971), 35.

VALUES

Values are anything that an individual considers to be important. They are learned by an individual and are influenced by his family, social, and cultural background. Each individual defines his own value system, which influences his behavior and decision-making processes. As one's circumstances change throughout life, so values may change also. An individual faced with identical choice situations at different times in the life cycle may make very different decisions because of changes that have taken place in his or her value priorities. Personal values are important in one's concept of well-being, for they provide a standard by which to assess the extent of satisfactions in and with life.

Although values in themselves are intangible and abstract in character, they manifest themselves concretely in the behavioral patterns of individuals, especially in the realm of rationalization of behavior, providing both justification and explanation for it. Because of the cause-and-effect relationship between values and behavior, understanding a person's values may shed light on his behavior and, conversely, his behavior may reflect more accurately his declared values.[2]

When groups of people or a nation agree on common values, those values become *ideals* and serve to unite people in a common effort to bring about what is best for the majority. Often the ideals form the basis for laws which regulate the behavior of all the people within the group. Usually the laws function in the best interest of the majority of the people, but sometimes the same ideal can influence the passage of two related laws which conflict in their scope. This is the situation that has developed in the conflict between the environmentalist, who wants to conserve the purity of the water supply, and the textile technologist, who is concerned with providing flame-retardant clothing and textile products. The crux of the problem lies in the use of phosphates in detergents, which tends to pollute the water supply, thus contributing to making it unsafe for human consumption. On the other hand, flame-retardant finishes currently applied to cellulosic fiber clothing and home furnishings may become ineffective if they are laundered in nonphosphate detergents. Laws have been passed requiring that certain textile products be made flame-retardant, while some states have passed other laws banning the use of phosphates in detergents. The

---

2. Nicholas Rescher, "What Is Valuing?" *Forum*, J. C. Penney Co., Inc., New York (Spring/Summer 1972), 3.

overall desire for a safe environment motivates the behavior of both groups and yet they are in conflict with each other.

NEEDS

The level of social development of an individual, a group of people, or a nation may reflect needs at that point, which in turn influence values. According to Maslow's theory of motivation,[3] human needs are organized in a hierarchy of predominance, and only after lower-level needs relating to the basic drives of hunger, thirst, and sex are satisfied do other needs come into play. These include safety and the need for security and protection from physical harm; love and the need for friendship, affection, and acceptance; esteem, related to self-respect, respect of others, and recognition; and ultimately the need for self-actualization. In the process of examining the various levels of human existence that may be found within the world today, it may be possible to find individuals or groups who live at all levels of need satisfaction.

Applying this theory to textile-product consumption, then a visitor to a community of people who live in the most primitive way in a year-round mild climate might notice a complete absence of textile products. Only if these people suffer from attacks by wild animals or from disagreeable climatic conditions might they find textile fibers such as those available in plant leaves or animal skins useful for clothing and shelter purposes. As people become more sociable and interact with others, they tend to desire mutual acceptance, expressed in the form of friendship and affection. Then textile products become useful as catalysts for social interaction, stimulating the need for the acquisition of appropriate clothing for entertaining guests or adequate furnishings to facilitate group gatherings. An individual may derive esteem and recognition from peers because of the kind and monetary value of textile products possessed. The acquisition of antique furnishings or creations from original designer houses may be contemporary ways to achieve the desired prestige. Self-actualization, or reaching one's potential, may be experienced by using textile products as a means of creative expression—for example, when a person constructs a self-designed garment or uses original

---

3. A. H. Maslow, *Motivation and Personality*, Harper and Brothers Publishers, New York, 1954, pp. 80–106.

ideas to make a wall hanging, just for the sheer enjoyment of doing it.

VALUE CLARIFICATION

It may be difficult for an individual to identify values or to decide whether something considered important is actually a value. The following questions may be used to help clarify one's values. A "yes" answer to all questions indicates a value.[4]

1. Has it been freely chosen by the individual?
2. Has it been chosen from among alternatives?
3. Has it been chosen after thoughtful consideration of the alternatives?
4. Is the individual happy or proud of the choice?
5. Is the individual willing to publicly affirm the choice?
6. Does the individual act according to how the choice dictates?
7. Does the individual make this specific choice repeatedly and consistently?

Selecting Textile Products

Table 11-1 can be used as a check list for selecting textile products. The answers to the questions may help make decisions that will result in more satisfaction from the product. The wise consumer is willing to spend some time evaluating products before buying, for by so doing it often is possible to avoid unnecessary or inappropriate purchases. Many clothes closets contain at least one "white elephant" purchase that could have been avoided had more time been spent in product evaluation beforehand.

Quality in Fabric and Construction

Quality is not necessarily dependent on place of purchase or price, although both may be a help at times. Often, famous-name manufacturers or nationally known stores may not offer products of the finest quality, although their prices may be among the highest. The consumer who knows how to judge quality may be able to shop skillfully almost anywhere and make substantial savings.

---

4. Thelma Frame, "In Choosing Values Today's Children Need Practice," *The Delta Kappa Gamma Bulletin* (Fall 1969), 33–36.

TABLE 11-1 *Check List for Selecting Textile Products*

	Yes	No

1. Does the textile product meet my individual needs?
   a. It is appropriate for my life style.
   b. It will coordinate with other articles I have and will be used with them.
   c. It will maintain an acceptable appearance during a reasonable period of use.
   d. It will fit within my budget.		

2. What facts do I know about the textile product?
   a. The quality is compatible with the price.
   b. The label information is adequate and meets the legal requirements.
   c. The brand is one that has a reputation of general consumer satisfaction.
   d. The product has passed some end-use testing, according to information on the label.		

3. Do I fully understand the recommended procedure required to maintain this product?
   a. It can be laundered at home either by machine or by hand.
   b. It can be dry cleaned professionally or in a coin-operated machine.
   c. It can be spot cleaned successfully.
   d. It requires no special attention before cleaning (such as button or trim removal).
   e. The entire garment, including trim, can be cleaned in the same manner.		

4. What facts do I know about the retailer?
   a. The store has a professionally trained salesperson to assist me in making my selection.
   b. The store has a standard procedure for returning unusable or defective products.
   c. The store has a long- or short-term payment plan that meets my needs.
   d. The store has an acceptable reputation within the community.		

5. Do I know about the following aspects of the item?
   a. Fiber content
   b. Fabrication method (woven, knit, etc.)
   c. Finishes used
   d. Fabric trade name		

6. Does the product compare favorably with similar products available elsewhere in the following respects?
   a. Quality of workmanship
   b. Price
   c. Required care		

FABRIC

Firmly woven fabric usually is more durable and will keep its shape better than fabric that is loosely woven. Therefore, if the garment to be purchased will receive heavy wear, a firm, closely woven fabric is the better choice. Fabrics with open or novelty weaves may be preferred for certain articles, to create a desired effect. In clothing, coolness might be wanted. Loosely woven fabrics usually are used for glass curtains, to allow more light to enter the room and to give an "airy" atmosphere.

Double knits tend to have more body and durability than single knits. Where durability and service are important factors, a double knit would deliver more wear. On the other hand, single knit is desirable for items where softness and comfort are wanted, as in underwear.

Finishes such as Sanforization for shrinkage control and Zepel and Scotchgard for stain and spot resistance extend the life and service of the product. Additionally, since these finishes are not inexpensive, manufacturers of cheap products are less likely to use them. Therefore, an item carrying tags or labels for these finishes may well be of better quality than one without them.

Fabric and design grain of all pieces should be true, and all parts of the garment or product should be checked for this point. On-grain cutting gives the best appearance and also wears longer. Good-quality fabric should be guaranteed by the manufacturer or retailer for colorfastness to light, perspiration, washing, dry cleaning, and crocking, as the case may be. Fabric should have no weak or thin places. If there is any doubt on this point, a garment can be held up to the light. On larger items such as upholstered furniture, thin sections in the fabric can sometimes be felt by running the fingers very carefully over the section that is suspected of being weaker.

GARMENT CONSTRUCTION

Learning to recognize quality construction takes time and experience; it does not come overnight. However, there are a number of points which can be checked.

1. The fabric is suitable in weight, color, pattern, and texture for the garment. For example, a pair of pants for everyday wear in cool weather probably would be made of medium-weight fabric, in a sturdy weave or knit, to stand up to wear. The color might be a solid, basic one, to go with a range of tops; the pattern of the fabric might be a stripe, plaid, or check. Since this pair of pants would be worn a good deal, a smooth-textured fabric, with no loops or nubs, would deliver the best service because it would not snag or catch on objects.

2. When the garment is on the store hanger, all the seams are smooth and flat. Puckers and wrinkles at seam lines usually indicate hasty construction methods. They will not disappear when the garment is worn: often they indicate problems in fit.
3. Seams are finished in some way, especially if the fabric ravels easily. If the seam edges show loose threads of the fabric before the garment is purchased, the condition can only worsen during wear.
4. Seam allowances are at least one-half inch. Skimpy seam allowances often indicate cheap construction and they are one of the easiest points to check. Seams are pressed open and flat, with each seam pressed before it is crossed by another seam. Bias seams in loosely woven or knit fabrics have tape reinforcements, in order to prevent stretching.
5. Stitching is smooth and even, and the stitches are the correct length for the fabric. Uneven stitching, varying between long and short, indicates fast construction, usually with little attention to correct construction. Thread ends are tacked, to prevent the seam from working loose. Stitching in knits should have some give, to allow for the fabric's flexibility in wear. Seams in knits that are made with too-tight stitches may split open when strain is put on them. Topstitching, when used as decoration, is made with the same length of stitch in all areas of the garment.
6. Thread is of good quality. Garments made with weak, sleazy thread should be left in the store. Thread color matches the fabric closely. Threads of manufactured fibers (such as nylon) and core-wrapped threads (such as cotton-covered polyester) tend to be stronger. Also, they have some stretch, which makes them desirable for use on knit fabrics.
7. Hems are invisible and properly taped or finished. Dress hems, for instance, should have good-quality seam tape if tape is used. Lined coats and jackets may not have taped hems, particularly if the fabric does not ravel, but the hem should be tacked to the outside fabric in enough places that it will not sag.
8. Linings in coats and jackets are well made and fit the garment properly. If the lining sags when the garment is on the hanger, it may not fit the garment correctly. A lining that is too small for the garment will pull it out of shape.

9. Plackets and other openings lie flat and smooth, are inconspicuous, and are long enough to fulfill their purpose with ease. The fasteners are sturdy and sewn on well with matching thread.
10. Trimmings are appropriate in style and design for the product and are securely attached. They can be cleaned in the same way as the product.

Time spent checking the quality of construction in an item is never wasted. A poorly constructed product almost always will turn out to be a waste of money, since it will not give the service expected.

This section of the chapter has dealt primarily with decision making in the purchase of clothing, but the same general guidelines and approach can be used for other textile products. In addition, the consumer would need measurements, such as the length of curtains or size of bath towels required, before setting out on a shopping trip.

FIGURE 11-2 *A trademark used over one hundred years ago. (Courtesy of Levi Strauss & Co.)*

Trademarks

A trademark is a symbol owned by a manufacturer. Frequently, it is used as a special type of label or tag on his products. It may be a word that has a logical connection with the product; it may be all or part of the company name; it may combine a word and a drawing.

All United States trademarks must be registered with the United States Patent Office. Registration is indicated by the small R in a circle, ®, used with the trademark. To obtain the right to use a particular trademark, a manufacturer must comply with all the requirements for registration. Considerable time and effort are involved, and once the right to use the trademark forever has been granted, the holder is careful to guard against its misuse.

Trademarks have been used in the United States for many years. An early one, used over one hundred years ago, is shown in Figure 11-2. A redesigned version of this early trademark is still used by the company as the "Two-Horse Brand Ticket," a leatherlike label that is sewn onto the waistband of each pair of Levi's® basic jeans, which are made of the original heavyweight (14 ounces per square yard) denim and also bear the red tab on the right rear pocket (Figure 11-3). Levi's® jeans have become famous worldwide, and other producers have attempted to copy the product. Today, all authentic jeans and other garments produced by this

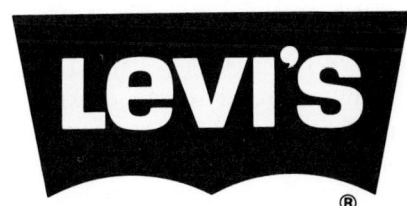

FIGURE 11-3 *This trademark appears on all jeans and other garments produced today by Levi Strauss & Co. (Courtesy of Levi Strauss & Co.)*

11 / Guidelines for Purchasing

FIGURE 11-4 *A dealer in the Flea Market in Paris offers genuine Levi's® jeans.* (Steve Ettlinger)

company and its licensees bear the trademark shown in Figure 11-3, in white letters on a red ground. International respect for this trademark is indicated by the scene shown in Figure 11-4.

Most trademarks apply to a particular product, but those shown in Figures 11-5 and 11-6 apply to a process used in manufacture of woven or knit fabric, rather than to the product itself. They are particularly important to anyone who plans to buy a product made of 100 percent cotton: they guarantee that the product will not shrink more than 1 percent by the federal government's standard test. Thus, if the product carries a label showing this mark, the consumer may be sure that shrinkage after washing will be minimal.

FIGURE 11-5 *This trademark applies to a process used in manufacturing fabric of 100 percent cotton.* (Courtesy of the SANFORIZED COMPANY, A Division of Cluett, Peabody & Co., Inc.)

Part Three / Selection

Generally speaking, the presence of a registered trademark on a product means that the manufacturer has tried to provide merchandise of high quality. Such a manufacturer is interested in maintaining the company's reputation and sets certain standards for its products. During manufacture, the item receives more care and attention than a product turned out rapidly by a company whose only interest is in high profits. The consumer should remember that a product bearing a label with a registered trademark (with the ®) is far more likely to provide satisfaction than one without such a label (Figure 11-7). Again, the consumer should remember to follow the care instructions provided with the product, to ensure best service.

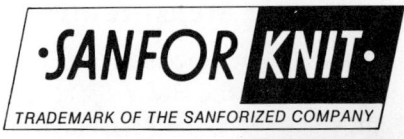

FIGURE 11-6 *The trademark on the top is found on men's knit undergarments; the mark on the bottom applies to jeans made of cotton. Both of these trademarks indicate shrinkage control and no-iron characteristics and apply to processes rather than to the products.* (Courtesy of the SANFORIZED COMPANY, A Division of Cluett, Peabody & Co., Inc.)

FIGURE 11-7 *A variety of trademarks found on textile products in the United States.* (Courtesy of McGregor-Doniger Inc., Buster Brown Textiles, Inc., West Point Pepperell, Ship'n Shore, Inc., Cannon Mills, Inc., Wamsutta Mills/Pacific Home Products, and The Manhattan Shirt Company)

11 / Guidelines for Purchasing

Metric Measurement

A bill introduced in the House of Representatives and approved by the House Space Committee in September 1973 provides for a voluntary metric conversion program to be implemented over a ten-year period. A major concern of business is the cost of the change,[5] while for individual Americans, who for so long have purchased fabric by the yard and made an ideal of the "size 10 dress," the change to meters and centimeters for measurement and size determination will require a whole new way of thinking. For example, the size 10 dress *may* have the equivalent Continental size 38, although no decision has been made. Once the simple formulas for converting measurements from the customary to the metric system are memorized, a little practice allows one to think automatically in terms of meters and centimeters. Table 11–2 may be a help.

TABLE 11-2 *Approximate Conversions for Changing to Metric Units*

When you know:	You can find:	If you multiply by:
Inches	Millimeters	25.0
Inches	Centimeters	2.5
Feet	Centimeters	30.0
Yards	Meters	0.9
Miles	Kilometers	1.6
Millimeters	Inches	0.04
Centimeters	Inches	0.4
Meters	Yards	1.1
Kilometers	Miles	0.6

Source: U.S., Department of Commerce, *Report to the Congress, A Metric America*, U.S. Government Printing Office, Washington, D.C., 1971, p. 32.

To date, there has been no indication of how changing to the metric system will affect sizing of ready-to-wear clothing, but considerable thought has been given to metrification and fabric manufacturing. A major problem for textile mills is that the standard sizes for making fabric are determined by existing looms and knitting machines. Although machinery will probably be developed using the meter as the standard of measure, machines in operation today are based on the yard. The current thought is that the present widths will

---

5. *Textile World* (December 1973), 15.

continue to be used but will be expressed in terms of centimeters rather than inches. In order to make this conversion, the consumer needs only to multiply inches by 2.5 to determine the equivalent fabric width in centimeters (see Table 11-3). In the future fabric will be purchased in meter lengths instead of yards. To convert fabric requirements to meters, multiply the number of yards by 0.9. For example, for a pattern requiring $2\frac{3}{4}$ yards of fabric, $2\frac{1}{2}$ meters ($2\frac{3}{4}$ yards multiplied by 0.9 equals 2.475 meters) probably will be needed.

TABLE 11-3 *Conversion of Fabric Widths to Centimeters*

Fabric width in inches		Centimeters
36	× 2.5	90.0
45		112.5
48		120.0
54		135.0
60		150.0

Some pattern companies already list measurements in both inches and centimeters (Figure 11-8). Dual listing of body measurements might appear like this for a size 16 pattern: bust, 38 in. and 97 cm.; waist, 30 in. and 76 cm.; hip, 40 in. and 102 cm.

Study Questions

1. What are values? Name five personal values you hold.
2. What factors determine the values an individual holds at any given time during a lifetime?
3. The text cites the conflict between the ban on phosphate detergents and laundry requirements for nonflammable fabrics as being based on laws enacted for the protection of consumers. Explain how this is so. What other examples can you cite of laws that are in conflict with each other? What is the best way to resolve such conflicts?
4. Explain Maslow's theory of need. How do needs influence decisions relating to selection of textile products?
5. State ten shopping practices that can help the consumer make wise choices and economize when buying textile products.
6. State and explain seven factors that help the consumer to evaluate textile products for quality.

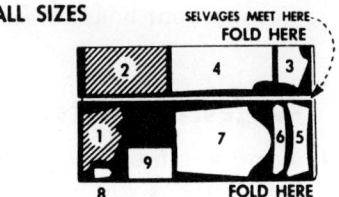

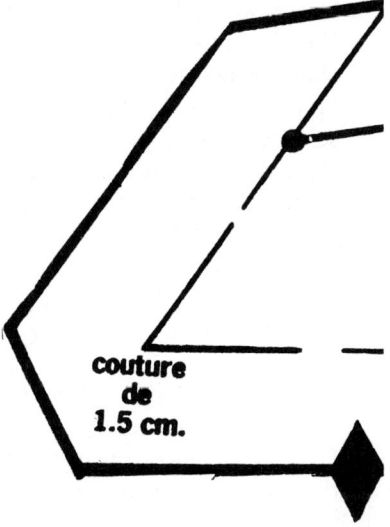

FIGURE 11-8 *Some pattern companies are already incorporating metric measurements, as shown by this illustration from McCall's pattern 4354. (Courtesy of The McCall Pattern Company)*

7. If a pattern required 2 yards of 45-inch fabric, how many meters would be needed? How wide would the fabric be in centimeters?
8. Convert your body measurements to metric units.

Suggested Activities

1. Identify your own personal values. How do they influence the decisions you make?
2. Verify the above list of values by using the value verification check list.
3. Select two or three of the shopping guidelines suggested in the text and deliberately put them into practice as you shop for textile products.
4. Prepare a bulletin board or a display on tips to follow when selecting textile products.
5. Visit several ready-to-wear clothing stores and examine clothing items for features that relate to quality.
6. Work with a group of elementary or high school age students, such as a 4-H Club, on the topic of looking for quality in ready-made clothing. Include a visit to a local ready-to-wear clothing store to examine quality features in clothing.
7. Write a news story for the local paper on the metric system of measurement.
8. Prepare a display on converting from the customary to the metric system of measurement.

Part Four
Family Clothing

Chapter 12
Preferences in Clothing

CHANGING LIFE STYLES, technological developments in textiles, and international trade have brought about changes in the clothing preferences of today's consumers. As families have become less formal in their mode of living, the manner of dress has become more casual. Pantsuits, at one time limited mostly to recreational use, now may be worn by women at any type of function. The fabric seems to be the chief factor that determines the occasion for which pants are worn, and flared-leg jumpsuits made of elegant white satin may be the choice of many brides for a traditionally formal church wedding.

People today tend to have more multipurpose clothing and fewer items that are worn only to special occasions such as church or formal events. Formal attire for women has changed from the elaborate and expensive evening dress to include almost any type of garment that is floor-length. Except for the rare, highly formal occasion requiring a tuxedo, a man may be appropriately dressed for work or for dinner in the same business suit, with merely a change of shirt.[1]

---

1. Marilyn J. Horn, *The Second Skin*, 2nd ed., Houghton Mifflin, Boston, 1975, pp. 406–411.

FIGURE 12-1 *A wardrobe consisting of two skirts, three sweaters, five blouses or tops, three pairs of pants, three lightweight jackets, and one fleece jacket, made of wool, cotton, and polyester/cotton blend, which could be mixed and matched according to your needs and whim.* (Courtesy of Cotton Incorporated—first photograph; Pendleton Woolen Mills—second and fourth photographs; The Wool Bureau, Inc.—third photograph; and Ship'n Shore, Inc.—fifth photograph)

12 / *Preferences in Clothing*

FIGURE 12-2 *Coordinating garments for men to mix and match as desired: (a) two-button sport coat in 100 percent polyester double knit; (b) slacks in Dacron® polyester double knit; (c) 100 percent polyester double-knit casual suit; (d) Dacron® polyester knit shirt; (e) and (f) patterned and plain casual suits, in textured and smooth polyester.* (Courtesy of McGregor-Doniger Inc.)

12 / *Preferences in Clothing*

With shorter workweeks, families have more time for recreational activities. Camping has become an important way of life, influencing the selection of separates and coordinates as clothing preferred by both sexes (Figure 12-1 and 12-2). Designers and manufacturers capitalize on this by supplying separates—pants, skirts, jackets, blouses, and tops—that may be purchased individually but that coordinate into a variety of ensembles of as many items as desired by the person. One such coordinated outfit could meet the major portion of the wardrobe needs for a weekend of recreational activities that included sightseeing, shopping, and informal dining (Figure 12-3).

People tend to be more fashion-conscious now than in past years and even those of limited income are now able to have clothing of high fashion through careful shopping or home

FIGURE 12-3 *A Harris tweed suit and matching turtleneck. These three garments could be worn together, as a complete outfit, or the skirt and turtleneck could be combined with other garments, since the tweed is a monotone background with flecks of color woven in. (Courtesy of The Harris Tweed Association)*

sewing. Most major pattern companies today feature designs by well-known American and European designers, and the international market has promoted competition in fashion trend setting between the Old and New Worlds. While Europe, and particularly Paris, was once the fashion center of the world, the United States now is an equal competitor.[2]

More women work away from home for pay, and the increased family income allows more money for the clothing budget. However, working women have less time to spend on clothing maintenance and prefer those items that require the least amount of care. Minimum-care finishes applied to fabric or ready-made clothing increase the cost and thus the consumer pays more money for fewer clothing items. People seem to prefer to pay more for clothing in order to have more time for leisure or other activities.

Homes provide year-round comfort with controlled temperatures, so that certain seasonal clothing items may not be as essential as they once were. Except for heavier outer garments that are needed in extremely cold climates, much of today's clothing can be worn during a greater portion of the year (Figure 12–4). Additionally, homes are often built with a minimum, if not inadequate, amount of storage space, and the proper care for stored clothing items during out-of-season times of the year can be a problem for a family of any size. Clothing that can be worn year-round reduces both storage needs and the cost of the wardrobe that is required to clothe the family adequately.

Consumers tend to prefer clothing that is comfortable. Styles are such that a minimum amount of fabric is used in constructing the garments, and the lighter-weight fibers used in fabrics make clothing that feels lighter to wear and thus more comfortable. Manufactured fibers weigh much less than natural fibers, which, however, become lighter when blended with manufactured fibers. Clothing that stretches with body movement contributes to comfort also. Many of today's fabrics provide stretch because of fiber properties, yarn processes, fabric construction, or fabric finishes. This partly explains the popularity of knit garments.

Clothing preferences can influence consumer choices, but actual ownership is determined by the amount of money the family has to spend and, more specifically, the amount allocated for the clothing budget. Family income and size, age of family members, life style, and place of residence determine clothing expenditures.

---

2. Horn, *The Second Skin*, pp. 342–351.

FIGURE 12-4 *A coat like this one can be worn almost all year around, particularly if it has a zip-in lining for colder weather.* (Courtesy of Misty Harbor Ltd.)

In brief, the consumer of today tends to prefer clothing that is aesthetically attractive, socially acceptable, physically comfortable, psychologically gratifying, economically obtainable, and, at the same time, easily maintained. In order to achieve these goals, the consumer needs to improve his knowledge and skills in comparative shopping, alterations, budgeting, and care of clothing.

Clothing Values

Clothing is one means of value expression used by individuals, families, and society as a whole. The family adopts those values approved by the larger society and transmits them to the child through the socialization process. Other agencies that contribute significantly to the process of value clarification and adoption include the school, church, movies, television, and all other forms of mass communication.

Studies show that groups and individuals attach importance to clothing, and the attitudes most often associated with clothing relate to values, such as desires for conformity, self-expression, aesthetic satisfaction, prestige, social participation, physical comfort, and economy. Individuals often hold competing or conflicting values, making it difficult for them to decide in matters relating to clothing choices. When one value is placed above another, the individual is usually able to resolve the conflict.[3]

The following procedure is only one of several that might be used by an individual or group to identify clothing buying values. It includes three steps: (1) an initial ranking of what the individual perceives his values to be; (2) a second ranking of values after conditioning and explanation; and (3) a final ranking after an exercise in which each value is compared with every other value, requiring a choice to be made.

A SCALE FOR IDENTIFYING VALUES IN CLOTHING BUYING

DIRECTIONS   Look through the list of garment descriptions below, decide which one you would best like to buy, and put a *1* in the blank beside that one. Look through the list again and write *2* by the one you like the next best. Continue until you have placed a number beside *each* one. (There should be ten numbers when you finish.)

1. A garment that fits perfectly.   _____
2. A garment that is well constructed.   _____
3. A garment that requires minimum care. _____
4. A garment that is becoming.   _____
5. A garment that is economical.   _____
6. A garment that has a famous name brand. _____
7. A garment that is fashionable.   _____
8. A garment that is versatile.   _____
9. A garment that is comfortable.   _____
10. A garment that is original in design. _____

Now read what is said about every garment. When you have finished you will have a chance to rate them again.

1. *This is a garment that fits perfectly.* You will not need to alter it in any way before you wear it. It may not be your favorite color or your most becoming style, and it

---

3. *Ibid.*, p. 94.

may not be as fashionable as you would like, but it is a perfect fit.
2. *This is a garment that is well constructed.* Superior workmanship has been used in making it. All the pieces fit together just as they should and fabric designs are perfectly matched. It may not be comfortable and it may not fit very well, but it is well constructed.
3. *This is a garment that requires a minimum amount of care.* It may be washed by hand or in the automatic washer and requires little or no ironing. It may not be fashionable or have a famous name brand but it does require only a minimum amount of care.
4. *This is a garment that is becoming.* The color and style suit you perfectly and bring out your best features. It may require more care than other garments and its price may not be economical, but it really becomes you.
5. *This is a garment that is economical in price.* It is one you can afford to buy. It may not reflect any special individuality or be very becoming, but it is economical.
6. *This is a garment with a famous name brand.* It was designed by a well-known designer and has an impressive label to prove it. It may not be becoming or economical and may be difficult to care for, but it has a famous name brand.
7. *This is a garment that is fashionable.* It is in keeping with the latest trends and styles in clothing. It may not be becoming and it may not fit without extensive alterations, but it is fashionable.
8. *This is a versatile garment.* It can be worn for many different occasions and with various accessories. With this garment you can be appropriately dressed for most occasions. It may not be very original in design or very becoming, but it is versatile.
9. *This is a comfortable garment.* It permits free movement of the various parts of the body. It does not pull or feel tight anywhere and is cool in summer or warm in winter. It may not be fashionable in design or well constructed, but it is comfortable.
10. *This is a garment that is original in design.* No other garment has been made exactly like it. It may be neither well constructed nor economical, but it is original.

Now that you know more about these garments, please rank them again in the order that you think you would choose them.

First choice	_____	Sixth choice	_____
Second choice	_____	Seventh choice	_____
Third choice	_____	Eighth choice	_____
Fourth choice	_____	Ninth choice	_____
Fifth choice	_____	Tenth choice	_____

What you have done so far has shown what kind of garment you think you prefer, but you cannot be sure until you compare each one with every other garment. Now you will have a chance to do just that. If you were shopping for a dress, shirt, pants, coat, or other item of clothing, *which one in each pair would you probably buy?* Draw a circle around the number of the garment you prefer in each pair. It may be difficult to decide at times, but *you must make a choice in each case.*

1 The garment that fits 2 The garment that is well constructed	1 The garment that fits 3 The garment that requires minimum care
2 The garment that is well constructed 3 The garment that requires minimum care	2 The garment that is well constructed 4 The garment that is becoming
3 The garment that requires minimum care 7 The garment that is fashionable	4 The garment that is becoming 9 The garment that is comfortable
8 The garment that is versatile 9 The garment that is comfortable	6 The garment that has a famous name brand 8 The garment that is versatile
7 The garment that is fashionable 9 The garment that is comfortable	1 The garment that fits 5 The garment that is economical
2 The garment that is well constructed 10 The garment that is original in design	3 The garment that requires minimum care 5 The garment that is economical

1 The garment that fits	3 The garment that requires minimum care
8 The garment that is versatile	10 The garment that is original in design
4 The garment that is becoming	5 The garment that is economical
7 The garment that is fashionable	9 The garment that is comfortable
7 The garment that is fashionable	8 The garment that is versatile
10 The garment that is original in design	10 The garment that is original in design
6 The garment that has a famous name brand	5 The garment that is economical
9 The garment that is comfortable	10 The garment that is original in design
1 The garment that fits	2 The garment that is well constructed
4 The garment that is becoming	8 The garment that is versatile
5 The garment that is economical	1 The garment that fits
7 The garment that is fashionable	6 The garment that has a famous name brand
3 The garment that requires minimum care	7 The garment that is fashionable
4 The garment that is becoming	8 The garment that is versatile
4 The garment that is becoming	3 The garment that requires minimum care
5 The garment that is economical	8 The garment that is versatile
9 The garment that is comfortable	1 The garment that fits
10 The garment that is original in design	7 The garment that is fashionable

5 The garment that is economical 6 The garment that has a famous name brand	1 The garment that fits 10 The garment that is original in design
2 The garment that is well constructed 7 The garment that is fashionable	4 The garment that is becoming 6 The garment that has a famous name brand
2 The garment that is well constructed 5 The garment that is economical	3 The garment that requires minimum care 9 The garment that is comfortable
6 The garment that has a famous name brand 10 The garment that is original in design	1 The garment that fits 9 The garment that is comfortable
4 The garment that is becoming 8 The garment that is versatile	5 The garment that is economical 8 The garment that is versatile
6 The garment that has a famous name brand 7 The garment that is fashionable	2 The garment that is well constructed 6 The garment that has a famous name brand
4 The garment that is becoming 10 The garment that is original in design	3 The garment that requires minimum care 6 The garment that has a famous name brand
2 The garment that is well constructed 9 The garment that is comfortable	

Now, count the number of times that you have chosen each garment and rank them in the order of your choices, from the highest number of times selected to the lowest number. (See page 210.) This indicates your final value hierarchy.

First choice	_____	Sixth choice	_____
Second choice	_____	Seventh choice	_____
Third choice	_____	Eighth choice	_____
Fourth choice	_____	Ninth choice	_____
Fifth choice	_____	Tenth choice	_____

Now compare this list with the two you did earlier. What changes do you notice?

Fit in Ready-made Clothing

How to buy clothing that fits is probably one of the more difficult shopping skills which the consumer has to develop. In part, the concept of fit varies from one individual to another and is somewhat influenced by personal taste and preference (Figures 12-5 and 12-6). Some people prefer clothing that is snug, while others like the carefree feeling of

FIGURE 12-5 *Good fit in men's clothing makes the difference between good and poor appearance. This slim jacket and trousers made of cotton corduroy fit well, yet have sufficient ease for comfortable movement by the wearer.* (Courtesy of Cotton Incorporated)

FIGURE 12-6 *An example of excellent fit in pants. These pants hang from the waist with no bulges or wrinkling. The creases run correctly, straight up and down. The length of the pants is also correct—just brushing the shoe tops. (Courtesy of Bobbie Brooks, Inc.)*

loosely hanging garments. Poorly fitting clothing may be either too large or too small, but the cause of the problem is that the garment is either the wrong size or not properly proportioned for the wearer.

Nothing positive can be said of clothing that fits badly. Not only is it unattractive and uncomfortable for the wearer, but its usefulness may be shortened or impaired because of strains that develop in fabric and seams. If poorly fitting clothing is purchased, garment manufacturers and retailers run the risk of losing customer goodwill and patronage, since their reputation is directly related to customer satisfaction, and clothing brands that fit poorly (unless extensive alterations are made) are often passed up by the discriminating shopper.

In past years, getting a good fit in ready-made clothing was a serious problem, and people who sewed usually felt they could make clothing that fit better. Much of the difficulty was due to the fact that each manufacturer used his own sizing system, which was based on a study of measurements involving a very limited number of people. This trial-and-error approach to sizing meant that garment sizes varied greatly from one manufacturer to another, and few garments fit without alterations.

Today an individual has a much better chance of buying clothes that fit with little or no alteration needed. Through the joint efforts of the Department of Agriculture, the Department of Commerce, and educational institutions, actual body measurements were taken from enough men, women, and children to make possible the development of commercial standards for sizing.

SIZE STANDARDS

Commercial standards are of three types, and each contributes to fit in a different way. *Body-measurement standards* refer to those taken over underwear or foundation clothing. *Model-form standards* represent special length and girth modifications of body-measurement standards for the purposes of garment fit. *Garment-size standards* give dimensions for specific items of clothing and additionally are based on the body-measurement standards. Body-measurement standards are probably more important to the consumer than the other two. They are of interest to the person who sews also, since this is the basis for commercial pattern sizing.

Under body-measurement standards there are four classifications of women's sizes and nine different body types, representing the most comprehensive of the standards in use. The size classifications are Misses', Women's, Half-size (for shorter women), and Junior. Body types are divided into tall, regular, and short, and each height group has three bust-hip categories. In each bust-hip category, the bust measurement is the same but hip types are described as slender, regular, and full. The slender group is designated with a minus, and the full, with a plus. In putting all this information together, then, the size number, although based on the bust measurement, is not numerically equal to it, and the symbols combined with it complete the size designation. For example, 14R refers to a size 14 bust of a regular or average height and hips, while 14T− identifies a size 14 bust, tall in height, of a slender-hip type, and 14S+ indicates the size is

14 in bust, short in height, and of a full-hip type.[4] In Chapters 15 and 16, standard sizes are given for all age groups and both sexes.

Study Questions

1. What factors influence consumer preferences in clothing?
2. Which factors determine the amount of money a family can spend for clothing?
3. What types of knowledge and skills can help consumers achieve their personal or family clothing goals?
4. How are clothing values acquired by an individual?
5. What are eight clothing values that might influence consumer choices?
6. How does an individual know when a garment fits properly?
7. With reference to commercial sizing of ready-made clothing, what would the designation 14S+ mean on a garment?

Suggested Activities

1. Look through current fashion magazines and identify the factor(s) that influenced the clothing styles and types featured.
2. Interview other students and or nonstudent consumers about their preferences in clothing styles, fabrics, and so forth. Write a report on your findings.
3. Make a bulletin board or display to illustrate values you feel are important when buying clothing.
4. Prepare a bulletin board or an exhibit or write a news story about proper fit in ready-made clothing.
5. Discuss with a group of friends the ways in which their personal feelings about clothes affect their choice of particular garments.

---

4. U.S., Department of Agriculture, *Consumers All*, The Yearbook of Agriculture, U.S. Government Printing Office, Washington, D.C., 1965, pp. 341–345.

Chapter 13

Clothing the Individual

AT DIFFERENT STAGES of life, individuals have different needs in clothing. These needs are common to all human beings, are manifested in the clothing worn, and may be classified as physiological, sociological, and psychological.

Basic Human Needs in Clothing

PHYSIOLOGICAL

Physiological growth and development make varying demands on clothing (Figure 13-1). During the first years of life, the individual undergoes the greatest growth rate in the shortest period of time. Therefore, clothing for children must allow proper growth to take place. Adolescents grow taller and change in body proportions, size, and appearance. By age 18 or so, the young person usually has developed the physical appearance of an adult, except that muscles generally are firmer and skin is more nearly free from wrinkles. The person in the twenties and early thirties will probably change very little physically, provided weight is maintained.

FIGURE 13-1 *Crisply tailored separates that could be worn by any age.* (Courtesy of Bobbie Brooks, Inc.)

As individuals approach middle age, gradual but definite physical changes may be noted in body contour and proportions, due to increased weight and fat deposits around the waist, stomach, and hips. Wrinkles and loose skin present problems in selecting clothing to minimize these changes. As old age approaches, the body tends to grow shorter, and posture and mobility changes are noticeable. Obesity often is a problem for the elderly, and the expanding waistline causes the figure to appear fairly straight from shoulders to hips.

The physically handicapped, at whatever age, require special attention in selecting clothes, for their garments can either minimize or intensify the handicap. Disabled or handicapped individuals should not be grouped together, for the clothing needs of the blind are different from those of the person who is confined to a wheelchair.

SOCIOLOGICAL

Social growth and development are required of the individual at each stage in life if he or she is to become a functioning member of society. Generally, society defines what is appropriate dress at each age, and the individual is either accepted, tolerated, or rejected according to conformity to these standards. Dress codes are related to concepts of decency and appropriateness, and unacceptable deviations from these standards usually bring about ridicule, condemnation, and social isolation for the individual who chooses not to conform. Factors such as age, sex, occupation, social status, geographic location, and economic level determine the standards in dress for an individual at any given time in the life cycle.[1]

PSYCHOLOGICAL

Each individual develops a self-concept based largely on interactions with other people. Acceptance or rejection by society is related to habits of dress, regardless of the personal reasons for clothing choices. First impressions are formed by others according to their reactions to how an individual is dressed, and acceptance or rejection by one's peers contributes to the feeling of personal worth or lack of it. All through life, individuals consciously or subconsciously choose clothing that will obtain a positive reaction from the other people who are significant in their associations.

Clothing for Children

Babies and very small children do not consider clothes as such. So far as is known, comfort is the main concern of babies: if they are too warm or too cool, they convey their unhappiness by crying. Many very young children seem to regard their clothes as a nuisance and often they would prefer to dispense with any covering, as many parents have found to their chagrin.

As a rule, clothing items for these two age groups are purchased by their families, with attention to the details of comfort, care, and becomingness to the particular child.

Older children tend to be unconcerned whether a particular garment or combination of garments is becoming to them.

---

1. Marilyn J. Horn, *The Second Skin*, 2nd ed., Houghton Mifflin, Boston, 1975, pp. 189–212.

They may become especially fond of a particular item, for reasons that may not be apparent to other family members. Other than this, most children are content. However, since habits formed early in life are apt to stay with an individual, children should be taught to pay some attention to their appearance. The age at which this learning may start will depend upon the individual child, and, in all cases, the matter should not be overemphasized. Good taste in clothing can be developed by providing items of apparel that suit the child in both style and color, and the merits of the design can be pointed out to the child in passing.

Clothing for the school-age child, however, should be considered from additional viewpoints. For instance, when a child is dressed in a way that makes him look different from his peers, he is often unaccepted and rejected by them, which can have long-lasting effects. The child who is too tall or too short or who has a weight problem is often ridiculed. Whatever corrections are possible should be made. Little can be done to increase or decrease height, but the child who is either too fat or too thin may be helped by an improved diet and eating habits.

If a child has any physical defect which might cause him to look different, proper selection of clothing is very important and can be a way of detracting from the defect. Chubby little girls look even more chubby when they wear full, gathered skirts and loosely fitting blouses. One-piece dresses with flared or A-line skirt designs give the same freedom of movement required for activity and help the girl appear taller and more slender. Thick bulky fabrics increase apparent size, while lighter-weight fabrics have a slimming effect on the child.

When a child has strong likes and dislikes about clothing, this may reflect satisfactory or unsatisfactory reactions from members of his peer group. The age-old expression describing one quality of friendship, "I like myself when I am with you," applies to childhood relationships as well as to those of adults. As much as anything else, the point of acceptance may often be found in the realm of clothing, exemplified in expressions such as, "My shoes are just like yours." Being dressed adequately and appropriately for school helps to keep a child performing well in his work and enables him to receive self-satisfaction and peer-group recognition.

These factors all should be kept in mind when family members or relatives are purchasing clothing items for children, with any particular considerations made as needed for the child involved (Figure 13–2).

FIGURE 13-2 *Three appropriate, comfortable, and easy-care outfits for youngsters: (a) cotton denim jacket, appliqué-embroidered, combined with a pull-on skirt; (b) cotton knit jersey and corduroy jeans; (c) cotton corduroy jacket and pants, with appliqué matching the shirt.* (Courtesy of Cotton Incorporated)

a

b

c

Clothing for Adolescents

The adolescent years can be divided into two periods: early adolescence, ages twelve to fifteen; and adolescence, ages fifteen to twenty. The first half corresponds roughly with junior high school age, and the latter includes high school and early college or career years. Growth rates for the two periods vary greatly, and the implications for clothing are very important.

EARLY ADOLESCENCE

During these years, growth may be very rapid, as the body begins to take on adult characteristics. Further, the growth rate for different parts of the body may be uneven, particularly in boys. It is not unusual for boys to outgrow their

FIGURE 13-3 *A long denim skirt and a plaid shirt, both Western-styled, would coordinate well with other garments in a wardrobe.* (Courtesy of Levi Strauss & Co.)

13 / Clothing the Individual

FIGURE 13-4 *One sportsuit and tops to wear with it: (a) cotton denim topper and wide-leg pants, either of which could be worn with other outfits; (b) pure wool, machine-washable and dryable sweater; (c) striped cotton sweater in three colors; (d) ribbed, zippered cotton sweater, cardigan style; (e) speckled vest and cardigan in cotton knit.* (Courtesy of Cotton Incorporated [a], [c], [d], [e], and The Wool Bureau, Inc. [b])

a

b

c

d

e

clothing rather than wear it out; many parents despair at the problems presented.

During this period, youths grow away from their families and develop more interest in forming friendships with peers. Both sexes seek peer-group acceptance, which helps them develop a certain amount of self-acceptance and esteem.

ADOLESCENCE

Both sexes seek increased approval from peers, especially members of the opposite sex. They become more conscious of grooming and personal appearance, particularly in terms of what will attract more attention from an admired boy or girl friend. Peer-group acceptance and popularity often are equated with physical attractiveness and adequate wardrobes.

DESIRABLE CLOTHING PROPERTIES

Clothing is very important during this period, and fit is a major problem. For girls, dresses rapidly become too short-waisted and too tight across the bust, and skirts require frequent lengthening. Pants and shirt or coat sleeves that become too short add to the already awkward look of boys, who always need new clothing to replace items they have outgrown.

Coordinated separates, such as matched tops, pants, skirts, and jackets, may be one solution to the problem of fit (Figures 13-3 and 13-4). The recently developed junior and teen shops are an effort by manufacturers and retailers to recognize that clothing designed for adult figures does not meet the needs of adolescents any more than does clothing designed for children.

Comfort is a primary consideration for adolescents and often explains why some clothing items are worn constantly, while others may not be worn at all. Knit fabric for pants, tops, dresses, and shirts is comfortable, and its stretch properties let the garment "grow with the individual," up to a point, without feeling tight or binding.

Both fabric and construction should be durable enough to withstand whatever vigorous activities the adolescent participates in. Denim jeans usually are well constructed of fabric that stands up to hard wear. Unless the adolescent is responsible for the maintenance and upkeep of his clothing, easy-care features may not be a concern. Garments with finishes for stain resistance and wash-and-wear properties launder more easily and keep a fresh appearance (Figure 13-5).

The adolescent's concept of beauty often puzzles the adult, for the young person is attracted by the styles, fabrics, and patterns worn by friends. Clothing fads are most prevalent during this age period, and the adolescent feels the importance of being dressed just like his or her friends. The popularity of decorating jeans with all kinds of embroidery, appliqués, feathers, and sequins is an example. Such fads usually are short-lived, and whatever may be "in" this season is likely to be modified or changed completely the next year. For this reason, students entering college for the first time often are advised not to purchase clothing in quantity until they are actually on the campus and can see firsthand what the current clothing fad may be.

As dress codes are relaxed or eliminated on high school and college campuses, adolescents have more freedom to decide what they will wear, although incidents associated with the "streaking" craze indicate that society does limit

FIGURE 13-5 *Jeans-type styling in faded-look 100 percent cotton corduroy makes for comfort in wearing and ease in laundering.* (Courtesy of Cotton Incorporated)

this freedom. Most parents are familiar with the almost impossible task of trying to select clothing items that meet the approval of their adolescent children; hence much of the buying power today is in the hands of youth.[2]

Clothing for Adults

The transition from adolescence to adulthood is steady and gradual. The legal age for becoming an adult ranges from eighteen to twenty-one, but the responsibilities often associated with adulthood may be assumed at almost any time before, during, or after these years. By the early twenties the individual generally has reached maturity in physical growth. Maximum height has been reached and all sex characteristics are developed more or less to their potential. The resulting physique probably will be maintained throughout the adult years (Figure 13–6).

As a person advances in age, and energy needs become less, a real problem may be that of maintaining a weight appropriate for body build. Overweight and obesity impair physical well-being and can be a liability in professional advancement. The trim and well-kept adult figure is easier to clothe, and an attractive physical appearance contributes to a good self-concept and good mental health.

The clothing needs of the adult are influenced by several factors such as socioeconomic level or income, age, sex, place of residence, occupation, and social participation.[3] People in higher-income brackets have more money to spend on clothing than do low-income individuals. Young adults tend to want clothing changes more often than they may when they reach the middle or older years. Women are considered to have more interest in clothing than men, but recent trends in men's fashions lead one to believe that men are just as clothes-conscious as women.

---

2. Mary Shaw Ryan, *Clothing: A Study in Human Behavior*, Holt, Rinehart and Winston, New York, 1966; Horn, *The Second Skin*; Mildred Thurow Tate and Oris Glisson, *Family Clothing*, John Wiley & Sons, New York, 1961; Joanne B. Eicher and Eleanor A. Kelley, with Betty Wass, *A Longitudinal Study of High School Girls' Friendship Patterns, Social Class, and Clothing*, Research Report 222, Home and Family Living, Michigan State University Agricultural Experiment Station, East Lansing, 1974; Eleanor A. Kelley, Caroline W. Daigle, Rosetta S. LaFleur, and Lenda Jo Wilson, *Clothing Acquisition and Use Practices of Early Adolescents*, Home Economics Research Report No. 2, Louisiana State University and Agricultural Experiment Station, Baton Rouge, June 1973.

3. Ryan, *Clothing*, p. 120.

FIGURE 13-6 *A coat for any age male, for wear in almost any climate.* (Courtesy of Harbor Master Ltd.)

At one time, residence in rural or urban areas helped determine the kind and amount of clothing needed, but today there is a less noticeable difference between rural and urban dwellers in their manner of dress. Occupation may still make a difference in clothing needs. Police personnel wear uniforms; farm workers need sturdy, durable clothing; and, in many colleges, male professors are expected to wear coats and ties and the appropriate attire for women includes shoes with high heels and attractive dresses. Women who join the work force in middle years must often consider whether the cost of additional, appropriate clothing outweighs the salary. The adult who leads a very active social life and the outdoor sportsman need very different types of clothing. Geographic location and climatic conditions influence the type of clothing needed, too.

FIGURE 13-7 *With styling derived from basic jeans and work jacket, these garments could be worn together, as shown, or with other pants and tops.* (Courtesy of Levi Strauss & Co.)

DESIRABLE CLOTHING PROPERTIES

Durability, fit, style and color, cost, and cleaning qualities are among the aspects that adults may consider important in clothing.[4] Durability is particularly important to people who are engaged in manual labor, such as construction work or farming, where clothing must stand up under heavy wear and strain. Overalls or jeans of cotton denim and work shirts often are worn for such jobs, because of their durability. On the other hand, many adults want durable clothes so they can be worn for several years (Figure 13-7).

---

4. Patsy Ruth Alexander, "Problems and Practices of Rural and Urban Homemakers in Clothing Construction and Buying, Bossier Parish, 1964," Master's thesis, Louisiana State University, Baton Rouge, 1965.

Part Four / Family Clothing

Fit is important for both comfort and good appearance. Garments of knit fabrics are popular because their stretch properties make them comfortable. Knit garments also are less likely to show poor fit during periods of weight loss or gain. Along with a good fit, adults want their clothing to be comfortable in relation to temperature. Some people find polyester and other manufactured fibers too hot to wear in summer, and they select cooler fibers such as cotton or blends. Others can wear manufactured fibers all year round. Still other people wear wool in winter, manufactured fibers in the spring and fall, and cotton or blends in the summer.

Generally speaking, a majority of adults are aware of the fact that the style and color of their clothing can improve their appearance. Therefore, they are interested in having a wide variety of styles, colors, fabrics, and patterns from which to make the selections best suited to their individual figure requirements and preferences. Cost is quite often a major consideration for adults when they are purchasing clothing. Some adults are interested in buying less-expensive items that lack style, while others pay more for clothing with more style and wear it for a longer time.

Cleaning qualities may or may not be a concern. Life style, availability of laundry equipment and dry cleaners, personal preference, and income affect selection and enter into decisions. Adults who travel quite a bit, either for pleasure or as a part of their work, find that clothing with wrinkle-resistance and minimum-care features is very desirable. These qualities may be found in fabrics made of manufactured fibers, or of natural fibers with these finishes applied. Clothes with these properties are also time- and energy-savers for people whose work or social responsibilities keep them away from home much of the time.

Clothing for the Elderly

As people grow older and reach retirement age, they often encounter problems in finding suitable clothing. Most of the clothing industry focuses on pleasing the younger set, and the needs of those in the upper age bracket are largely unmet.

While elderly people still interact with others and lead a productive life, clothing is important to them (Figure 13-8). It is only when individuals feel they have lost all meaningful relationships with other people that they totally disregard their personal appearance. From a social standpoint, the elderly still need to feel accepted by their peers. Just like

FIGURE 13-8 Many older people lead very active lives, and comfortable, easy-to-care-for clothing is just as important to them as it is to younger age groups. (Courtesy of U.S. Department of Health, Education and Welfare and *Aging* magazine)

younger people, they enjoy receiving approval for their beautiful hair, lovely complexion, youthful figure, or fashionable clothing. They want their clothing to fit, to be stylish, to be made of beautiful fabrics, to be comfortable, easy to put on, and easy to care for. They especially resent the uninteresting styles which society seems to think are appropriate for them.[5] However, the physical changes which gradually occur over the years finally become major figure defects and do pose problems in dress. In general, older people become stooped in the shoulders, thicker in the waist, larger in the bust, and tend to develop a protruding abdomen. Clothing must be especially designed to minimize these defects.

---

5. Marjorie Y. Baker, *Clothing for the Elderly*, The Oklahoma State University Cooperative Extension Service, Stillwater, Okla., Publication E-811, November 1969.

Older people often wear clothing that is too large, not necessarily because it is comfortable, but because it fits a little better than other garments available or because they can get in and out of it without assistance. Clothing that is easy for the elderly to put on and take off needs fasteners which can be manipulated by fingers that may be unsteady or crippled by arthritis (Figure 13–9). Such features include pull tabs on zippers, magnetic fasteners, Velcro tape (Figure 13–10), large flat buttons with thread shanks, large hooks and eyes, and snaps. Clothing that opens down the front with fasteners, like fly-front zippers and Velcro, and wraparounds are preferred by elderly people. Usually short sleeves will provide more freedom and safety, but older people often prefer longer sleeves, especially if they have a tendency to feel the cold. Both slim and full skirts should be avoided, since slim skirts ride up and full skirts get in the way. Skirts of A-line style may be more serviceable and comfortable. Short wraps may be easier for the elderly to handle than long coats. Shirts and blouses with underarm gussets may be more com-

FIGURE 13-9 *Velcro patches, inconspicuously attached to garments, avoid problems with buttons or snaps.* (Courtesy of Vocational Guidance & Rehabilitation Service)

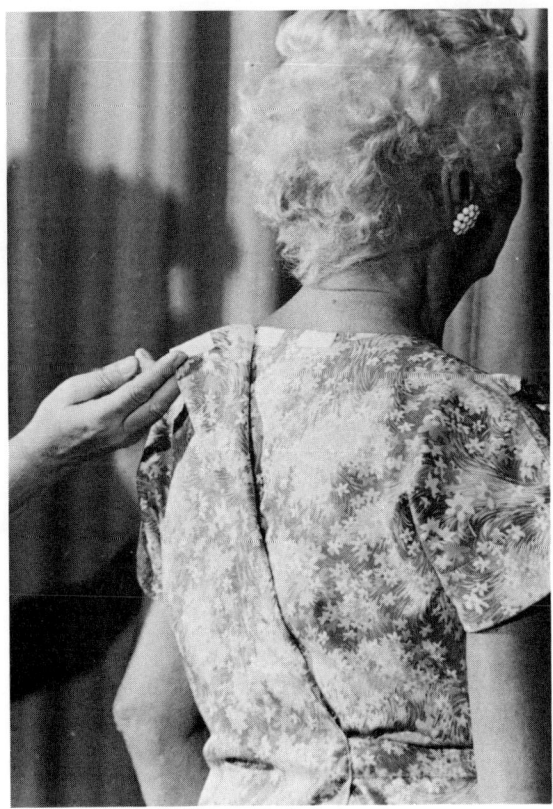

13 / Clothing the Individual

FIGURE 13-10 *This self-fastening tape comes in a range of colors and shapes for different types of garments.* (Courtesy of Velcro Industries Ltd.)

fortable for reaching, and dresses with pleats across the back may provide more ease in movement.

DESIRABLE CLOTHING PROPERTIES

Clothing should be well made, since it is usually subjected to much strain, and fabrics should be durable. Minimum-care and spot-resistant finishes make stain removal and laundry easier. Lightweight clothing, such as that made of knit fabric, is usually less tiring and more comfortable, especially if it provides warmth also. Knit fabrics provide stretch comfort. Fabrics should be soft and nonirritating for individuals who may have sensitive skin.

Safety is a serious matter for the elderly. Long, flowing garments may restrict mobility, especially for persons who are not agile and sure-footed. Fabrics that are flameproof and flame-resistant should be chosen whenever possible.

Clothing for the Physically Handicapped

Many of the clothing problems of the elderly are identical to those experienced by the physically handicapped. The rehabilitation of physically handicapped or disabled persons centers on helping them become self-reliant, particularly in the area of tending to their clothing needs. They need clothing that is easy to manipulate, safe to wear, comfortable and attractive, and easy to clean. It also should be adapted to the particular disability. Wheelchair users especially need clothing that is comfortable for long periods of sitting in one position. Fabrics should be nonirritating to the skin, absorbent, soft, and stretchable to permit body movements. Garment styles need to be those that will permit normal body movements, especially from the waist upward. Clothing should be made with adequate fabric for comfort, but not so much that it becomes bulky and unmanageable. Skirts or trousers that are too long and loose around the bottom should be avoided lest they become caught in the wheels. Garments should have conveniently placed openings with fastenings that are manageable by the person. Short wraps that end above the waist will provide the needed extra warmth and eliminate sitting on excess fabric bulk. Pants made of knit fabrics are preferred by many wheelchair individuals. Garments need to be of a style and fabric that are attractive and easy to clean. Spot- and stain-resistant finishes aid in removing spots due to occasional spilling accidents. Fabric that is wrinkle-resistant maintains a fresh and unmussed appearance for longer periods of time than fabric that is not.[6]

Clothing for the Blind

Blind persons have clothing problems that are somewhat different from those of other individuals. Except for loss of sight, blind people are usually very normal individuals in all other ways and rehabilitation programs focus on helping them function adequately in today's society. Many of their problems lie in misunderstandings that sighted persons have regarding the normality of the blind, who are too often

---

6. Clarice L. Scott, *Clothes for the Physically Handicapped Homemaker*, U.S. Department of Agriculture Home Economics Research Report No. 12, Agricultural Research Service, U.S. Government Printing Office, Washington, D.C., 1961, 0-575135.

prevented from developing independence and self-reliance by overly protective family and friends.

Most blind people develop a high degree of sensitivity to touch, especially in the fingertips, and this is a very important part of clothing recognition. They learn to recognize certain garments by feeling the design lines and the fabric texture. Through the help of sighted friends, they memorize color and texture concepts and the various ways of combining them. They soon learn to distinguish between the rough texture of tweed fabric and the smooth feel of satin or between the stretch of knit fabrics and lack of stretch of woven fabrics. Special identification marks can be sewn around the neckline of a dress to help a blind girl distinguish her clothing from that of a friend. The fingers of blind people are usually nimble and they are able to handle even tiny fasteners without too much difficulty. The main problem lies in first learning to recognize what type of fastener they are dealing with and how to manipulate it. Once they have mastered the mechanical workings, they can fasten grippers, snaps, buttons, and zippers with ease.

Safe clothing is particularly important. Fabrics should be flame-resistant and garments that might snag or catch on objects should be avoided. Clothing that is treated for wrinkle resistance, minimum care, and stain resistance will cut down on maintenance, which presents a different type of problem to a blind person.

In general, clothing for a blind person can be selected according to personal preference and needs, subject to the above precautions. Once the style, color, and fabric are learned by the person and the fastenings mastered, no special problem is encountered.

Study Questions

1. Give some specific examples of physiological, sociological, and psychological needs of individuals that are manifested in the clothing they wear.
2. Why do college students dress as they do?
3. What features in clothing relate to the physical changes that occur in adults as they reach maturity?
4. What specific clothing needs do elderly people have?
5. What concept do you have about the kind of clothing elderly people should wear? Why?
6. Why does a person in a wheelchair have particular clothing needs?
7. How do blind people learn to dress themselves?

Suggested Activities

1. Select one or more of the following locations to study the clothing needs of people there: a nursing home for the elderly, a state school for the blind, a rehabilitation center for the physically handicapped.
2. Observe elderly men and women as you move around your area. How are they dressed—for comfort, or for style? Without being rude, can you note any physical infirmities that might explain their clothing selections?
3. Visit local ready-to-wear clothing stores to observe any techniques used to help any of the following individuals find suitable clothing: persons in wheelchairs, persons with physical disabilities such as loss of an arm, elderly persons with crippling arthritis. Note what you observe and explain your findings.
4. Prepare a display of clothing items designed to help physically handicapped persons dress themselves. Consider specific disabilities when you plan this display.

Chapter 14

Apparel for Children

A COMPARATIVELY RECENT development in the clothing industry has been the expanded production of clothing for children, particularly those under school age. This came about because the number of pre-school-age children has increased and because their young mothers are highly clothes-conscious. Many mothers work outside the home and have little or no time to sew. Also, in recent years, greater emphasis has been placed on style in clothing designed for children.[1]

From the time of birth and during the preschool years, physical growth is rapid in the young child: by the age of six, body proportions are much like those of an adult. During these early years, the child is concerned with physical developmental tasks such as sitting, creeping, reaching, standing alone, walking, pulling, and climbing. The very young child is often happiest without clothing and is not concerned with clothing at all, except as it is related to comfort.

---

1. Mildred Thurow Tate and Oris Glisson, *Family Clothing*, John Wiley & Sons, New York, 1961, pp. 169–173.

Sizing

The body-measurement standards for clothing sizes for infants, babies, toddlers, and children contain few measurements. Height is the standard more than anything else. Babies are considered from the viewpoint of their size—small, medium, large, and extra large—which is a combination of height and weight specifications. Toddler sizes range from 1 through 6X. Children's sizes range from 2 through 6X.

A current mail-order catalog from Sears, Roebuck and Co. uses a measurement system based on body development. The consumer is instructed to order by size, not by age, with height cited as the most important measurement. Growing girls' sizes are divided into girls', slim girls', and chubby girls' (see Table 16-1). Boys' sizes are charted under the categories "boys" and "students" (see Table 15-2). Slim, regular, and husky indicate body development.

The Infant

Clothing for the infant should provide comfort in terms of warmth, freedom of body movement, and hygiene (Figures 14-1 and 14-2). Healthy infants usually are content if the room temperature is agreeable, their clothing is not binding or irritating to the skin, and they are kept clean.

The most suitable fiber for infants' clothing is cotton because it is soft, not unnecessarily binding, and can be kept hygienically safe by washing in extremely hot or boiling water. Knit fabric garments stretch with body movements and are easy to put on the infant. Openings all the way down the front or back make dressing simpler. Ties or flat fasteners are more comfortable; drawstring necklines are not recommended because the infant might become caught in the strings. Clothing should be absorbent and permit ventilation, for inadequate air circulation can cause skin irritation and contribute to discomfort. For these reasons, infants should not be left in plastic pants for long periods of time.[2]

Shirts and diapers are the standard clothing for infants for the first five or six months of life. Depending on the season and the local climate, sweaters may be included in the infant's wardrobe, and these should be easily washable. Coveralls of stretch or knit fabric and sleepers (with or without feet) may be required. After the baby has begun to creep about, more clothes are required, partly for safety's sake.

FIGURE 14-1 *This matching set (print creeper and sandbox hat), made in polyester and cotton blend seersucker, is typical of infants' wear on the market.* (Courtesy of Buster Brown Textiles, Inc.)

FIGURE 14-2 *Made in the same polyester and cotton blend seersucker, this little dress for sizes 6 to 24 months has matching panties.* (Courtesy of Buster Brown Textiles, Inc.)

---

2. Ibid.

Overalls are the simplest form of garment for both sexes, especially those with snaps in the crotch for ease in diapering.

At this age, a snowsuit may be needed for cold weather, and a hooded type is most satisfactory. A lightweight, wind-resistant, and washable fabric such as nylon poplin is desirable for this garment.

Shoes, socks, and training pants may be worn by children in this age bracket. Both shoes and socks should be long enough for comfort, but not so long that the child will trip when she or he attempts to walk. Training pants of knit fabrics are desirable, since they will give as the child moves about, and the stretch inherent in the fabric will allow for some degree of growth.

The Toddler

The toddler needs clothing that provides maximum freedom for all the activity usual at this age. Again, overalls are preferred, especially if they have wide shoulder straps that are long enough for adjustment as the child grows (Figure 14–3). Creepers, one-piece garments with gripper openings at the legs or crotch, are commonly worn by toddlers, although one-piece clothing is soon outgrown, because of the rapid growth in this period. Nevertheless, during the creeping and toddling years, one-piece pajamas are usually safer and neater than two-piece ones. Cotton knit fabrics, which fit closely to the body and can be finished for flame resistance, provide safety factors that should be considered in pajamas particularly.

Shoes are probably the most important clothing item for a child of this age. A properly fitting shoe is $\frac{1}{2}$ to $\frac{3}{4}$ inch longer than the foot, measured from the end of the big toe. Shoe fabric should be flexible enough not to bind the foot, while soles should be firm, to give support as the toddler begins to walk. Shoes that lace above the anklebone provide additional support for the feet. Because of the speed of growth, shoes may be outgrown every two or three months, so they can be a major expense. However, because of the potential damage to the foot and the whole skeletal frame, children never should be permitted to wear shoes that have become too short.

The Preschool Child

Clothing for the pre-school-age child may become a major problem for the family because it is expensive, yet is used

FIGURE 14-3 *Cotton knit overalls with gripper crotch provide warmth, protect the knees, and make diaper changing quicker.* (Courtesy of Buster Brown Textiles, Inc.)

for only a short time. It should be selected to help the child develop self-reliance, practice social skills, and interact with peers. Garments should be flexible, comfortably warm, easily cleaned, soft, durably constructed to encourage self-reliance, convenient for frequent toileting, adjustable to the rapidly growing body, and attractive in design and fabric (Figure 14–4). Children of this age also need make-believe clothing to accommodate their dream-world fantasies. Such garments are usually very expensive to buy, are of poor-quality fabric and construction, and give limited wear. However, clothes handed down from adults make good substitutes. Costumes such as those worn at Halloween are often hazardous near fires and should be flame-retardant for safety.

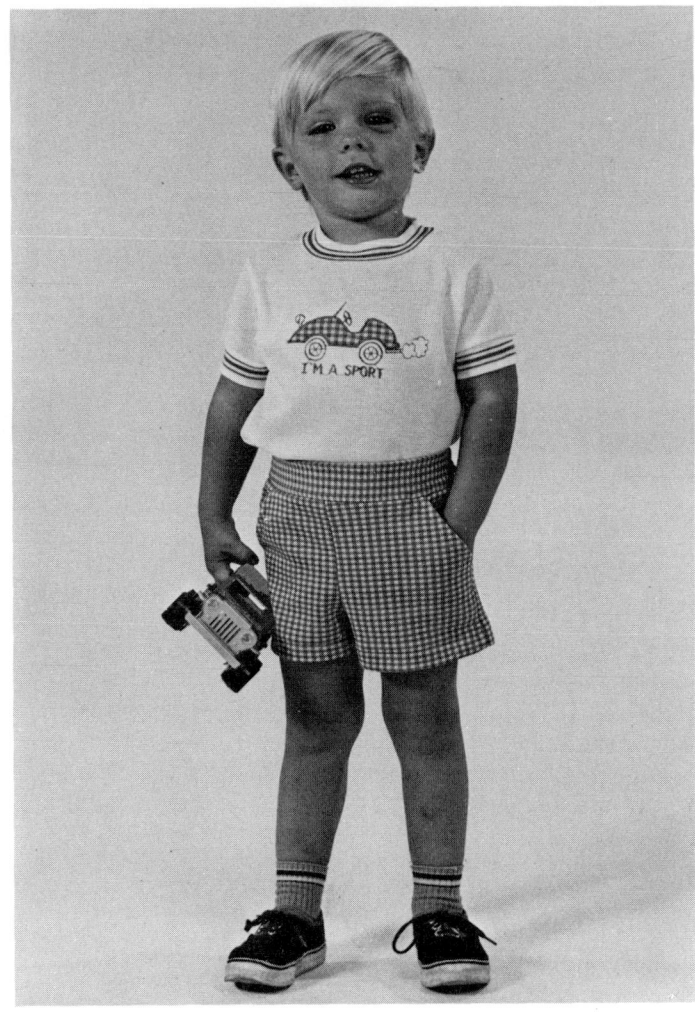

FIGURE 14-4 *Double-knit shorts and single-knit polo shirt with matching trim, both made in a polyester/cotton blend fabric, are comfortable to wear, yet easy to keep clean.* (Courtesy of Carter's)

FIGURE 14-5 *This heavyweight Fortrel polyester sleeper has nonskid soles, extra waist snaps to allow for growth, and elasticized ankles for ease in use. It also has a flame-retardant finish.* (Courtesy of Carter's)

The preschool child needs clothing that fits close to the body and is free from dangling ties or ornamentation that might catch on things. It should fit fairly loosely at the waist or, preferably, hang from the shoulders. Fabrics of manufactured fibers such as nylon and polyester are ideal because they are lightweight and also provide warmth and protection.

Clothing for outdoor wear should repel water and resist stains. All washable garments should be preshrunk (preferably Sanforized) for longer wear. Crease-resistant and minimum-care finishes are useful care features. By law, nightwear must be flame-retardant (Figure 14–5).

The child who is nearing school age should have clothing with good design features resembling those found in adult clothing. Garments should be simple and allow adequately for growth, self-help, ease of care, and comfort (Figures 14–6 and 14–7). Clothing also should be well constructed and have

FIGURE 14-6 *This three-piece set in matching floral-printed corduroy, of 100 percent cotton, is simply styled but very attractive. Large buttons and the straight front closing make it easier to put on and remove.* (Courtesy of Cotton Incorporated)

FIGURE 14-7 *Comfortable overalls made in all-cotton corduroy, with an elasticized waist, crisscrossed straps, and large buttons.* (Courtesy of Cotton Incorporated)

TABLE 14-1 *Clothing Needs Related to Activities*

Age	Activities	Clothing needs
Infant (birth to 8 or 9 months)	Sleeps, eats, looks about, moves hands and feet; has little muscle control; requires frequent changes; grows rapidly	Soft, absorbent, lightweight fabrics for comfort; easy-to-launder, no-iron fabrics; easy on-off design; simple design; room for growth
Creeper (8 or 9 months to 1 year)	Moves about, starts exploring, crawls and creeps, reaches for things, tries to walk	Action features; loose-fitting, simple styles; easy on-off design; reinforcement at points of strain; sturdy fabrics; properly fitted shoes
Toddler (1 to 2 years)	Becomes more active; begins to dress self; gets impatient when clothes are hard to get on and off; grows rapidly, then slowly; likes to be outdoors	Sturdy, well-fitted shoes; self-help features; warm, waterproof outer garments; durable clothes; fit and style that will not hamper activities
Preschooler (2 to 4 years)	Continues to be active; dresses self; becomes interested in clothing; likes to dress up like adults; wants to be dressed like friends	Action and self-help features; wants opportunity to make clothing choices; clothing like what friends wear; dress clothes; play costumes (cowboy outfits, fireman's hat, nurse's cap)

Source: Helen M. Gray, "How to Select Clothing for Children," *What's New in Home Economics* (November 1969), 37. Copyright © 1969 Dun-Donnelley Publishing Corporation. Reprinted by special permission.

a reasonable life expectancy. Table 14–1 is helpful in understanding children's clothing needs in relation to their activities.

The School-age Child

The child entering school has several basic needs that relate to clothing. Comfort, durability, acceptance and security, and self-concept are the primary considerations (Figure 14-8). Adequate and appropriate dress is comfortable and protects the child from temperature and weather changes. Garments should be made of fabric that does not irritate the skin and cut with ample fabric to prevent binding. Design features and fasteners that are large and simple to manipulate

FIGURE 14-8 *A cotton jersey turtleneck and ribless cotton corduroy pants provide style and comfort for the school-age boy. (Courtesy of Cotton Incorporated)*

allow the child to dress and undress to go to the toilet. Fabrics that resist soiling and wrinkling let children appear reasonably neat and well groomed even after hard play during recess period. Garments need to be well constructed and durable so they can stand up well under a reasonable amount of strain during wear.

The way a child is clothed for school plays a part in determining how well she or he will adjust to the new environment. Clothing should be of a style and fabric that permit and encourage participation in play and physical activity. To this end it should fit well without binding and be simple in design and decoration.

In general, when buying clothing for children, consider these guidelines:

1. Quality construction is important if clothing is to wear well, fit properly, and be comfortable. Look for fabrics that are colorfast, preshrunk, and firmly woven or closely

knitted. Seams should be finished to prevent raveling and stitching should be secure. All fasteners and decorative trims should be firmly attached and stitched securely to lie flat.

2. The garment should fit the child properly and allow for adequate ease of body movements. Properly sized garments do not gape, bind, or rub.
3. Features that allow for rapid growth make it possible for garments to be worn longer (Figure 14–9). Growth features include deep hems that can be let out and straps that can be adjusted as the child grows taller. Kimono or raglan sleeves, as well as sleeveless garments, are less binding as the child develops across the shoulders. Wide seams can be let out, and stretch fabrics like knits allow for expansion.
4. Safety is an important consideration and includes garments made of fire-resistant fabrics. This is especially important for costumes of the type worn for Halloween events. Safe garments are also free of any long dangling strings that might catch on objects while the child is playing.
5. Garments should be of a color and style that become the child and are similar to those worn by other children of the same age (Figure 14–10). Small children may be quite clothes-conscious and their clothing should contribute to their feeling of self-worth.
6. Self-help features enable the child to learn independence (Figure 14–11). Garments with front openings and large plackets featuring medium-sized smooth buttons and easy-to-operate zippers encourage children to handle their

FIGURE 14-9 *Growth features, such as tucks that can be let out and straps and waistbands that can be fastened in several places, increase the length of time a garment can be worn.* (Drawing by Eleanor Hotte)

FIGURE 14-10 *Children's clothes can be simple and comfortable and still have style, as these three garments show. (Drawing by Eleanor Hotte)*

FIGURE 14-11 *Front openings, big buttons, and zippers help children learn to dress themselves. (Drawing by Eleanor Hotte)*

clothing problems themselves. For the child who visits away from home or attends nursery school, tops with large slipover necklines and boxer-style pants with elasticized waists are a help, also.
7. Care features of clothing may be of more importance to parents than to the child. Fabrics that are colorfast, shrink-resistant, permanent-press, and treated for soil resistance contribute to easy care, as does durable workmanship.

Not all of the clothing worn by children need be purchased new for them, but neither should a child be expected to wear only clothing items passed down from older children. Individuals learn early whether they are regarded as being important. Having clothing that adequately meets their own special needs is one way children learn they are important individuals.

Study Questions

1. What are the main considerations for clothing for infants? Why?
2. How is clothing for children sized?
3. At about what age do children begin to need shoes? Why are shoes important?
4. Is safety ever a matter of concern in children's clothing? Why?
5. Do school-age children have any preferences in clothing? Why?
6. State seven points to remember when selecting clothing for children.
7. What clothing features help a child to develop independence?

Suggested Activities

1. Visit a nursery school or kindergarten and note the types and styles of clothing worn by the children. Can you tell the fabric construction of these items? List the types you see.
2. Make a survey in the different types of stores in your town to note the types of clothing for children of different ages. Are the items well constructed? Do they look durable? Do they have features that will allow for growth?
3. Discuss shoes for small children with a salesperson in a local shoe store.

4. Talk with young mothers you may know about the problems encountered in dressing small children. Have they worked out ways to keep up with the rapid growth common in this age bracket? Note your findings and report to the class.
5. On the basis of what you learned in the above activities, write a report that might be printed in your local newspaper.

Chapter 15

Apparel for Men and Boys

FOR MANY YEARS, women have been the victims of high costs and fast, planned obsolescence in clothing. Finally, these manipulative tactics of the fashion industry have filtered into fashions for men. Evidence of high fashion in men's wear is seen in the high prices of clothing that carries the labels of top designers such as Pierre Cardin, Givenchy, and Cassini. Rapid fluctuations between narrow and flared trousers, narrow and wide coat lapels, and extremely wide to string-width ties all have been accompanied by sharp price increases.

Many American men are aware of these fashion influences, but they are not anxious to be peacocks. Others are value-conscious, either from personal preference or from necessity. The consumer who knows how to judge quality and how to take advantage of sales can achieve the degree of fashion he wishes and make definite savings at the same time. This chapter will give basic information on specific items of men's clothing, to serve as a foundation for informed buying.

Sizing

Clothing for men and boys is manufactured in a standard range of sizes. The range of sizes and instructions for measurement, as used by Sears, Roebuck and Co., are shown in Tables 15-1 and 15-2. Items from some manufacturers vary from these standards, and such garments may not fit properly. This is especially likely in less-expensive clothing, when the manufacturer has skimped on fabric. Therefore, garments should always be tried on and checked for correct fit before purchase.

Shirts can present a size problem when they are offered at special sales. Such merchandise may be slightly off standard size. As a general rule, manufacturers of brand-name shirts hold closely to standard sizes, so their shirts need not be tried on.

Suits, Jackets, and Slacks

First of all, a suit should be becoming to the wearer. The effects of the artistic principles of line, color, and design on total appearance should be considered. The color should be becoming to the skin, hair, eyes, and size, and the cut of the suit should emphasize the wearer's best features.

FABRIC

Fabric, especially fiber content, is a very important consideration. Traditionally, wool has been the fiber most often used in men's suits, because of its exquisite tailoring qualities. Worsted wool fabric takes a sharp crease and holds its shape better than softer woolen fabric. Gabardine and sharkskin are worsted fabrics often found in men's suits, but the softer tweeds, flannels, and homespuns are commonly used.

Manufactured fibers are widely used in men's suits, especially the polyesters, acrylics, rayons, and blends. Polyester suits usually take creases and retain pressing very well, while those made of acrylic often do not retain creases quite as well. However, acrylic fabrics may be warmer than polyester ones. Rayon often is blended with wool or with other manufactured fibers to lower cost and to make it possible for minimum-care and durable-press finishes to be applied.[1]

---

1. Ruby Taylor Miller, *Young Man—Dress Right/Look Right*, North Carolina State University at Raleigh and the U.S. Department of Agriculture (4-MC-6-3), State College Station, Raleigh, North Carolina, 1966, pp. 4-7.

TABLE 15-1 *Range of Sizes and Measurement Instructions for Men's Apparel*

Men's Apparel

Chest Well up under arms across shoulder blades and over fullest part. Hold tape firm but not tight. Be sure tape is straight across back and keep it level. Stand naturally.

Neck On a dress shirt of the same style that fits well, lay collar flat. Measure from center of collar button to far end of button hole.

Sleeve Measure from middle of back of neck, across the shoulder and around point of elbow to wrist.

Waist Measure waistband of well-fitting slacks of same style or measure over shirt (not over trousers) at position you normally wear your slacks.

Inseam Measure well-fitting slacks of same style along seam from crotch seam to bottom of leg. Flares should be worn approximately 1-inch longer than regular leg models. Cuffed pants and styles worn with higher heels require extra length.

Height Measure in stocking feet. **S** (short) 5'3" to 5'7", **R** (regular) over 5'7" to 5'11", **T** (tall) over 5'11" to 6'3", **XT** (extra tall) over 6'3".

Slacks and Jeans Here's how to select your style

Full Cut
Worn at normal waistline
Fuller in seat, thigh, and leg
Designed for the man with huskier than average build

Trim Regular
Fits slightly below waistline
Trim (not snug) in seat, leg
Designed for the man with average build

Trim 'N Tight
Low rise, will ride on hip bone
Snug fit follows contour of body
Designed for the young man with a slim build

Sportcoats, Blazers .. Order correct suit size or use chart.

Order Size	37	38	39	40	42	44	46
If Chest Measures	36½-37	37½-38	38½-39	39½-40	40½-42	42½-44	44½-46
And Waist Measures	30-32	31-33	32-34	33-35	35-37	37-40	39-42

Topcoats, Jackets, All-weather Coats .. Order correct suit size or use chart.

Order Size	34	36	38	40	42	44	46
If Chest Measures	32½-34	34½-36	36½-38	38½-40	40½-42	42½-44	44½-46

Shirts

Neck, inches	14½	15	15½, 16	16½, 17
Sleeve, inches	32, 33	32, 33, 34	32, 33, 34, 35	33, 34, 35

Source: Courtesy of Sears, Roebuck and Co.

TABLE 15-2 *Range of Sizes and Measurement Instructions for Boys' and Students' Apparel*

Boys and Students Apparel
Sizes 6 to 24

We're all the same height

I am a 10 Slim   I am a 10 Regular   I am a 10 Husky

1. **To find size** (6, 8, 10, etc.), measure **Height** without shoes.
2. **To determine if Slim, Regular or Husky**, check his **Weight** in that size. Inseam measurements are the same for Slim, Regular and Husky in each height range.
3. **Chest** for tops and **Waist** for bottoms are check points in the chart; adjust across chart for big differences.

For example:

For Height	Order Size	If he weighs	If he weighs	If he weighs
54 in.	10	60 lbs.	73 lbs.	81 lbs.
		He is a 10 Slim	He is a 10 Regular	He is a 10 Husky

	FOR HEIGHT (Inches)	ORDER SIZE	SLIM			REGULAR			HUSKY		
			Weight	Chest	Waist	Weight	Chest	Waist	Weight	Chest	Waist
Boys Sizes 6-12	44½-47	6	Under 47	23-24	19½-21	47-51	24½-25½	21½-23	—	—	—
	47½-50½	8	Under 52	24½-25½	20½-22	52-61	26-27	22½-24	62-69	27½-28½	24½-26
	51-54½	10	Under 62	26-27	21½-23	62-75	27½-28½	23½-25	76-83	29-30	25½-27
	55-58½	12	Under 76	27½-28½	22½-24	76-89	29-30	24½-26	90-97	30½-32	26½-28
Students Sizes 14-24	59-61½	14	Under 90	29-30	23½-25	90-103	30½-32	25½-27	104-115	32½-33½	27½-29
	62-64	16	Under 104	30½-32	24½-26	104-118	32½-33½	26½-28	119-133	34-35	28½-30
	64½-66	18	Under 119	32½-33½	25½-27	119-129	34-35	27½-29	130-146	35½-36½	29½-31
	66½-68	20	Under 130	34-35	26½-28	130-141	35½-36½	28½-30	142-159	37-38	30½-32
	68½-70½	22	Under 142	35½-36½	27½-29	142-155	37-38	29½-31	156-173	38½-40	31½-33
	68½-70½	24	Under 156	37-38	28½-30	156-169	38½-40	30½-32	170-189	40½-41½	32½-34

Student Size Pants are sold by **Waist** and **Inseam** measurements.
1. **To determine Size**, measure boy's waist at natural waistline. This is a body measurement; not the top of a pair of pants.
2. **To determine Inseam**, measure the inseam of a pair of well-fitting jeans or slacks.

Note: Inseams on flares and baggies are styled approximately 1 inch longer than stated inseams to cover shoe tops.

Helpful Hints .. Boys & Students

Height and Weight are key to finding correct size.

Height is the key factor when ordering boy's garments which do not have a Slim, Regular or Husky designation.

Tops (Shirts, Jackets, Sportcoats, etc.) .. order size closest to height, weight and chest.

Bottoms (Pants, Jeans, Slacks, etc.) .. order size closest to height, weight and waist.

Swimwear, Underwear, Briefs .. order size closest to weight and waist.

Underwear Tops .. order size closest to weight and chest.

The Waist is a boy's body measurement, not the top of a pair of pants.

Source: Courtesy of Sears, Roebuck and Co.

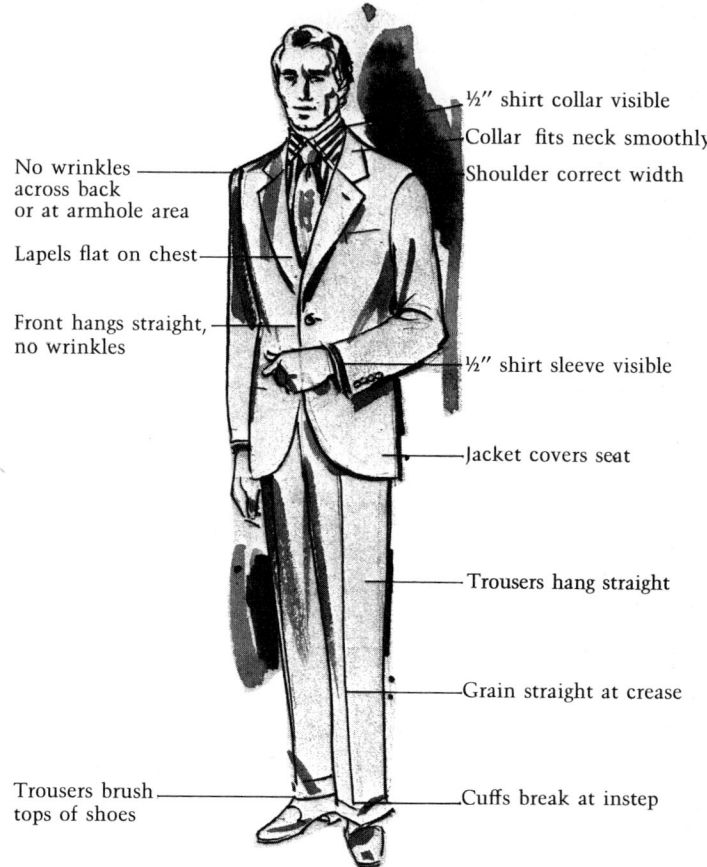

FIGURE 15-1 *The different points to check for correct fit in a man's suit.*

CONSTRUCTION

Quality construction includes good workmanship, and the following points should be checked before purchase. All pieces of the suit should be cut on the true fabric and design grainline. Patterned or plaid fabrics should match exactly at all seams; pocket flaps should match the pattern of the body section.

Jacket linings, full or partial, should be of a firm, durable fabric. Twill-woven linings are the most satisfactory. Buttonholes should be closely and evenly stitched, with reinforcements at both ends. Buttons should be firmly attached with strong thread. Jacket fronts should be interfaced, to hold the shape. The lapels should spring back to their original smooth appearance after being crushed in the hand. Armholes should be taped, to prevent stretching. Pockets should be deep and roomy, and made of a sturdy but lightweight fabric. They should be double-stitched and reinforced.

Trousers, which may or may not have cuffs, should have ample seam allowances for any necessary refitting. The waist should be interfaced; front facings should extend to reinforce the crotch, to prevent stretching. Pockets should be deep, roomy, and reinforced, and the pocket facings should be wide enough that the lining does not show. The zipper should lie flat and smooth, with no puckering. Belt loops, if used, should be firmly stitched, with ends either extended into the waistband or neatly folded under and stitched.

FIGURE 15-2 *Two very different styles in men's jackets: on the top a double-knit jacket of 100 percent polyester with the look of seersucker; and on the bottom a short jacket of polyester/cotton blend, with a Scotchgard® Rain Repeller finish.* (Courtesy of McGregor-Doniger Inc.)

FIT

The fit of a suit is a very important part of appearance and comfort. Both trousers and jacket should be tried on, and inspected carefully. Figure 15-1 shows the specific points to be checked.

Generally speaking, a suit that fits well will hang straight and will not pull or appear baggy anywhere (Figures 15-2 and 15-3). The shoulders will lie flat and smooth, with no looseness or strain. The collar will hug the neck, lying smooth and unwrinkled, and the lapels will be smooth, with no gaps apparent. Jacket fronts will hang even and straight when they are buttoned. Armholes will allow full arm movements, with no constriction or strain. Trousers will hang straight and even, with the creases running straight up and down. The waist will fit snugly, and the waistband, if any, will not gap or roll over.

FIGURE 15-3 *Cotton denim fabric and Western styling make an easy jacket and slim jeans. Both would be comfortable to wear and easy to take care of.* (Courtesy of Cotton Incorporated)

FIGURE 15-4 *A three-quarter-length coat such as this one would provide comfort and durability for colder climates, since it is made of all-cotton corduroy.* (Courtesy of Cotton Incorporated)

Overcoats and Topcoats

In recent years, men have changed their preferences in topcoats. Few men today own really heavy overcoats, and most men prefer jackets or car coats of different weights (Figure 15-4).

Usually identified with cold-weather wear, these coats are made from fabrics such as wool, camel and wool, fleece, heavy tweeds, reversible double-cloth, worsted covert, and melton. Collars and linings may be made of fake-fur fabrics. When such coats are to receive hard wear, the more desirable woolen fabrics are tweed, cheviot, homespun, and mackinaw. Harris tweed, a varicolored and rough-surfaced woolen, is one of the strongest tweeds. It is made in Scotland and must have a label bearing the name for it to be a true Harris tweed.

Topcoats (lightweight overcoats) should be roomy enough to fit comfortably over other clothing without looking baggy. Good workmanship and fabric are important, since they mean longer service.

"Suburban" or "car" coat is the name given to a three-quarter-length coat that is suitable for high-school, college, or suburban wear by all age groups. Fabrics used for these coats include cotton gabardine, wool or cashmere fleece, tweed, corduroy, or melton. Some coats have fleece linings, and often the fabrics are finished for water repellency (Figure 15–5).

Jackets, especially the zip-up style, are popular for everyday and sports wear. Fabrics suitable for winter wear in cold climates include leather with sheep's wool lining, heavy wool fleece, and melton. Lightweight nylon-and-cotton blends,

FIGURE 15–5 *A car coat for all-season wear, rain or shine.* (Courtesy of Harbor Master Ltd.)

FIGURE 15-6 Men's shirts are available in a wide range of styles and fabrics, similar to those shown: (a) dress shirt of Indian-print polyester/cotton blend, permanent-press finish; (b) dress shirt of 100 percent polyester, with permanent-press finish, intended for evening wear; (c) short-sleeved shirt for dress or casual wear, permanent-press polyester/cotton blend; (d) knit sport shirt in polyester/cotton blend. (Courtesy of The Manhattan Shirt Company)

a

b

c

d

rayon, acetate, corduroy, poplin, and heavy wool plaid shirts are suitable for milder weather. Laminated nylon or polyester make rugged lightweight jackets.[2]

Shirts

One of the most important parts of a man's wardrobe is his shirts. Texture and color contrast in interesting ways with other garments, and attention is directed to the face through the emphasis provided by color or pattern.

A shirt style is selected according to its appropriateness for the occasion—leisure, work, business, or dress. Fabric determines the comfort and care of the shirt. Fabric that is smooth in texture, absorbent, and can be laundered easily will contribute to comfort during wear, and it also will help keep suit coats or sport jackets fresh. A man's self-confidence and comfort are increased when his shirt is clean, neat, fresh, and well fitted.

STYLES

Shirt styles are determined by the color and type of fabric used, in combination with the cut of the collar, cuffs, and closure (Figure 15-6). Typical styles for collars are shown in Figure 15-7, and for cuffs in Figure 15-8.

Dress shirts should be selected according to collar point and cuff styles. Collar points may be short, medium, or long, with tips that are either pointed or rounded. The spread between the points may be narrow, medium, or wide, and should be selected to complement the shape of the wearer's face. The shirt body may be full-cut, straight, or tapered; choice depends upon body build and personal preference. Cuff styles may be barrel, convertible, link, or French.

Sport-shirt collars are generally softer and more flexible than those on dress shirts and are of three basic styles—Ivy, convertible, or pullover. Shirt sleeves may be either long or short, and barrel cuffs are commonly found on long-sleeved sport shirts. A sleeve is usually finished with a hem, vent, placket, or cuff.

---

2. Sidney Margolius, *The Consumer's Guide to Better Buying*, 2nd ed., The Benjamin Company, New York, 1972, p. 127; Helen G. Chambers and Verna Moulton, *Clothing Selection*, 2nd ed., J. B. Lippincott Company, New York, 1969, pp. 225–226; Isabel B. Wingate, *Textile Fabrics and Their Selection*, 6th ed., Prentice-Hall, Englewood Cliffs, N.J., 1970, pp. 500–501.

Regular

Spread

Button-down

Short point

Medium point

FIGURE 15-7 *Some basic styles in collars for men's shirts.*

FABRICS

Dress-shirt fabrics are either 100 percent cotton broadcloth or oxford cloth (with or without minimum-care finishes) or 65/35 percent polyester/cotton blend broadcloth. A wide range of fabrics is used for sport shirts (Figure 15–9). Gabardine and other twill weaves, gingham checks and stripes, percale, oxford, madras, flannel, corduroy, and knit fabrics are common. The most common fibers are wool, acrylic, polyester, rayon, and cotton, and they may be used in 100 percent forms or in blends or combinations.

Work shirts are made for durability and often have features such as double-fabric reinforced elbows, no-rip gussets in the lower side seams, and double- or triple-stitched seams, bartacked at points of strain. Other details that may be included for practical reasons are pockets with pencil slots,

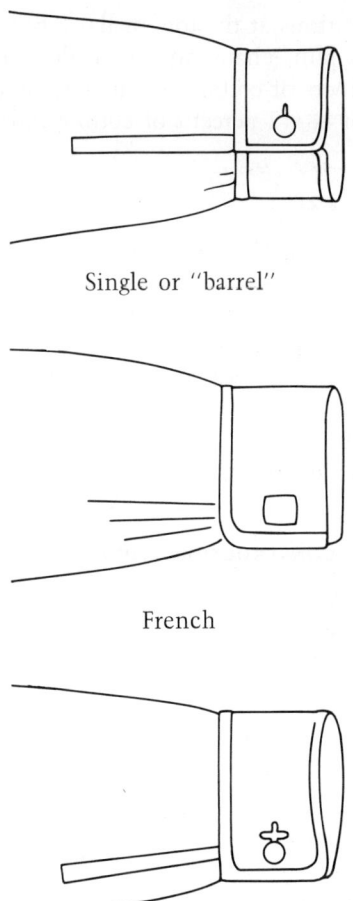

Single or "barrel"

French

Convertible

FIGURE 15-8 *Styles of cuffs found on men's shirts.*

FIGURE 15-9 *A plaid shirt in cotton flannel provides warmth and comfort.* (Courtesy of Cotton Incorporated)

buttons at the top, or flaps. Fabrics used most often include poplin, chambray, twill, denim covert, and drill cloth, in fibers of cotton, nylon, acrylic, and polyester. A twill blend of 88/12 percent of cotton and nylon also is popular.

SIZES

Dress-shirt sizes are based on neck measurements and, for shirts with long sleeves, the length of the sleeve measured from the center back of the neck, across the shoulder, and over the bent elbow to the wrist. Sport-shirt sizes for woven fabric correspond to the neck measurement and are grouped in body sizes—small, medium, large, and extra large. Knit sport shirts use chest-measurement sizes, which range from small to extra large.

CONSTRUCTION AND FIT

Construction features are important, since shirts receive very hard wear. All sections of the shirt should be cut on

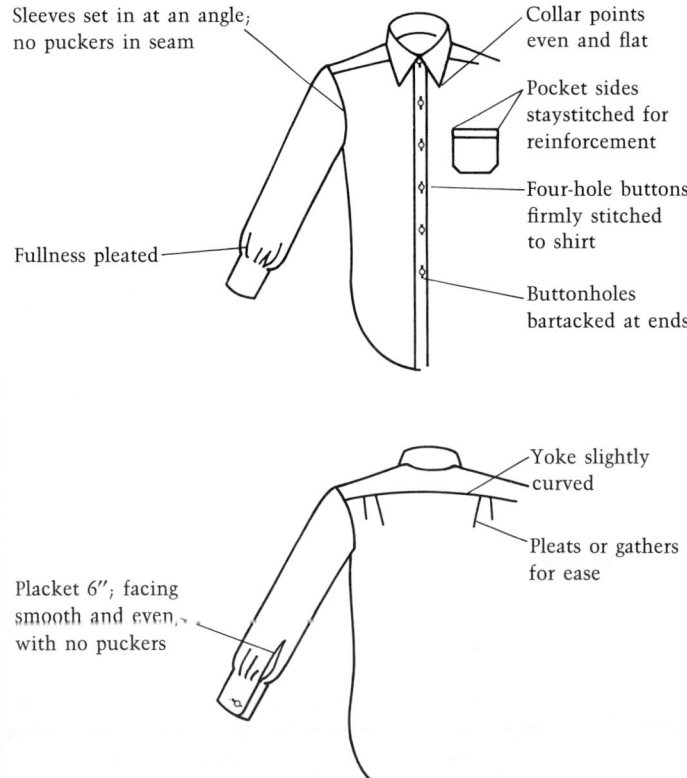

FIGURE 15-10 *The points to check for fit of a man's shirt.*

the true fabric grain. Patterned fabrics and plaids should match at sides, fronts, pockets, and collar fronts. All seams should be evenly stitched and lie smooth, without puckers. All topstitching on the collar and any other areas should be uniform. Collar points must be even and lie flat. Buttonholes should be evenly stitched and reinforced or backstitched; buttons should be sewn on well.

The yoke depth is proportioned to the neck size and sleeve length, and a deep yoke gives freedom of movement. Sleeves set into the shirt body at an angle also allow easy arm movement. Sleeve plackets should be smooth, with an opening of at least six inches on dress shirts. Permanent-press shirts usually have a continuous facing at the sleeve placket, and these facings should not pucker.[3] Points to check for fit in shirts are shown in Figure 15–10.

Jeans

Jeans were first designed to be worn by boys and men, but today anyone who wants a rugged durable garment may select jeans or dungarees. They were originally made from a darkblue, all-cotton, denim fabric (Figure 15–11), but recently they have become a fashion garment, and the dark-blue denim fabric no longer is synonymous with the garment style. Fabric colors now include descriptions such as "chocolate, berry, forest green, and skipper blue." Fabrics are now blends of cotton with either polyester or nylon, and the pants are lighter in weight, stronger, and more abrasion-resistant than the former all-cotton ones.

CONSTRUCTION

Quality construction in features such as the waistband, side pockets, and fly zipper should be looked for when selecting jeans. Multiple rows of stitching and double-stitched seams are signs of durable construction. The bottom of the zipper insert should be examined to make sure no raw edges have been left that might make the pants uncomfortable to wear. Zipper teeth made of stainless steel or brass are usually

---

3. *Men's Dress Shirts*, J. C. Penney Company, Inc., New York, n.d.; Margolius, *The Consumer's Guide to Better Buying*, pp. 128–130; Fae Roark, Bobbie L. McFatter, and R. Elizabeth Williams, *Shopping for Shirts*, Publication no. 1397, Baton Rouge, Louisiana State University Cooperative Extension Service, 1971.

FIGURE 15-11 *The basic blue jeans. Notice the manufacturer's trademark label at the waist and the tab at the edge of the right pocket.* (Courtesy of Levi Strauss & Co.)

more durable than those made of aluminum, and zipper pull tabs should be self-locking. Check hip pockets for reinforcement features such as a firm thread bartack or rivet.

STYLE

Jeans offer a wide variety of style choices. Legs may range from the tapered to flared bottom. They may be cut to fit the normal waistline or to ride low on the hips. The individual should check this style feature especially because it helps to determine garment fit. Jeans are usually purchased according to the inside leg seam length and the waist measurement.

CARE

Care instructions for jeans should be noted on the label before purchase and carefully followed when the pants are laundered. Generally, jeans shrink very little today because of durable-press finishes and blends of fibers. They also retain their color rather well through several washings. The popular faded look can be obtained by buying all-cotton jeans, which lose their color more rapidly than jeans that are made of blended fibers.

The zipper should be closed completely before laundering, to protect it. To prevent abrasion, jeans should be turned wrong side out before washing. Dark-colored jeans should be laundered only with other dark-colored clothing, and white or light-colored jeans with similar colors. This practice will prevent discoloration.

Leather Apparel

Because it is made from the outside covering of an animal, leather is not a true textile. However, it has been used for clothing for thousands of years, and modern methods of treatment result in leathers that can be handled like textiles. Many items of apparel such as coats, skirts, jackets, pants, and dresses are made from the softer, thinner leathers. In this section, discussion will be limited to aspects important for leather apparel. Further information on leather, and leather terms, will be covered in Chapter 17 in connection with shoes.

Leathers made from deer and sheep skins are widely used in items of apparel because they are soft and supple. Sheepskins may have some of the fleece left on them, for use as linings or outside trimmings on jackets and coats. Suede, which has been so popular for ladies' coats and jackets in recent years, is not a particular kind of leather. It is a finish, in which the surface of the hide is treated in a process called *napping*. The process raises the very small fibers on the surface, thus creating the soft, velvety feel of the leather. Either side of the hide may be napped in this way, and napping on the outside of the hide produces suede which is more durable than that on the inside of the hide.

Good leather is characterized by its softness, pliability, and firmness, whereas poor leather feels flabby and stiff. Good-quality leather is never inexpensive, and cheap leather will almost always turn out to be a bad investment because of its tendency to tear or crack at points of strain.

When considering clothing made of leather, the quality of the leather, construction of the garment, and fit are important. Garment sections should be checked for even thickness, softness, and flexibility, since variations in these qualities can cause the garment to fit or hang badly. Flexibility is important, to prevent cracking in areas where the garment bends, such as the elbow. The color should be even in all sections of the garment, with no streaks or spots.

As in fabric garments, construction details to be checked are ample seam allowances and firm, even stitching throughout. Buttons should be sewn on with a smaller button as reinforcement on the inside, to prevent tearing; stout shanks for the buttons are desirable to allow the garment to adjust to the wearer's movements.

The fit at shoulder, elbow, and hip, depending upon the garment involved, should be checked by trying on the item over the type of apparel that will be worn beneath it. Coats and jackets need ample room through the shoulder and sleeves, and skirts and pants require ease to allow for sitting and walking. Since leather is an excellent insulator, a little extra ease in the fit of an outer garment is desirable to retain any trapped air.

The durability of a leather garment depends partly upon the care it receives after purchase, to prolong its softness and flexibility. If the leather is allowed to become too dry, it may split, thus rendering the garment useless. Therefore, leather items should never be left near radiators or other sources of heat. If they get damp, they should be placed on hangers and hung in a well-ventilated place, away from heat.

Leather apparel should be cleaned only by dry cleaners who are thoroughly experienced in handling this type of work. Suede garments should be brushed with a bristle brush, not a wire brush, which might tear the small raised fibers and leave a bald spot on the surface. Leather apparel should be stored in a cool, dry place, since it is subject to attack by mildew.

Sweaters and Jerseys

Males of all ages find knit tops both comfortable and useful. A wide range of styles is available, from sleeveless garments for informal summer wear, through medium-weight, short-sleeved jerseys for sportswear, to heavy, bulky-knit sweaters which can double as jackets. Sweaters may button down the front, in cardigan or V-neck style, or they may be pullovers.

Full

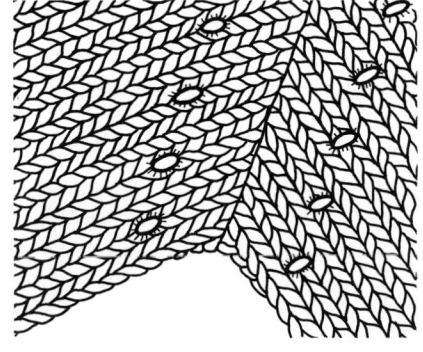

False

FIGURE 15-12 *The difference between full fashioning and false fashion marks, as they appear on the body of a sweater at the armhole.*

FIGURE 15-13 *Typical of those on the market, this sweater is made of acrylic, and the jersey is knit of 100 percent nylon. Both would require minimum care and keep a good appearance if properly laundered.* (Courtesy of McGregor-Doniger Inc.)

Generally speaking, jerseys and sweaters are selected according to chest measurements, which correspond to small, medium, large, and extra large. However, the length of long sleeves must be checked, since some variations among manufacturers can be expected. Many of these garments are worn over a shirt, and this fact must be considered at the time of purchase. In all cases, the jersey or sweater should not bind or constrain the wearer at any point.

Sweaters should be cut full-size, with armholes large enough for easy movement. A *full-fashioned* sweater, which has stitches knitted together along the sides of the armhole, is much more satisfactory than one that has only *false fashion marks* (Figure 15–12). Full-fashioned sweaters have sections that are knit to shape, then sewn together. Sweaters with false fashion marks use sections that are cut from knit fabric and then sewn together. False fashion marks are stitches made to look like full fashioning: no stitches really are dropped. Full fashioning, with the altered stitches, indicates a quality sweater that will not bind the wearer around the armhole.

Fibers used in jerseys may be 100 percent cotton or wool, manufactured fibers such as acrylic or polyester, or blends of various types (Figure 15–13). Fiber weights vary. Garments of manufactured fibers usually can be machine washed and dried, which makes them particularly useful for boys. However, these fibers may not be warm enough for cold-weather use, and they may make the wearer feel clammy in warm weather. All-wool sweaters can be hand washed, with great care, and they do provide additional warmth for colder climates. The need for protected off-season storage may be a factor to consider before purchase. In all instances, fiber and care labels should be read carefully, and cleaning instructions followed.

Socks

Socks should coordinate with clothes and shoes. Plain knit or rib socks are appropriate for dressy wear, while wool or bulky ones may be chosen for sport or casual wear. Cotton and wool socks are popular because their absorbency makes them comfortable, but the heels and toes should be reinforced with nylon for longer wear. Nylon socks can be washed and dried quickly, but some people find them hot or clammy, especially when worn in warm weather, because nylon is not absorbent.

Both stretch and nonstretch socks are available, and proper size is important in each type. Size is determined by measuring the distance from the point of the toe to the end of the heel. Stretch socks will cover several sizes, such as 10 to 13, while the nonstretch variety fits only one foot measurement. The elastic in the top of the socks should be strong enough to hold them up. Some styles are longer, with a ribbed top to help them stay up securely.[4]

Underwear

Several types of undershorts are available, and the style most comfortable is the one the consumer should choose. Knits allow for plenty of stretch, while boxer shorts have either full elastic waistbands or elastic in the side front or side back. The elastic should be of a quality to last the lifetime of the shorts. Colorfastness and shrinkage control should

---

4. Miller, *Young Man—Dress Right/Look Right*, pp. 12–13.

be checked for longer service. Construction details are important, and places of potential strain should be reinforced.

Shorts are sold by waist measurement. The knit type ranges from 28 inches to size 50, while the woven type usually goes up to size 54. Height is also important, and a very tall person may need a larger size in order to have a proper fit.[5]

Undershirts are of two types: the *athletic shirt*, with a low oval neck, deep-cut armholes, and no sleeves; and the *T-shirt*, which has a high neckline and sleeves. V-neck openings are popular because they do not show if the shirt collar is unbuttoned. In T-shirts the neck edge is bound with rib knit, which allows the neckline to return to its original shape. Sometimes the neck edge is reinforced with nylon for extra strength. Undershirts may be sized according to chest measurement as small, medium, large, and extra large, or in even numbers ranging from 34 to 54. Sanforized or preshrunk shirts will retain their size and shape longer than those not so labeled.[6]

Pajamas

Pajamas for men and boys may be made of woven or knitted fabric. Broadcloth and plissé are widely used for summer wear, and flannelette and knits are common for colder weather. Fiber blends such as cotton and polyester are usual, and flame-retardant finishes are highly desirable for all ages.

A standard range of sizes is produced, and personal preference for comfort usually determines the size of pajama selected. Generally, pajamas should be large enough to prevent any constriction of the wearer. They should be well constructed, with reinforced stitching at points of strain such as waist, crotch, and shoulder. Good quality in both fabric and construction ensures longer service from pajamas, which receive hard wear as the sleeper turns and bends. Fiber and care labels are as important as for other garments.

Study Questions

1. What changes have taken place in men's wear in the past ten years?
2. What design features are important for men to consider when buying clothing?

---

5. *Ibid.*
6. *Ibid.*

3. What types of fabric are best for suits? Why?
4. What are marks of good workmanship in clothing for men?
5. What terms are used to identify overcoats and topcoats for men? What are the distinguishing features of each?
6. What factors determine shirt styles?
7. What measurements are used to purchase dress shirts? Sport shirts? Knit sport shirts?
8. What features determine quality in jeans?
9. What fibers are popular in men's socks? Why?
10. What features should one look for in undershorts and undershirts?

Suggested Activities

1. Study the fashion changes in men's clothing over the past fifty years.
2. Survey men in different types of work, such as professionals, farmers, and businessmen, and find out what they like and dislike in men's clothing today.
3. Make a display or bulletin board on features to consider when buying men's clothing such as a suit, shirt, or coat.
4. Write a news story on the changing scene in men's clothing today.
5. Assist a man in selecting some clothing items and point out factors to consider relating to style, fabric selection, care features, and so on.
6. Visit a local men's clothing store and talk with the merchant about the factors that influence him in selecting items for the store stock.

Chapter 16

Apparel for Women and Girls

THE WOMAN OR GIRL who wishes to dress attractively within the limits of her budget needs to plan her wardrobe and be able to judge the quality and construction of the clothing she buys. The range of items needed in the basic wardrobe depends on the life style and activities of the individual. A college student, for example, would not have the same clothing needs as a woman with a full-time professional job.

The goal should be wardrobe flexibility. Simple styles that are suitable, with or without accessories, for a range of occasions are the answer. The best buys are usually classic styles in basic colors. Extremes of length, very bold or brilliant prints, exaggerated cut or style, or other short-lived fads should be avoided. Simplicity in styling affects maintenance costs, too, for nondetachable collars, ruffles, bows, or other trims increase cleaning costs or require special handling. Versatility can be achieved through selection of mix-and-match coordinates. Jumpers, two-piece dresses, and unlined suits lend themselves to different combinations. If the wardrobe is built on one or two basic colors, fewer accessories are needed, and overall cost is kept down.

TABLE 16-1 *Range of Sizes and Measurement Instructions for Girls' and Teens' Apparel*

Growing Girls Apparel

Girls' Sizes 7 to 16 | **Slim Sizes 7s to 14s** | **Chubby Sizes 8½ to 16½**

Girls' Sizes 7 to 16
School girls whose figures are lengthening and have acquired a straightness, but still undeveloped in bust and hips.

Height (in.)	49½-51½	52-53½	54-55½	56-58	58½-60½	61-63
Order Size	7	8	10	12	14	16
If Chest is	26-26½	27-27½	28-29	29½-30½	31-32	32½-33
If Waist is	22-22½	23-23½	24-24½	25-25½	26-26½	27-27½
If Hips are	27½-28	28½-29	29½-30½	31-32½	33-34½	35-36

Slim Girls' Sizes 7s to 14s
School girls whose figures are slimmer, but still undeveloped in bust and hips.

Order Size	7s	8s	10s	12s	14s	—
If Chest is	24½-25	25½-26	26½-27½	28-29	29½-30½	—
If Waist is	20½-21	21½-22	22½-23	23½-24	24½-25	—
If Hips are	25½-26	26½-27	27½-28½	29-30½	31-32½	—

Chubby Girls' Sizes 8½ to 16½
School girls whose figures are heavier, but still undeveloped in bust and hips.

Order Size	—	8½	10½	12½	14½	16½
If Chest is	—	29-29½	30-31	31½-32½	33-34	34½-35½
If Waist is	—	26-26½	27-27½	28-28½	29-29½	30-30½
If Hips are	—	31-31½	32-33	33½-35	35½-37	37½-39

Helpful Hints . . Growing Girls

Dresses, Coats, Shirts, Blouses, Sweaters . . order by height and chest measurement.
Skirts, Slacks and Shorts . . order size closest to your waist measurement.
All other Growing Girls' Fashions . . order by height and hips.
Height is the deciding factor when height and chest or hips fall into different sizes.

Young Teens Apparel

Sizes 6J to 16J

Young Teens Sizes 6J to 16J
Girls whose figures are beginning to develop. Height 4 ft. 11 in. to 5 ft. 5 in. in stocking feet.

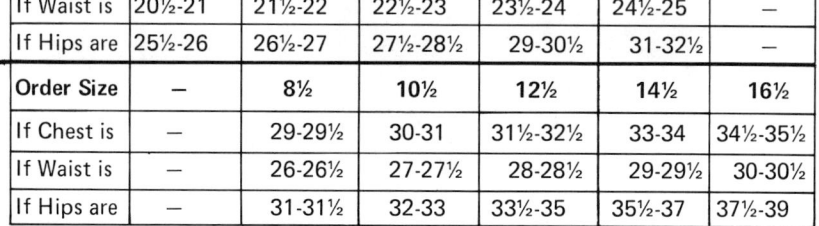

Height (in.)	59-60	60½-61	61½-62	62½-63	63½-64	64½-65
Order Size	6J	8J	10J	12J	14J	16J
If Bust is	28½-29	29½-30	30½-31	31½-32½	33-34	34½-35½
If Waist is	22-22½	23-23½	24-24½	25-25½	26-26½	27-27½
If Hips are	31-31½	32-32½	33-33½	34-35	35½-36½	37-38

Helpful Hints . . Young Teens

Shirts, Blouses, Sweaters. . order size closest to your bust measurement.
Skirts, Slacks and Shorts . . order size closest to your waist measurement.
Sheath Dresses . . order size closest to your hip measurement.

Source: Courtesy of Sears, Roebuck and Co.

TABLE 16-2 *Range of Sizes and Measurement Instructions for Women's Apparel*

Women's Apparel Measuring Charts

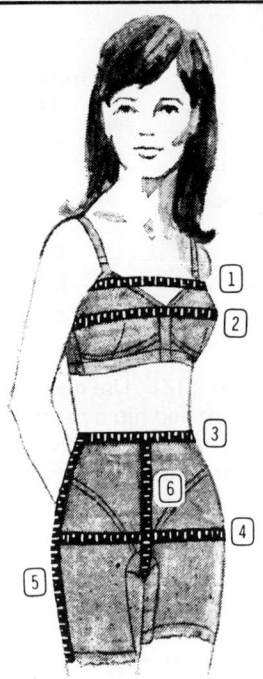

Measurements should be taken carefully over whatever type of foundation garments you normally wear.

> **For Women's Clothing use measurements 2, 3, 4**

1. **Chest**... Well under arm and above bust.
2. **Bust**... At the fullest part, but hold tape gently.
3. **Waist**... At the smallest part.
4. **Hips**... At the fullest part.
5. **Length**... At side from the waist down to where you want garment to end.
6. **Rise**... From waist at center front, down through crotch and up to waist at center back.

> **For Bras and Foundations use measurements 1 thru 6**

HOW TO DETERMINE SIZE FOR:

Dresses...Sheaths or Slim Styles, order size closest to hip measurement (see measurement 4).

Dresses...Flared, Skimmer, or "A" Line Styles, order size closest to bust measurement (see measurement 2).

Blouses...Shirts, order size closest to bust measurement (see measurement 2).

Sweaters...Shells, order size closest to bust measurement (see measurement 2).

Coats...Jackets, order the size closest to bust measurement (see measurement 2).

Skirts...Slacks...Shorts, elasticized waists, order by hip size (see measurement 4)...band top waists, order by waist size (see measurement 3).

Panties... order size closest to hip measurement (see measurement 4).

Half Slips...Pettipants, order size closest to hip measurement (see measurement 4).

Slips, Misses and Larger, order size closest to bust measurement (see measurement 2). Juniors, order size closest to dress size.

Nightwear, order size closest to bust measurement (see measurement 2).

Robes...Loungewear, order size closest to dress size.

Pantyhose.....	P, A, T SIZES P(petite); A(average); T(tall). *State* P, A, or T.	EXTRA-LARGE SIZE XL (fits women over 165 to 200 lbs.)	QUEEN SIZE XXXXL (fits women over 200 to 250 lbs.)		
Stockings.......	PETITE Sizes A(8-9) B(9½-10½)	SHAPELY Sizes A(8½-9½) B(10-11)	CLASSIC Sizes A(8½-9½) B(10-11)	TALL Sizes A(9½-10½) B(11-12)	STATUESQUE Sizes A(9½-10½) B(11-12)

TABLE 16-2 (cont.)

BRAS AND FOUNDATIONS

For Bra Size — The size you order is chest measurement No. 1.
For Cup Size — Subtract chest measurement 1 from bust measurement 2.

If Bust Measurement (2) is:	Order Cup
same or less than bra size (Measurement 1)	AAA
up to ½" larger than bra size (Measurement 1)	AA
up to 1" larger than bra size (Measurement 1)	A
up to 2" larger than bra size (Measurement 1)	B
up to 3" larger than bra size (Measurement 1)	C
up to 4" larger than bra size (Measurement 1)	D
up to 5" larger than bra size (Measurement 1)	DD
over 5½" larger than bra size (Measurement 1)	F

GIRDLES, PANTY GIRDLES AND BRIEFS...

Take measurements 3, 4 and 5. The size you order is measurement 3...your WAIST SIZE. Use measurement 4 to determine your Hip Size. The difference between your waist measurement and hip measurement will give your hip type. Measurement 5...Length, is your measurement from waist down to where you want the garment to end. All waist down measurements for garments represent measurements when worn on figure.

- Order by Waist Size...being sure that Hip Size and Length are right for you.

PROPORTIONED GARMENTS...

Take measurements 3, 4 and 5 as noted under Girdles, Panty Girdles and Briefs. Also, take measurement 6...Rise, for your torso type.

- Order by Waist Size...being sure that Hip Size, Length and Rise (torso type) are right for you.

ALL-IN-ONES...

Take measurements 1, 2, 4 and 5. The size you order is chest measurement 1...which is your Bra Size. Your cup type is found the same as for bras (see Bras above).

- Order by Bra Size...being sure that Cup Type, Hip Size and Length are right for you.

Source: Courtesy of Sears, Roebuck and Co.

A good general rule to keep in mind when planning clothing purchases is to buy the best quality that the budget will allow. Good fabric, high-quality construction, and correct fit in any garment mean better service over a longer period of time. Good fabrics will not shrink, fade, or tear. Good construction will help the garment hold its shape and stand up under the stress received during wear. Correct fit will improve personal appearance and add to self-confidence. Clothing for women and girls is manufactured in standard sizes; the sizes used to order Sears, Roebuck and Co. apparel are shown in Tables 16-1, 16-2, and 16-3.

Selection of clothing for women and girls is a wide topic. Whole books have been written on the subject, some covering generalities, others dealing with specifics. Among the

TABLE 16-3 *Misses, Junior, Half Sizes, and Women's Sizes*

Determine if you are a regular, tall or petite by measuring your height in stocking feet.

Misses Sizes .. For the figure of average proportions.
Average Misses.. Height is 5 ft. 3 in. to 5 ft. 6½ in. in stocking feet.
Petite Misses.. Height is 5 ft. 2½ in. and under in stocking feet. Garments are proportionately shorter than average misses'.
Tall Misses.. Height is 5 ft. 7 in. to 5 ft. 11 in. in stocking feet. Garments are proportionately longer than average Misses'.

Order Size	6	8	10	12	14	16	18	20
If fullest part of bust is	31½-32	32½-33	33½-34	34½-35½	36-37	37½-38½	39-40½	41-42½
If waist is	22½-23	23½-24	24½-25	25½-26½	27-28	28½-29½	30-31½	32-33½
If hips are	33½-34	34½-35	35½-36	36½-37½	38-39	39½-40½	41-42½	43-44½

Junior Sizes .. Smaller, more defined waist. Higher bustline. Slightly shorter from shoulder to waist than Misses'.
Average Juniors.. Height is 5 ft. 2 in. to 5 ft. 6 in. in stocking feet.
Petite Juniors.. Height is under 5 ft. 1½ in. in stocking feet. Garments are proportionately shorter than average Juniors.
Tall Juniors.. Height is 5 ft. 6½ in. to 5 ft. 11 in. in stocking feet. Garments are proprotionately longer than average Juniors.

Order Size	3	5	7	9	11	13	15
If fullest part of bust is	30-30½	31-31½	32-32½	33-33½	34-35	35½-36½	37-38
If waist is	21-21½	22-22½	23-23½	24-24½	25-26	25½-27½	28-29
If hips are	32-32½	33-33½	34-34½	35-35½	36-37	37½-38½	39-40

Half Sizes .. Medium to heavy frame. Shorter from shoulder to waist than Women's.
Half Sizes .. Shorter Women's Sizes.. Height is 5 ft. 4 in. and under in stocking feet. Garment waist length and overall lengths are shorter than Women's Sizes.

Order Size	14½	16½	18½	20½	22½	24½	26½
If fullest part of bust is	37-38½	39-40½	41-42½	43-44½	45-46½	47-48½	49-50½
If waist is	29-30½	31-32½	33-34½	35-37	37½-39½	40-42	42½-44½
If hips are	38-39½	40-41½	42-43½	44-45½	46-47½	48-49½	50-51½

Women's Sizes .. For the fuller, more mature figure. Longer from shoulder to waist and waist to hem line than Half Sizes.
Women's Sizes.. Height is 5 ft. 4½ in. to 5 ft. 6½ in. in stocking feet. Garment waist length and overall lengths are longer than Half Sizes.

Order Size	38	40	42	44	46	48
If fullest part of bust is	41-42½	43-44½	45-46½	47-48½	49-50½	51-52½
If waist is	33-34½	35-37	37½-39½	40-42	42½-44½	45-47
If hips are	42-43½	44-45½	46-47½	48-49½	50-51½	52-53½

Source: Courtesy of Sears, Roebuck and Co.

FIGURE 16-1 *The classic styles of women's coats, which range from formal designs like the clutch or tuxedo to casual styles like the balmacaan.*

Princess

Coachman

Chesterfield

Polo

16 / *Apparel for Women and Girls*

aspects considered are basic dress design; use of line, color, and texture; expression of individuality; fashion, style, and fad. This book does not attempt to deal with such material; specific books that will serve as introductions to these topics are listed in the Bibliography. This chapter deals with textiles, standards, and types and quality of clothing available to the consumer.

Coats

Fashions in coats change, but certain classic styles for cloth coats remain basically the same. Brief descriptions of these styles are given below, and they are illustrated in Figure 16–1.

BALMACAAN Loose and flaring, with small collar and raglan sleeves.

BOX Full-length style, with straight lines and collar.

CHESTERFIELD Tailored overcoat, originally single-breasted with concealed buttons.

CLUTCH OR WRAP Straight coat without buttons, often with a shawl collar. May or may not have a belt.

COACHMAN Heavy, fitted coat, double-breasted and buttoning high on the chest. Back may have pleated or flared skirt; usually has a wide collar and large revers.

POLO Casual topcoat, made of camel hair or an imitation, tailored in style.

PRINCESS Long coat, darted and seamed to give a close fit through the waist; usually has a gored skirt that flares at the hem.

REEFER Close-fitting, usually double-breasted style; long or short.

TRENCH Overcoat, usually waterproof or water-resistant; may be double- or single-breasted and belted all around. Often has a detachable lining (Figure 16–2).

TUXEDO Unfitted, long or short coat with flat, turned-back collar that continues in a band down the front to the hem. Usually has no fastening, but may tie with large, sash-type belt.

Fabrics for coats vary greatly, depending on style, degree of formality, and climate. Broadcloths, tweeds, meltons, and fleeces are used to make heavy coats for cold-weather wear. Lighter poplins, flannels, twills, and corduroys are common, as well as knits of various types, and lightweight summer coats may be of almost any suitable fabric. The fibers used for these different fabrics range from heavy pure wool for cold climates to cotton and manufactured fiber blends for all-weather wear. Fake fur of manufactured fibers is frequently used for coats or for linings.

FIGURE 16-2 *This coat, a variation of the trench-coat style, would be a useful addition to many wardrobes. Made of 100 percent cotton corduroy, it could be worn with both pants and skirts.* (Courtesy of Cotton Incorporated)

Heavy coats are usually lined and interlined. Lining fabrics range from taffetas and crepes to cotton and manufactured blends, while interlinings are often made of a lightweight, quilted fabric of either natural or manufactured fiber. Acrylic pile linings are widely used in sports and car coats and jackets. These heavier pile linings may be removable, for all-season service from the coat.

A good cloth coat without fur trim is usually a better buy than an inexpensive one with trim. Since two layers are warmer than one heavy layer, the warmest cloth coat is considered to be one made of new wool, with a heavy woolen inner lining.

CONSTRUCTION

Checking construction details before purchase presents problems, since many of them are concealed. However, good construction within the coat often is indicated by certain finishing details. The buyer should look for the following.

On heavy coats, buttons should have stout thread shanks or be reinforced with smaller, flat buttons on the inside of the coat. Buttonholes should be firmly and evenly stitched, and reinforced. The lining should be neatly set into the coat and it should hang evenly and smoothly, with no puckering or gaps. It should have a pleat or tuck in the back and in the shoulder seams of both fronts, to allow movement without ripping or pulling out. The lining should not show at the hemline or sleeve ends; in these areas, it should be loosely sewn to the coat fabric, to allow ease. A slippery lining is desirable, since it allows the coat to be put on or removed easily.

All sections of the coat should be cut on the true fabric grain. Patterned fabric should match exactly at all seams, collar, and lapels. Seams at the sides should run straight to the hem. Stitching, where it can be seen, should be even, firm, and without bunching.

FIGURE 16-3 *This all-weather coat in 100 percent polyester, raschel warp knit, shows the effect of Oriental design on American fashion. Side vents provide plenty of room for walking; easy shoulders suggest room for a light suit underneath.* (Courtesy of Misty Harbor Ltd.)

FIGURE 16-4 *Worn together, this double-knit pure wool blazer and long skirt make an effective combination. Both garments could be combined with other blouses or sweaters, and with other skirts and pants, for a variety of effects. Jewelry and scarves could also change the appearance.* (Courtesy of Pendleton Woolen Mills)

FIT

A coat is a major purchase, and the buyer should consider a number of points on fit (Figure 16-3). Since a coat is worn over other garments, it should be tried on over a dress or suit, as the case may be. The amount of ease around the armhole and in the sleeves should be checked, as well as the amount of fullness needed through the body of the coat. It should hang evenly, with no wrinkles or bunching at any point. The fronts should meet evenly when the coat is buttoned or wrapped. Sleeves should hang smoothly, with no tendency to pull forward or back, and sleeve length should be adequate.

Coat length should be checked carefully. As a general rule, a full-length coat should be approximately one inch longer than the dress or skirt. If alteration will be needed before the coat can be worn, seams should be checked, especially any complicated seaming or construction technique, where seams may have been trimmed close to the stitching.

Suits

A basic, becoming suit often is regarded as a wardrobe foundation. Suits can be worn with a blouse or without, as two-piece dresses. Simplicity in styling is highly desirable, so that a suit can be worn with scarves or jewelry for formality or worn without accessories for informal occasions. A simple, well-tailored suit, of good fabric, will provide longer service than a dressy suit with more intricate lines and decoration (Figure 16-4).

A wide range of fibers and fabrics is used for suits—polyesters, wool, cottons, and blends of natural and manufactured fibers, in flannels, tweeds, corduroys, knits, denims, and twills. Suits made of blends are less expensive on the whole than those of wool, and they can be worn for longer periods of the year in some climates.

FIGURE 16-5 *The different areas to check when inspecting a woman's suit for correct fit.*

Jacket linings may be crepes, taffetas, or twills of natural or manufactured fibers. Lightweight suits, like those of denim or poplin, often are unlined. As in the case of coats, a slippery lining fabric makes putting on or removing the jacket easier.

To fit properly, the jacket must be cut full enough that the arms can be raised without undue pulling at the seams (Figure 16-5). Large armholes and curved underarm seams are particularly important fitting details. The collar should fit the neck smoothly; both lapels should be the same width and roll back smoothly and evenly. When the jacket is buttoned, no gaps or signs of strain should be evident, and the fronts should overlap or meet evenly when the jacket is fastened. If a belt is included in the design, it should not hang free, but should be attached at the sides or run through loops or slides. Jacket shoulders must be smooth and the correct width for the wearer.

The skirt should hang smoothly from the waistband or waistline, with no bunching or wrinkling over the hips. Side seams should run straight, with no slant toward back or front. A straight skirt must allow for easy movement in walking and getting in and out of vehicles. Construction details to be checked are similar to those mentioned for coats.

Dresses

As with suits, a simply styled dress of good-quality fabric and good construction is a sound investment. With or without accessories, it can be worn for a wide range of events, and, depending on the climate, often for the major part of the year (Figure 16-6). Classic styles, such as shirtwaists and jumpers, in basic solid colors, lend themselves to combinations with jackets, sweaters, and blouses. Frequently it is more economical to buy one good-quality, basic dress than two or three of lesser quality for the same amount of money.

All types of fabrics are used for dresses (Figure 16-7), and the polyester knits and cotton blends are wearable almost year-round. Finishes for antiperspirant stain, permanent press, and wrinkle resistance help dress fabrics keep a fresh appearance for longer periods of time between washings, make washing easier, and reduce maintenance costs.

Dress sizes for girls and women, as used by Sears, Roebuck and Co., were given earlier, in Tables 16-1 and 16-2. They are typical of size standards and variations for body build and proportion.

FIGURE 16-6 *A simple cotton dress that could have many different accessories—belts, jewelry, and scarves. Depending upon the jewelry and shoes, it could be suitable for a party or for office wear.* (Courtesy of Cotton Incorporated)

FIT

Like coats and suits, a dress must be tried on before purchase. Because undergarments form the "underpinning" to a dress, it is always desirable to wear the appropriate undergarments when shopping for a dress, since they affect the way it fits and hangs. Similarly, shoes of the heel height planned to go with the dress should be worn, because heel height affects the overall proportions.

All sections of the dress should have enough ease for body movements during wear. Shoulders and sleeves should allow for reaching, with enough ease in the armhole and at the elbow, in long-sleeved dresses. There should be sufficient ease over the bust, in darts, fullness, or seaming, to avoid any appearance of strain on the fabric. The waistline, whether seamed or implied in the design, should lie at the wearer's waist, not just above or just below. The skirt should have sufficient ease or fullness to allow for body movement without constraint of any kind. If the skirt binds or tends to ride up, the dress should be left in the store, for it would be a constant aggravation to the wearer.

The neckline, collared or uncollared, should fit smoothly around the neck, with no gaps. A low or scoop neckline should fit snugly. Shoulders should be the right width for the wearer, and the tops of the sleeves should fit smoothly at the shoulder seam. Since necklines, shoulders, and sleeves are the most troublesome areas of a dress to refit, and often such work cannot be done properly, special attention to these parts is desirable.

The dress should not wrinkle or sag at any point; it should conform to body lines, depending on the styling. There should be no wrinkles in the sleeves when the arms are held naturally at the sides. Side seams should fall straight from the waistline. Pleated skirts should lie over the hips with

FIGURE 16-7 *This delicate and elegant party dress is made of 100 percent cotton. It would require careful hand washing, but many women would feel the design is so attractive that the dress is worth the care. (Courtesy of Cotton Incorporated)*

pleats folded. The hem should run evenly around the dress, with no sagging or unevenness.

CONSTRUCTION

Details of construction in dresses are comparatively easy to check, since most dresses are not lined in the same way that coats and suits are. Good construction is important for appearance, fit, and service.

A dress will wear best when the sections are cut on true fabric grain, with the design grain straight. The dress also should hang on the true fabric grain. Interfacings should be inconspicuous from the outside, appropriate in weight, and require the same type of cleaning as the dress fabric. These same criteria apply to linings.

All stitching should be secure, and, unless used for decoration, the thread should match the fabric color. Length of stitch should be appropriate to the fabric. Seams should be double-stitched at points of stress, and buttonholes made stoutly and evenly. Fasteners such as buttons, snaps, hooks, and zippers should be sewn on neatly, securely, and inconspicuously. Zippers, gussets, and facings should be smooth and flat, with no puckers and gaps. Seams should be ample, to allow for any necessary refitting, and they should be finished to prevent raveling. Collars should fit smoothly around the neck; the undercollar should not show. Set-in sleeves should have ample ease for comfort, with no puckers in either armhole seam or sleeve cap. Other types, such as kimono sleeves, need reinforcement along the curve of the underarm seam, as do sleeve gussets. Fabric designs such as plaids and stripes should match at all seams. Belts that are entirely covered on the fabric grain, with inconspicuous stitching, improve the outside appearance of the dress. Hem stitching should not be visible on the outside of the dress, and it should not cause the outside fabric to pucker or wrinkle. Any decorative trim such as braid, lace, or embroidery should be of good quality and capable of being cleaned in the same way as the dress fabric. Also, it should be appropriate for the particular dress.

Pants

Pants are available in so many styles and fabrics that only general guidelines will be mentioned in this section. Suitability of fabric to the particular style is important. Thus, a tailored pantsuit to be worn to work should be made of fabric

FIGURE 16-8 *Three styles in pants: (a) glen-plaid tailored pants, worn with a blazer and blouse; (b) soft separates for casual or semiformal occasions; (c) easy jumpsuit with pajama-style legs, for comfort at home or for parties, with jewelry added. (Courtesy of Pendleton Woolen Mills [a], Bobbie Brooks, Inc. [b], and Cotton Incorporated [c])*

a

b

c

16 / Apparel for Women and Girls

that will retain its shape, resist wrinkling, and hold the crease in the pants. Pajama-style pants for evening or festive wear, on the other hand, require a soft fabric that will drape and move gracefully with the wearer (Figure 16-8).

Fit is all-important, for both appearance and comfort. Pants should fit smoothly at the waist and over the hips, with no gapping, wrinkling, or bunching. The seat should not bag or wrinkle. Side seams should run straight up and down. Cuffs or hems, as the case may be, should hang clear of the ground, both to give a correct proportion to the figure and to avoid soiling and tearing during wear.

Ease of movement must be considered well before purchase. Pants should always be tried on and checked for adequate fabric in crotch and hip areas. Width of seams should be checked, in case refitting is necessary. Skimpy seams often indicate poor workmanship and inferior fabrics. Cotton pants should be Sanforized to avoid shrinkage.

The construction details to be considered are similar to those given for suits: even stitching, reinforcement at points of strain, sections cut on the true grain of the fabric, matched patterns, and smooth-lying zippers. Labels should be read and care instructions followed.

Blouses

Styles in blouses vary widely, from tailored shirt types to those which incorporate lace or ruffles in their design (Figure 16-9). Fabrics commonly used for blouses are washable polyester knits, woven permanent-press polyester/cotton blends, acetate or triacetate for more dressy styles, cotton broadcloth, and crepes. Satins and metallic fabrics are used in blouses for festive occasions or formal events.

Many of the points mentioned for buying dresses apply to blouses also, especially those pertaining to construction. Blouses are bought by bust size, but body and sleeve length must be checked before purchase.

Since washability is important in blouses, labels should be read carefully for care instructions. Sanforized or preshrunk fabrics, minimum-care finishes, and colorfastness should be sought out.

Sweaters

The sweater is an all-time favorite because of its versatility, warmth, comfort, and light weight. Whether knit or cro-

FIGURE 16-9 *The classic shirt in Qiana nylon knit.* (Courtesy of Ship'n Shore, Inc.)

cheted, a sweater can be used as part of a basic combination, like a sweater and skirt. It can also be a coat, a jacket, or an over-the-shoulder wrap.

Sweaters made of wool are satisfactory for both summer and winter wear. They can be hand washed, with great care in both laundering and drying, but often they are dry cleaned. Protective storage during off-seasons is required, since insects attack wool. Wool knit sweaters should be stored flat, since hanging loosely knitted fabrics (like sweaters) can cause them to undergo loop elongation, which results in garment stretching and distortion. In addition, since wool fiber is weaker than other sweater fibers, the weight could cause fiber and yarn damage.

Sweaters made of manufactured fibers such as polyester and nylon launder and dry easily and quickly. Polyesters, however, may be uncomfortable for some people, and they may not provide enough warmth in cold climates. They tend to attract static electricity and they pill readily. Nylon sweaters may cause the wearer to have a clammy feeling, because the fiber holds perspiration next to the skin. Since nylon tends to collect color and soil during laundering, white nylon sweaters must be washed separately. All labels must be checked before purchase and care instructions followed precisely.

Sweaters are bought according to bust size, but body and arm length must always be checked. A sweater that is too short in either area will ride up and wrinkle or bunch, constantly annoying the wearer. Generally, a sweater should be bought a size larger than the blouse size, to fit neither too snugly nor too loosely. For cold-weather wear, a sweater that is loose is warmer than a snug-fitting one, since the space between sweater and body serves as insulation. Construction details given for men's and boys' sweaters apply also to sweaters for women and girls, and full fashioning is equally desirable.

Foundation Garments

Personal preference dictates the type and style of undergarments worn by women and girls. These garments include panties, brassieres, slips, and girdles, and all are available in a variety of styles, fabrics, and colors. Correctly and carefully selected, they provide a comfortable "underpinning" for the outer clothing.

In all cases, some thought should be given to the outer garments under which foundation garments will be worn.

A slip, for example, should reach to just below the hem stitching of an opaque dress, so that the overall effect of the dress is not spoiled. Dresses or blouses with narrow shoulder straps or low fronts and backs require brassieres and slips cut accordingly. Similarly, foundation garments to be worn under clingy fabrics such as jerseys or thin crepes should have no bulky construction details that will form lumps or ridges. In other words, undergarments should be invisible.

As a rule, foundation garments should be soft, lightweight, and easy to launder. They should not stick or cling to the outer clothing, twist, or crawl. Proper size is extremely important, for these garments should stay in place, fit smoothly and comfortably, and not bind, irritate, or chafe the wearer.

FABRIC

Depending on the purpose of the garment, the fabric may be woven or knitted of cotton, rayon, acetate, nylon polyester, lastex, or spandex fibers. Spandex and lastex are elastic and are used where a high degree of stretch is required, as in girdles and brassiere sections that fit over the rib cage. Spandex is considerably lighter in weight and stronger than lastex, and it provides comparable control.

Knitted fabrics of cotton, rayon, acetate, and nylon are the most popular for panties. The knit construction provides enough stretch for comfort in body movement and it allows the garment to conform to the body for a smooth appearance. Cotton and rayon are more absorbent and thus more comfortable than other fibers. Nylon and polyester are popular because they dry quickly.

Slips are made of cotton, rayon, acetate, polyester, and nylon, of either woven or knitted construction. Polyester and nylon tend to accumulate static electricity and may cling to outer garments in cold weather. This problem can be reduced if the slips are finished to give antistatic properties; the Antron III type of nylon fiber is relatively static-free.[1]

Brassieres are made of cotton and manufactured fibers, either woven or knitted. They usually have some sections made of spandex, to allow for ease in movement and breathing.

---

1. R. Elizabeth Williams and Celia Hissong, *Foundation Garments*, Cooperative Extension Publication no. 1502, Louisiana State University Cooperative Extension Service, Baton Rouge, 1967.

SIZE

Foundation garments are available in a wide range of sizes. The sizes and measurement instructions used for Sears, Roebuck and Co. merchandise are shown in Table 16-2. They are typical of American manufacturers. Full slips usually need bust and length measurements; panties require waist and hip measurements; and girdles are bought by waist, hip, and torso length measurements. Brassieres require both garment-size measurement and cup size, which is determined by the degree of bust development. The woman who has difficulty in deciding her proper size may find it helpful to be fitted by a salesperson who is trained in fitting foundation garments.

STYLES

Slips are available in full-length and half-length styles. Within the full-length category are *regular* styles, which have the bustline fullness controlled by gathering or darting, or, in knits, with fabric stretch providing the needed fullness. *Chemise-style* slips are short, averaging about four inches above the knee, for wear under short skirts. *Bra-slips* give the same type of bust support as brassieres and eliminate the need for the extra garment. This style must be fitted with the same care as brassieres. *Midi-slips* reach to midcalf in length and usually are limited to evening wear. The *half-slip* provides fullness under a dress or skirt, as well as body under a soft fabric. It may also be worn to protect sheer fabrics.

Panties are available in five styles: the *bikini* is more comfortable for wear under girdles or pantyhose; the *brief* often is worn with pantyhose or garter belts. Women who desire extra coverage or have a chafing problem may prefer *boxer* or *long-leg* panties; and *petti-pants* may take the place of a half-slip.[2]

Brassiere styles may be *bandeau, three-quarter-length,* or *long-line* (reaching to the waist), depending on the amount of control desired around the rib cage. Styles with adjustable straps often are more comfortable.

Girdles may be crotched or without crotch; high-waisted or waist-high; boned or unboned; slip-on or zippered; or corselets, which are bra and girdle in one garment.

---

2. "Lingerie Follows the Fashion Lead for Fit and Fun," *What's New in Home Economics* (December 1968), 15-16.

CONSTRUCTION AND CARE

Durable fabrics and quality construction are important factors in choosing underclothing. Since they are worn next to the skin, these garments absorb perspiration, body oils, and odors and they must be laundered very frequently. Washing instructions should be read with particular care and followed exactly, to ensure good length of service. Some undergarments can be machine washed and dried, but others are best laundered by hand.

Construction details to check are fabric grain of the pieces, seams, and fastenings. Straps should have enough length to allow adjustments. Laces and other trims should be durable and well sewn to the basic fabric. Ideally, such trims should last as long as the basic fabric, but this seldom proves to be the case. Reinforced stitching in areas of strain, such as around zippers and other fasteners, is a very important feature.

Nightclothes

This type of apparel includes nightgowns, pajamas, bathrobes, brunch coats, and so on. Styles and fabrics vary widely, so that personal preference directs individual selection. The consumer's best course is to read labels and consider the amount and type of wear an item will receive. Good construction and fabric are important. Trims such as braids, embroidery, or lace should be of good quality and firmly attached, to stand up under the frequent cleaning the garment will receive.

Comfort for the wearer usually is the main concern with these garments, but safety must also be considered. Fire-retardant finishes are highly desirable, especially on girls' nightwear, and length should be checked, since a trailing garment can cause a fall.

Hosiery

Hosiery is an important accessory and should be selected with some thought, for comfort and attractive appearance. Most hosiery is made of nylon; it may be stretch or non-stretch, with or without seams, and made in either plain or mesh knit. A broken loop in a plain-knit stocking can cause a run. Mesh knit has irregularly patterned loops, which are more apt to tear than to run.

SIZE

Size is determined by shoe size for regular-length stockings. Proportioned stockings are sized according to foot size, weight, and leg size. Pantyhose, which combines stockings and panties in one garment, also requires hip measurement. The Sears, Roebuck and Co. size ranges for hosiery are shown in Table 16-2.

Correct hosiery size is important because stockings that are too large will wrinkle and bag and catch more easily on objects, while stockings that are too short are more likely to tear or run from strain. Poorly fitted stockings can be uncomfortable, and, if worn over a period of time, can contribute to foot problems.

CONSTRUCTION AND CARE

Quality stockings can be recognized by the following details (Figure 16-10):

1. Top welts that have enough stretch to allow for snug fit, without binding.
2. A row of run-stop stitches just below the welt, to stop runs in the welt from continuing down into the body of the stocking.

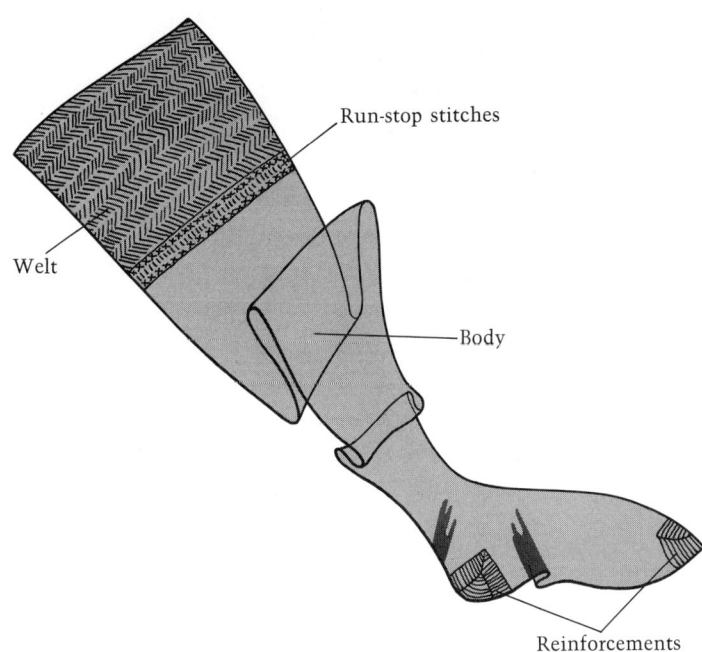

FIGURE 16-10 *The different parts of the stocking that should be checked before purchase.* (© 1969 J. C. Penney Co., Inc.)

16 / Apparel for Women and Girls

FIGURE 16-11 When we open a box or package of stockings, they lie flat and in a certain shape. This illustration shows the "boarding process" in hosiery manufacturing, which gives the unworn stockings their shape. (Courtesy of Burlington Industries, Inc.)

3. Enough fabric in the leg portion for a good fit (Figure 16-11).
4. Color that is even throughout the stocking and free of streaks.
5. Reinforced heels and toes, for longer wear.
6. Seamed stockings with neat, evenly sewn seams.

Stockings must be put on and taken off with a good deal of care, to ensure long wear. They will snag on chipped finger- and toenails, on rough places on the skin, and on rings or bracelets. The stocking should be gathered together, right down to the toe, and the foot inserted. Then the stocking can be drawn up, smoothly and evenly. Pantyhose requires adjustment, one leg at a time, all the way to the waist, for even fabric distribution. Stockings must be washed after every wearing, and they must be guarded from snagging during laundering. They should be dried away from direct heat.

Study Questions

1. What are the names of some classic styles in cloth coats?
2. What are the characteristics of a well-fitting suit?
3. What construction details should be checked in suits?
4. Describe the characteristics of quality construction in dresses.
5. Why should wool knit sweaters be stored flat rather than on hangers?

6. What is the difference between sweaters that are "cut-and-sewn" and "full-fashioned"?
7. What fibers are generally considered the most comfortable to wear for panties?
8. What body measurements are needed to purchase slips, panties, girdles, and brassieres?
9. What two types of knit construction are used in making stockings?
10. What are the marks of quality stockings?

Suggested Activities

1. Visit a women's ready-to-wear store and look for quality details in suits and coats.
2. Look through fashion magazines and see how many examples of the basic styles of coats are currently featured.
3. Look through your own sweaters and determine whether they are constructed in "full-fashioned" or "cut-and-sewn" style.
4. Interview other students and ask what fibers they prefer for their underclothing and the reasons for their preferences.
5. Interview students and/or customers in a store about their preferences in stocking styles and type of knit construction.
6. Develop a basic wardrobe plan for yourself, or for other family members.

Chapter 17

Shoes

CAREFUL SELECTION of proper shoes is vital for the feet, which are under constant strain and stress. During ordinary movement, as in walking, each foot in turn bears the total weight of the body. In active sports, the speed of the activity increases the suddenness of weight shifts and full-body turns. Shoes which do not support the foot adequately, or which do not fit properly, can lead to permanent foot damage, to say nothing of temporary discomfort. Shoes are thus one of the most important items that a person can have in his or her wardrobe.

Parts of the Shoe

Figures 17-1 and 17-2 show the parts of men's and women's shoes in considerable detail. The main parts are the *outsole*, or bottom; the *upper*, or top; the *heel*; and the *insole*. The front part of the upper is called the *vamp* and the back

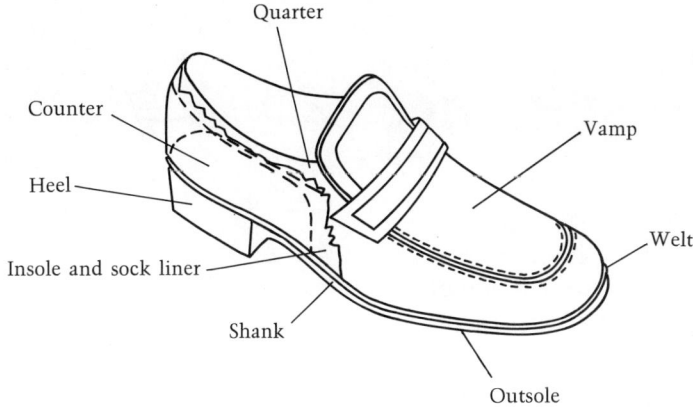

FIGURE 17-1 *The main parts of a man's shoe.*

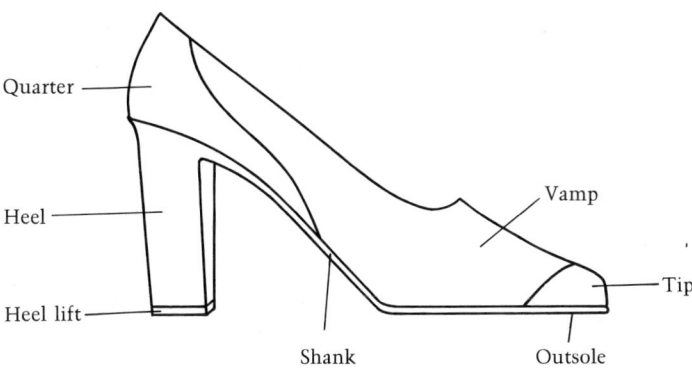

FIGURE 17-2 *The main parts of a woman's shoe.*

part is the *quarter*. A piece of stiffened material, the *counter*, is inserted in the back, between the quarter and the shoe lining, and serves to hold the shape of the back. Most shoes also have a *shank*, usually made of steel, running between the front of the shoe and the back, that serves as support for the foot. The shank, of course, is omitted in "soft" shoes like sneakers and certain types of sandals. The *welt*, a narrow piece between the sole and the upper, holds these two parts of the shoe together.

The lining of a shoe is more important, in some respects, than the outside. Lining materials are subject to the friction of the foot in wear and to moisture from perspiration, and therefore should be of good-quality materials. A good lining not only makes a shoe more comfortable to wear, it helps hold the shape and adds to the length of the shoe's life. In addition to the insole, mentioned above, the lining consists of the *sock liner*, a layer added for comfort and absorption.

Shoe Manufacture[1]

Three methods are currently used in producing shoes: sewing, cementing, and molding.

SEWING

Sewn shoes have always been considered to be the most desirable, partly because they are flexible. The different parts of the shoe are sewn together, which allows movement of the sections. However, sewn shoes are usually more expensive than those made by the other methods. The higher price results partly from the fact that this method uses a *last*, a plastic form that shapes the shoe. Figure 17–3 shows the range of shapes in lasts and the measurements used to make them. Whenever shoe shapes change significantly, a manufacturer of sewn shoes must obtain new lasts for the new shapes, in the entire range of sizes he makes, and schedule production around the style changeover. The cost of new lasts is reflected in the selling price of the shoe.

An additional cost arises from the fact that most sewn shoes are made of good-quality leathers. Leather in itself is more expensive than other substances, and it must be adjusted by hand in some manufacturing steps. For example, each hide must be cut separately, to avoid any weak places or breaks in the hide. This type of handwork also adds to the cost of the shoe. A cutaway diagram of a sewn shoe, made by the welt process, is shown in Figure 17–4 with a labeled diagram of the different parts.

CEMENTING

A shoe made by this method has a sole that is cemented to the upper, rather than sewn. A cross-sectional diagram of the parts of a cemented shoe is shown in Figure 17–5. Heat and pressure are used to assure a solid bonding of the sole and upper in this process.

MOLDING

Molded shoes are made in three different ways, by vulcanizing, by injection molding, and by the process of slush molding.

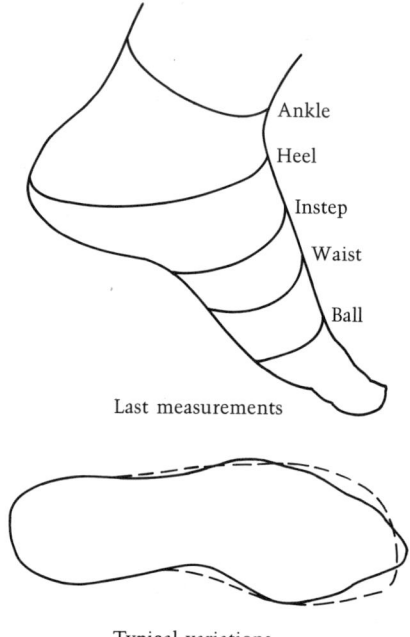

FIGURE 17-3 *The range of shapes and the measurements used for lasts.*

---

1. This section is based in part upon information furnished by the American Footwear Industries Association.

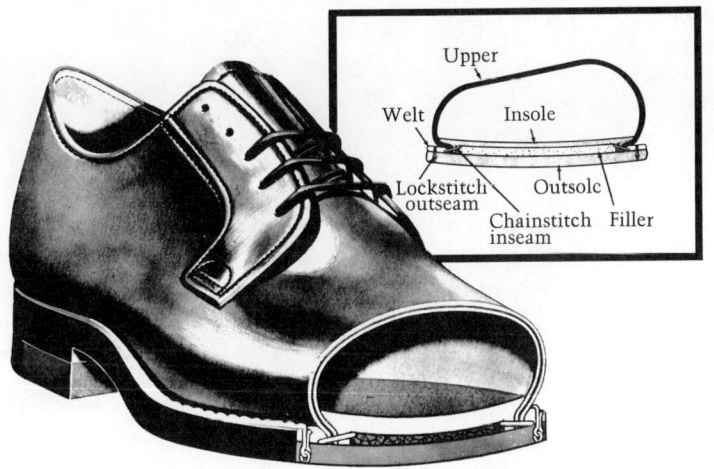

FIGURE 17-4 *Cross section of a sewn shoe showing the parts, which are labeled in the diagram.* (Prepared by USM Machinery Division, for use in "The Art and Science of Footwear Manufacturing," American Footwear Industries Association, Arlington, Va., 1974)

VULCANIZING This process is illustrated in Figure 17-6. On the left, the upper is positioned over the electrically heated mold, which is made to fit each last. On the right, the upper and the sole are joined, and the sole compound is being forced around the bottom of the shoe. Heat is applied in the mold, and pressure is used on all sides, as indicated by the arrows. This process can turn out either cleated or smooth soles, as desired.

INJECTION MOLDING In this method, the assembled upper is put into place in a machine that has a mold for the sole. Liquid soling substance is injected into the preheated mold, and pressure is applied. Figure 17-7 shows a cutaway diagram of an injection-molded shoe.

SLUSH MOLDING In this method, a hollow mold, electrically heated, is made in the exact shape and size of the shoe desired. A liquid mixture called *plastisol* is poured into the

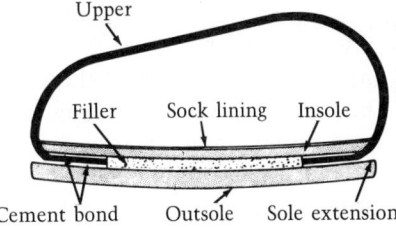

FIGURE 17-5 *Cross-sectional diagram of the parts of a cemented shoe. Notice that the cement is used only around the sides of the shoe.* (Prepared by USM Machinery Division, for use in "The Art and Science of Footwear Manufacturing," American Footwear Industries Association, Arlington, Va., 1974)

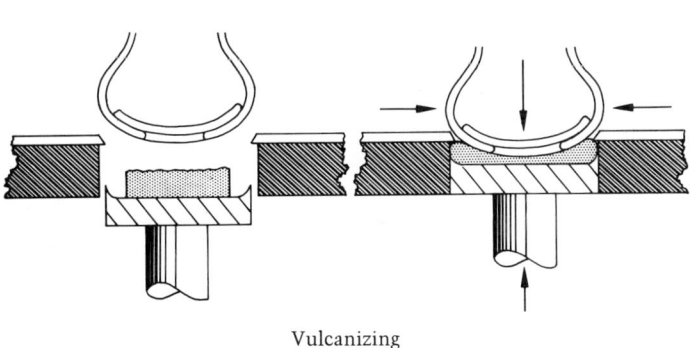

Vulcanizing

FIGURE 17-6 *The vulcanizing process.* (Prepared by USM Machinery Division, for use in "The Art and Science of Footwear Manufacturing," American Footwear Industries Association, Arlington, Va., 1974)

mold and the entire shoe is produced in one step. The plastisol is allowed to "cure," or set, to the thickness desired, before the shoe is removed from the mold.

Shoe Materials

Traditionally, the best and most satisfactory shoes have been made of *leather*. It has always been the preferred material because it gives a good appearance to the shoes, wears very well, withstands heavy use, and is flexible. It has additional assets: it will hold its shape, conform to fit the foot, absorb the foot's moisture without damage, and allow proper air circulation, and it serves to insulate the foot. Leather can be treated to resist water and some chemical substances, and it can be treated for scuff resistance and for additional wear.

Manufactured substances, made from sheet materials, also are used for shoes. These shoes tend to resist scuffing, need no polishing, hold their color, and are mostly satisfactory in other ways. However, one of these materials, Corfam, was found unsatisfactory for uppers because of its lack of flexibility and tendency to stretch after wear. Overall, the stiffness and rigidity of synthetic uppers have so far prevented wide acceptance in the market. Shoe soles of manufactured materials are widely used and wear much longer than leather.

Many other materials are used for shoes—paper, raffia, fabrics of all sorts, and furs. Women's elaborate evening shoes, which are decorative rather than durable, have even been made with uppers of feathers. But even in today's market, conditioned to substitute and manufactured materials, shoes of a good-quality leather are considered the best value.

FIGURE 17-7 *A shoe produced by the injection-molding method.* (Prepared by USM Machinery Division, for use in "The Art and Science of Footwear Manufacturing," American Footwear Industries Association, Arlington, Va., 1974)

Purchasing Shoes

Because shoes and boots are expensive, the wise buyer looks for the best fit possible in an affordable price range (Figure 17-8). Ill-fitting shoes are never a good investment; they will damage both the feet and the disposition of the wearer. Taking time to get the proper fit in shoes of good-quality materials is the best way to get value for the dollar.

CHECKING FIT OF NEW SHOES

Properly fitted shoes fit at the heel without slipping, hold the foot snugly at the sides, fit at the instep without bulging, and do not turn up at the toes. Shoes should support the three weight-bearing points of the foot: the ball of the heel, the ball of the great toe, and the ball of the little toe.

Children should always have their feet measured before any new shoes are purchased, to be sure of the correct size. Adults also should remember to have their feet measured fairly frequently, because they can change in both length and width over the years. A person whose job involves a great deal of standing or walking—a waiter or waitress, traffic director, or nurse—should have foot measurements made yearly.

Once the size is determined, shoes should be tried on and examined carefully. Any that feel too tight, cramp the toes, or pinch the heel should be rejected, despite the popular belief that shoes "loosen up" after wear. The buyer should aim for shoes that are comfortable at the very beginning, to avoid blisters now and, possibly, more serious foot trouble later. The buyer should consider the kind of wear the shoe will receive (Figure 17-9).

Both shoes should be put on, laced up or fastened, and the buyer should walk around the store, thoroughly testing the

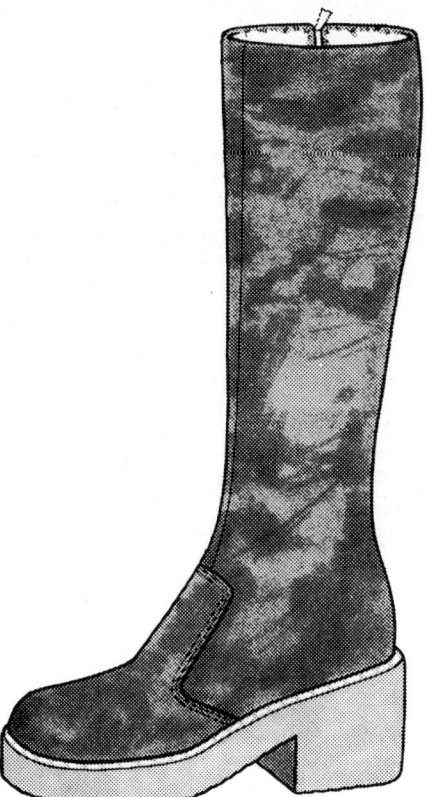

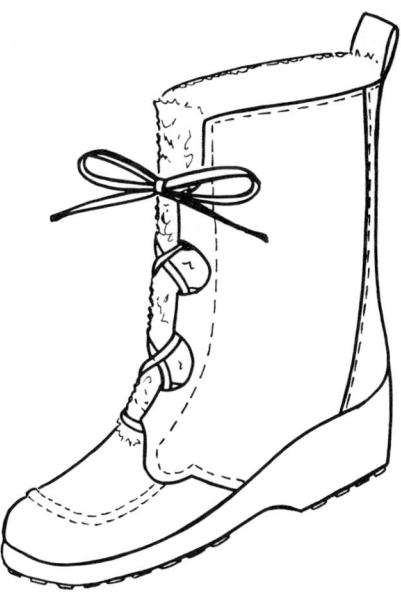

FIGURE 17-8 *Two styles of winter boots, typical of those available for colder climates.* (Courtesy of Sandler of Boston)

feel of the shoes. When a person stands up, the foot changes shape to accommodate the weight of the body. This change may be in length only, or in length and width, and each shoe must be tested in this way to see whether it has space for the foot's adjustment. Since both feet are not always the same length, shoes should be purchased large enough for the longer foot. Walking around in the store tests for this needed length, as well as for the general comfort of the shoes.

The best time to buy shoes is at the end of the day, because the feet become slightly larger as the day passes and they tire. Tired feet are more sensitive to shoes that fit poorly.

The salesperson often can give the customer guidance regarding the style, length, and width appropriate for the feet, but only the person who wears the shoes knows whether they fit comfortably. Shoes that fit properly do not need to be "broken in," but are comfortable from the first.

FITTING CLUES FROM OLD SHOES

Examining old or worn shoes can give clues as to whether they fit correctly. If the sole is worn unevenly, with more wear at the front, the shoe is too short: the sole should wear through at the center. If the sole shows wear at both edges, the shoe is too narrow, whereas wear on one side only means the foot is off balance. Uppers that bulge over the sole line indicate that the shoes are too narrow. If the heel pushes under, or new lifts are needed often, the shoe is too short. Heels should wear slightly at the back or outside line. When the heel wears on the inside, the arch is probably weak. The front tip of the sole may show wear if the shoes are too short. If shoes are out of shape, the size is wrong. Worn pockets for the toes in the inside sole indicate that the shoes are too tight. When the shoe puckers or wrinkles behind the ball of the foot, along the arch, the shoe is not long enough from ball to heel, although the overall length may be correct.

If your worn or old shoes show any of these signs, it is well to remember them on the next shoe-buying trip. Any care that can be taken when purchasing shoes is a good investment.

FIGURE 17-9 *Three shoe styles that would provide for a range of activites—a plain pump, a wedge moccasin, and a lace-and-tie.* (Courtesy of Sandler of Boston)

QUALITY

Judging the quality of a shoe is not easy, but often the price is an indication, since good materials are not inexpensive. There are a few specific points that can be checked, as outlined in the following paragraphs.

A good shoe is not stiff and unyielding: it is flexible and easy to bend. The degree of flexibility, of course, varies with the type of shoe—a man's heavy work shoe necessarily is less pliable than a woman's sandal—but the shoe should "give" when bent.

The shoe leather should feel soft and smooth to the touch, not hard or rough. Leather that is not properly treated during the tanning process, before being made into shoes, can harden. Later, after wear, the leather may split.

All parts of the shoe lining should feel smooth, with no rough seams or wrinkles. The materials of the lining should be of good quality, and the insole should be made of smooth leather.

The top edge should stand firm. It too should be smooth and fit closely and neatly against the foot with no gaps or bunches. If the shoe has a binding around this edge, any seams in the binding should be smooth and even.

Shoe Care

Shoes that are cared for properly will remain serviceable for a longer period than those that are ignored when not being worn. Added service means a better return on the original investment in dollars and a longer period before replacement is needed.

Basic rules for shoe care are simple. Once the reasons behind them are understood, they can be made a matter of habit.

1. Do not force the foot into a shoe. Use a shoehorn, to avoid breaking down the back of the heel.
2. Always unlace or unfasten shoes before removing them. The less stress and strain on the thread and component parts, the longer the shoe will serve you.
3. When you remove shoes, put shoetrees in them. Shoetrees are forms made to hold the shoes in correct shape between wearings. They can be adjusted to a range of sizes and will last for many years. Check the shoes for dirt. Oil and grease damage leather and should be removed as soon as possible.
4. Keep shoes in a well-ventilated place. Feet perspire and shoes usually are slightly damp inside after being worn.
5. If possible, do not wear the same shoes two days in a row. They need time to dry out and return to shape. Try to have enough shoes to allow at least a twenty-four-hour period between wearings.

6. Avoid getting shoes wet. Water tends to stiffen shoe leather, and wearing wet shoes can stretch them out of shape. Lightweight overshoes offer excellent protection to expensive leather. If shoes do get wet, stuff them with paper after removal and set them in a well-ventilated place, *away* from heat. Heat will stiffen the leather as it dries, increasing the chances of cracked leather, as well as discomfort when the shoes are worn again.
7. Replace heel lifts before they are worn down all the way. This will help keep the shoes in shape and in balance, thus prolonging their service.
8. Keep shoes cleaned and polished. A clean, well-polished shoe resists dirt and moisture and gives a much better appearance.

Shoes made of good-quality leathers often are worth resoling. A good shoe-repair shop that does quality work is not easy to locate, but is worth the search. Resoling can extend the life of shoes for a year or more.

Leather Terms

We are accustomed to using the terms "pigskin" and "cowhide" without realizing that the two names reflect the size of the animal from which the leather came. In the terminology of the leather industry, there is a difference. If the leather was made from the covering of a small animal like a pig or kid (young goat), it is called a *skin;* if made from that of a large animal such as a cow or horse, it is a *hide.*

Whatever the animal's size, the best leather is produced from the center back section, where the animal grew the heaviest covering as protection from the weather. The most durable leather for shoe soles, for example, comes from the back section of the hide.

Grain is another term frequently used in connection with leather; it refers to the pattern on the outer surface (the side away from the flesh) of the hide. This pattern is made by the hair follicles on the hide's surface and the chemical processes used in treating the hide make the markings more noticeable. The pattern does not show on the flesh side of the hide, and each kind of animal—horse, deer, pig, cow—has a different pattern.

A hide may be split into layers before it is used, and, in that case, the outer layer with the pattern on it is called *top grain leather.* This layer is considered the most desirable, because of the pattern and because it is the most durable.

Frequently, better grades of shoes are described as being made only of this quality leather.

Other names and terms used in connection with leather are given below.[2]

BUCKSKIN   From a deer or an elk; porous, cool, fine-textured, with a napped surface. Expensive, as only the outer skin with grain removed is genuine buckskin. Often imitated.

CALFSKIN   Pliable, smooth, fine; not easily scuffed or marred.

CORDOVAN   From the rump of horsehide; fine pores and smooth; very durable and takes a high shine.

DOESKIN   Name for white leather from lamb or sheep.

KID   Upper leathers from goat skins; fine, close-knit, resilient, porous.

NAP   The fine fuzzy finish on leathers like suede.

PATENT   Calf-, horse-, or kidskin, plastic-coated; finish is nearly airtight and watertight.

PIGSKIN   Leather made from skin of pigs or hogs; cool, comfortable; some types are washable, as in gloves.

SHEEPSKIN   Leather from sheep skin, used for slipper linings, etc.

SIDE LEATHER   The name for the two sections which result if the hide is cut along the backbone.

SPLIT LEATHER   Any layer of skin or hide other than the top or grain side; less durable than grain layer (top grain).

Study Questions

1. What are the main parts of a shoe?
2. Why is the lining material important?
3. What are the three most commonly used processes for making shoes?
4. What materials are commonly used to make shoe soles?
5. Why is leather traditionally considered the best and most satisfactory shoe material?
6. What are the characteristics of shoes that fit the feet properly?
7. How may old or worn shoes give clues to whether they fit correctly?

---

2. R. Elizabeth Williams, *Smart Shoppers for Smart Clothes*, Cooperative Extension Publication no. 1499, Louisiana State University Cooperative Extension Service, Baton Rouge, 1971, p. 39; and Norman V. Germany and Maribeth Cuccinelli, *The Art and Science of Footwear Manufacturing*, American Footwear Industries Association, Arlington, Va., 1974, pp. 6–21.

8. What factors may be used to judge quality in shoes?
9. What kinds of care should be given shoes for them to last longer?
10. What are ten leather terms that may be used to identify shoe materials?

Suggested Activities

1. Visit a shoe store and observe the various styles of shoes being worn today. Identify the major parts of the various shoes observed.
2. Look for examples of shoes made by the three most commonly used processes.
3. Question other students about their preferences in shoe materials and reasons for the preferences.
4. Arrange a display or bulletin board depicting the factors one should consider when buying new shoes.

Part Five
Textiles in the Home

Chapter 18

Home Furnishings

MANY FACTORS INFLUENCE consumers' choices in home furnishings. Geographic location, climate, and local customs affect decisions. Family income and the amount of money available for a given item are prime considerations. Family size, ages of children, and life style determine the amount and kind of wear and tear furnishings will receive.

Upholstered furniture, rugs and carpets, curtains and draperies, and slipcovers are major financial investments. They should be selected to harmonize in color, line, proportion, balance, and style, not as independent items unrelated to each other (Figures 18-1 and 18-2). Many decorating books are available for the reader who wants information on the use of art principles in furnishing the home. This chapter deals with fabrics used in constructing the items listed above.

When considering fabrics for use in homes, the consumer first should think about durability, ease of cleaning, color stability, soil and rot resistance, nonflammability, dimensional stability, and resistance to damage by sunlight. Most fabrics used in home furnishings have these properties. If certain of these factors are particularly important because

FIGURE 18-1 *Simple, modern styling in living room furniture. Patterned and plain upholstery fabric add contrast but provide overall coordination.* (Courtesy of Bassett, Upholstery Division)

FIGURE 18-2 *A sofa with a secret for a dwelling with limited space: this 74-inch-long sofa doubles as a bed. Sofa and matching bolsters and back cushions are covered in a tightly woven cotton print.* (Courtesy of Kroehler Manufacturing Co.)

of life style, climate, or age of children, careful reading of labels which must accompany the items will show which should be satisfactory. A couch for an open patio, for instance, should be more durable and weather-resistant than one intended for a covered, screened porch.

Quality construction is an important concern, for poor construction decreases serviceability, and the buyer pays more in the long run. However, if the item is intended for short-term usage, quality and durability may be less important than cost. Thus, if two college students are furnishing an apartment they intend to use for only a year or two, second-hand items may serve their temporary needs, but furnishings intended for long-range use should be both serviceable and durable.

FIGURE 18-3 *Traditional styling adapted for modern houses. Hardwood construction, with a walnut finish.* (Courtesy of Bassett, Upholstery Division)

Upholstered Furniture

Since appearance and quality do not always go together, several points must be kept in mind when upholstered items are considered. As a general rule, the buyer should select the best quality the budget will permit. Good quality means a solid framework, good filling, and durable fabrics throughout (Figure 18-3).

FRAMEWORK

The best frames are made from kiln-dried hardwood such as hackberry, elm, oak, maple, or birch (Figure 18-4). The strongest and most durable joints are double-doweled and corner-blocked. Webbing should be about four inches wide, firmly woven, and preferably of jute, which is stronger than burlap. Double-cone coil springs tied eight ways are one mark of superior quality in furniture. The filling may be of cotton, which gives good support and is strong and odorless. Other materials used may be fiberfill, foam rubber, urethane foam, and hair. These should be slip- or tear-resistant, crushproof, and lightweight. Padding materials, usually made of felted cotton or foam, go over the filling to give the final shape and are sometimes covered with muslin. One way to make a saving in furniture is to purchase it in the muslin stage and complete the slipcovering or upholstering at home.[1]

---

1. R. Elizabeth Williams and Verna D. Guillory, *Upholstered Furniture*, Cooperative Extension Publication no. 1546, Louisiana State University Cooperative Extension Service, Baton Rouge, 1970.

CONSTRUCTION

The upholstered piece should feel rounded to the touch, with no wood or metal framing noticeable. Exposed parts should be smooth and evenly finished. The outside arms should not be hollow, but should be webbed and covered with fabric and a layer of padding to soften the frame. Welt seams should be straight and neatly sewn; a small welt seam indicates furniture of higher quality. Seams should be well stitched with nine to eleven stitches per inch, as is appropriate for the type of fabric and seam. A small number of seams on a long sofa back is a sign of higher quality, since fewer seams cost the manufacturer more money owing to fabric waste. The sides should preferably be upholstered in one piece, but, if the fabric is pieced, it should be neatly done with the pattern well matched. The edge along the front under the cushions should be soft. Spring construction should be used in the front, where the pillow rests, for better wear. The back should be as attractive as the front, and legs or any exposed wood details should be well finished. Higher-priced pieces are often undercovered completely in muslin, making the outer fabric wear longer. Cushions should have neatly concealed zippers and straps to hold them in place.

The use of buttons or tufting in upholstery may or may not be desirable. On one hand, they help hold the filling materials in place. On the other hand, they may add to the initial cost of the piece, and reupholstering is more costly. Tufts and buttons tend to collect dust, so cleaning takes longer.

Since chairs and sofas are made to be sat on, the buyer should test the pieces, to be sure they are comfortable. An

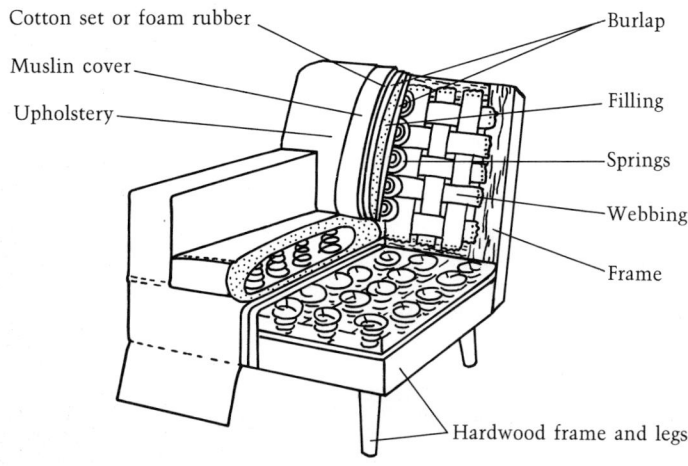

FIGURE 18-4 *Cross-sectional drawing of a well-constructed upholstered chair, showing the different parts and the way they are assembled.*

Part Five / Textiles in the Home

BASIC FABRIC EXAMPLES

FIGURE 18-5 *Examples of fabrics used for upholstery.* (The University of Mississippi, courtesy of R. G. Culp Associates, Inc.)

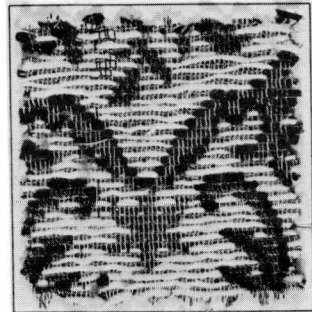

Damask · Jacquard

Matelassé · Print

Tapestry · Tweed

upholstered piece that is the right size for a short individual will probably be uncomfortable and unsatisfactory for a tall person. Therefore, height of arms, depth of seat, and shape of the back should be tested. Preference for softness or firmness should be considered.

18 / Home Furnishings

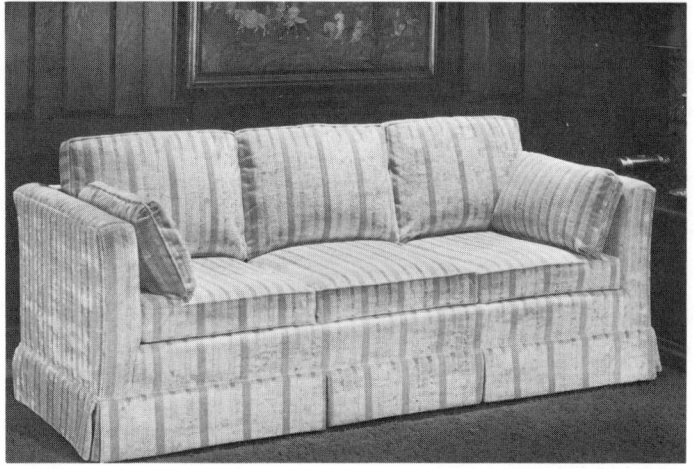

FIGURE 18-6 *A simple style in a sofa, with a look of luxury added by the upholstery fabric.* (Courtesy of American of Martinsville)

OUTER FABRIC

For best service, upholstery fabric should be strong, firmly woven, with all yarns about the same size (Figure 18-5). It should not pick, fuzz, show lint, or soil easily. Soil-repellent and soil-release finishes and protection against water spotting and staining help in cleaning the furniture.[2]

Deep-pile fabrics usually wear longer than flat-woven fabrics because the pile protects the base yarns. However, pile tends to collect dust, often mats down, and may require more frequent care. A tightly woven flat fabric may wear as well as a pile fabric and usually lasts longer than loosely constructed pile fabric of an inferior quality. Fabric manufacturers usually quality-grade their merchandise according to codes or numbering systems, which should be explained to the consumer by the salesperson. Quality varies within price ranges as well as among the various grades (Figure 18-6).

Fibers more commonly used in furniture fabric include cotton, flax, wool, silk, rayon, acetates, nylon, and, more recently, olefin. Vinyl has become popular where care is an important factor, and the olefin that is now available in upholstery fabric is very durable and stain-resistant.

Label information gives clues to the quality of merchandise under consideration for purchase. By law, upholstered furniture is required to have a label permanently affixed, listing all fibers used in the fabric and their percentage by weight. Fiberfill and cushioning materials must also be identified.

---

2. Williams and Guillory, *Upholstered Furniture*.

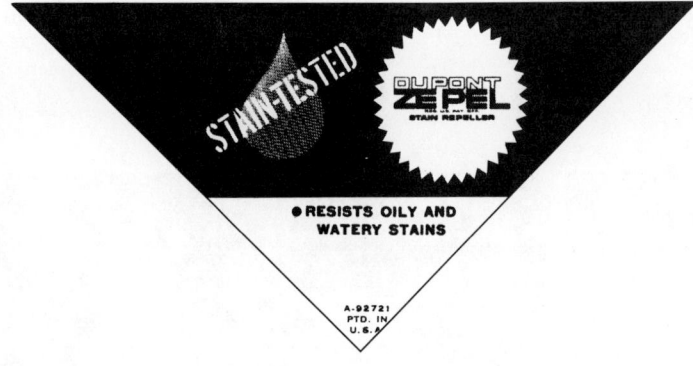

Information stating what the consumer may expect regarding colorfastness, flammability, and stain resistance is also helpful (Figure 18–7). Manufacturers often make construction guarantees or indicate expected wear length for fabric, and these should be noted by the consumer. Care instructions for removable parts such as cushion covers give clues on how to receive longer service from the product.

CARE

The covers on some upholstered pieces have zippers, which are used by the manufacturer to provide a smooth, even fit. Presence of a zipper does *not* imply that the covers can be removed and laundered. Laundering can cause fabric shrinkage and opened or distorted seams if the machine action is heavy. Dry cleaning can also harm fibers and fabric. In all cases, the instructions for care that are provided with the piece of furniture must be followed precisely, to avoid lasting damage and resulting dissatisfaction. If any doubt as to the proper cleaning method arises, it is best to consult the salesperson in the store where the purchase was made, or to write to the manufacturer, giving the style and model numbers of the piece and other pertinent details.

Proper care of upholstery includes frequent vacuum cleaning to prevent attacks by moths on wool, as well as to remove dirt. Fabric susceptible to moth damage should be treated with a mothproofing finish. Stains and spills should be removed as quickly as possible, and, if necessary, the piece should be taken to a reliable upholsterer for professional cleaning.

Two major problems with upholstered furniture are loss of fabric strength and color fading, caused by overexposure to sunlight. Upholstered furniture should be kept away from direct sunlight as much as possible.

FIGURE 18–7 *A label and hangtag found on home furnishing fabrics with this finish.* (Courtesy of E. I. du Pont de Nemours & Company)

FIGURE 18-8 *Three types of carpeting now on the market:* (a) *plain color, sheared;* (b) *variegated-color shag;* (c) *patterned plus.* (Courtesy of Bigelow-Sanford, Inc.)

a

b

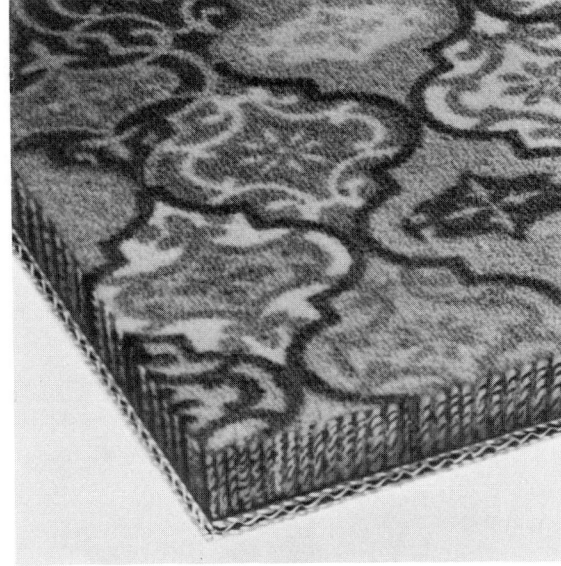

c

Part Five / Textiles in the Home

Rugs and Carpets

Consumers' decisions about their floor coverings are influenced by a number of factors: personal assessment of need for comfort and warmth is a major concern; floor coverings represent an investment of a large portion of the home furnishing budget; and cost is always a factor. Since the floor is a large surface, the color, texture, and design of the covering are considerations, because of their decorative effects (Figure 18–8). Durability and easy maintenance are very important because particles of dirt abrade the fibers when the covering is walked on.

Technically, *rugs* are finished on all four sides, and usually they are not fastened to the floor. They are produced in standard sizes, or are cut from various widths with the edges bound. *Carpeting* is woven in widths of from twenty-seven inches to eighteen feet or more. It is cut to room size and fastened to the floor. Broadloom is a type of carpeting over fifty-four inches wide and seamless.

FIGURE 18-9 *This label is sewn onto carpets and rugs that have this finish.* (Courtesy of E. I. du Pont de Nemours & Company)

FIBERS

Traditionally, wool has been the preferred fiber, because of its durability, springiness, and resistance to heavy traffic. It is used for floor coverings still, but manufactured fibers—polyester, olefin, nylon, and acrylic—also are used very widely. Cotton and rayon are made into rugs, but these fibers are not well suited to the purpose. Rayon is the least durable rug fiber and cotton is the least resilient.[3]

The most *durable* fibers are nylon and olefin, with polyester, wool, cotton, and acrylic rated next. Acrylic and wool rate the highest in *soil resistance*, followed by nylon, polyester, and olefin; rayon and cotton are rated lowest. Floor coverings can be given protective soil-resistant finishes (Figure 18–9).

Modacrylic is nonflammable and is sometimes blended with acrylic for increased flame resistance. Olefin is often selected when moisture resistance is an important consideration. Its resistance to chemicals and stains has increased its usefulness in carpets for outdoor areas and kitchens.[4]

---

3. R. Elizabeth Williams, Verna D. Guillory, and Celia S. Hissong, *Rug and Carpet Fibers*, Cooperative Extension Publication no. 1595, Louisiana State University Cooperative Extension Service, Baton Rouge, 1970.

4. *Ibid.*

QUALITY

Quality is determined by factors other than type and grade of fiber and includes yarn, method of construction, and pile density and height. Crimped and high-twist ply yarns give carpets a textured quality that does not show marks and footprints easily. A good single clue to quality is *density*, which refers to the height and closeness of carpet pile yarns. The best-quality carpets have long yarns set very closely together. Such yarns help support each other and resist bending and abrasion, further increasing their wear qualities. Dense carpets also are easily maintained, since the soil stays near the surface and is quickly picked up in the vacuuming process.

Tufted

FIGURE 18-10 *Basic rug construction.* (Courtesy of The Carpet and Rug Institute)

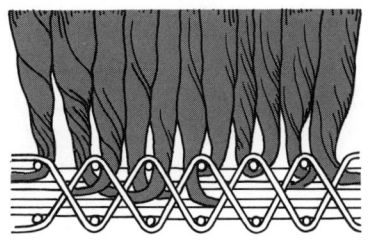

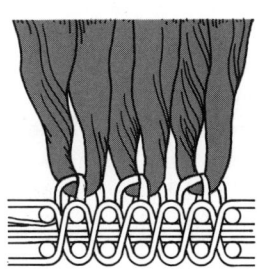

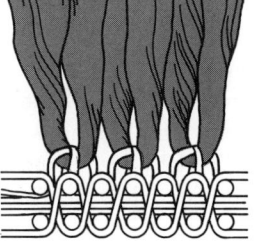

a b

c d

Woven: (*a*) *Wilton;* (*b*) *chenille;* (*c*) *velvet;* (*d*) *Axminster.*

Part Five / Textiles in the Home

CONSTRUCTION

Most of the rugs and carpets sold today are made by *tufting* (Figure 18–10). The fibers are sewn to a cloth backing, then secured in place by a coating of latex. Several different textures can be made this way. *Level loop* is durable, easy to take care of, and is ideal for heavy-traffic areas. *Random shear* is also very durable and has both cut and uncut loops. *Two-level and multilevel loop* have a sculptured or carved look and give a formal appearance to the surface. *Plush* is cut-pile construction that is best for formal, low-traffic areas. Its appearance is very luxurious and velvety, but such carpets show footprints. *Shag* carpets have very long, cut pile, and are best suited for informal, medium-traffic areas. *Splush* carpets are a combination of shag and plush. They can be used in more formal areas than shags because of the shorter, denser pile height.[5]

Woven carpets (Figure 18–10) include the Wilton, Axminster, velvet, and chenille types, made with either cut or uncut pile, depending on individual preference. None of these terms actually denotes quality, since a wide range of quality may be found within the cut-pile types like Axminster, velvet, and Wilton, or within the uncut-pile types.

Carpets are also made by needlepunching and flocking, although these methods of construction are not as commonly used today as are the other methods.

CARE

Carpets should be rotated periodically to lengthen their life. The right padding underneath extends their usefulness, too. Carpeting with a jute backing, installed over a separate padding, usually gives long service. Felt padding with added hair wears well and often is preferred. It is relatively inexpensive and durable and gives good support to the carpet.

Dirt is the worst enemy of rugs and carpets, since it drops in among the fibers and is ground against them. The pile may be cut by the sharp gritty edges. Daily care should include light cleaning with a carpet sweeper or vacuum cleaner to pick up surface dust, lint, and crumbs before they work down into the pile. Rugs and carpets need a thorough weekly cleaning, with a forward-and-back motion to remove both surface soil and any embedded grit. At least annually, carpets should

---

5. "Bright News in Carpets," *News Notes for the Home Economist,* Hercules Incorporated, Wilmington, Del. (Fall–Winter 1973).

be cleaned by a dependable rug-cleaning establishment or have a good home cleaning with an electric shampooer.[6]

Indoor-Outdoor Carpeting

Recently developed for outdoor use, this type of covering has introduced a new dimension of serviceability. Such carpeting is now found around swimming pools, on patios, and covering recreational areas such as football fields and tennis courts. Two manufactured fibers, olefin and acrylic, can withstand the effects of weather. They are strong and resist abrasion; are not affected by moisture, stains, or mildew; and are colorfast to sunlight. Acrylic can be made flame-resistant if a fire retardant is added during the solution-dyeing process. This is important if such carpeting is used near barbecue pits on patios or in kitchens.

These carpets are available in a wide range of colors and in heathers and tweeds. They offer an element of beauty to areas previously regarded as inappropriate for carpet.

For prolonged life and serviceability, indoor-outdoor carpets need frequent cleaning to keep dirt and grime from becoming embedded among the fibers, cutting them and shortening their life. Stains and spills should be sponged away as quickly as possible, using either detergent and water or a solvent, depending on the type of stain. Outdoor carpeting can be hosed down for frequent cleaning and it dries quickly. In addition, it can be cleaned by sweeping or vacuuming also.[7]

Curtains and Draperies

Although many people use the terms interchangeably, there is a difference between curtains and draperies. Generally, *curtains* are sheer, semisheer, or lightweight fabric hangings that hang next to the window and may extend over only part of the window, all of it, or from the top of the window to the floor. *Draperies* are made of heavier fabric and extend from the window top to the windowsill, below the sill to cover the apron, or all the way to the floor. Curtains and draperies may be used together, depending on the effect

---

6. Williams, Guillory, and Hissong, *Rug and Carpet Fibers.*

7. "Indoor-Outdoor Carpets," *Consumer Buying Guide,* J. C. Penney Co., Inc., Educational and Consumer Relations, New York, 1968.

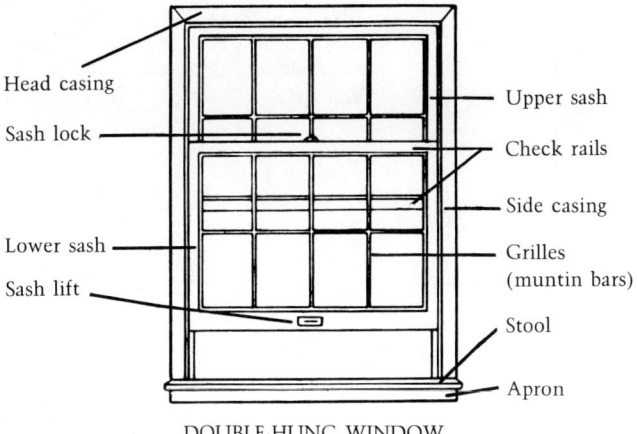

FIGURE 18-11 *Diagram of the different parts of a double-hung window.* (Courtesy of Andersen Corporation, Bayport, Minnesota)

desired. They are used to control light and air, to provide privacy, or simply to add decoration to the room.

Aside from what is in good taste or beautiful from the decorator's viewpoint, size, style, serviceability, and care are the main points to consider in selecting either curtains or draperies. Thorough reading of labels before purchase is always advisable.

SIZE

Curtains and draperies must be purchased according to the dimensions of the window, the desired length, and the amount of fullness wanted. The length should be measured from the level of the mounted fixture to the sill, apron, or floor, depending on individual preference and style. Width should be measured as the distance between the fixtures, as mounted on the frame or wall. The amount of fullness may vary from one and one-half times the window width to as much as three times the measured distance, depending on fabric sheerness and amount of fullness wanted.

Three types of windows are commonly found in houses. The *double-hung* window, shown in Figure 18-11, has been used for many years. Lengths and widths vary greatly, depending upon the architectural style and age of the dwelling. The other two window types, *horizontal gliding* and *casement* (shown in Figures 18-12 and 18-13), are of comparatively recent structural design, although earlier versions of casement windows have been in use for many, many years. Horizontal gliding windows may be combined with stationary sashes to make the large expanses of window walls found

FIGURE 18-12 *The different parts of a horizontal gliding window. (Courtesy of Andersen Corporation, Bayport, Minnesota)*

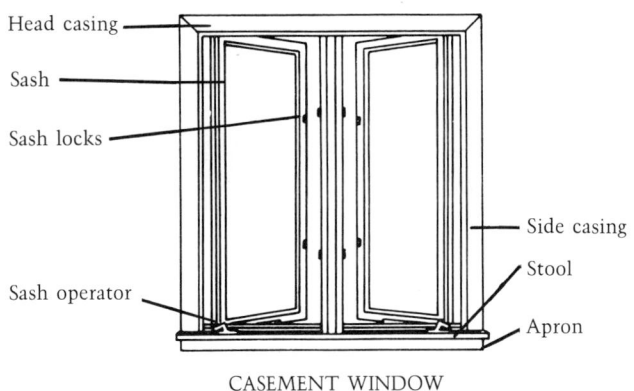

FIGURE 18-13 *The different parts of a casement window, labeled for identification. (Courtesy of Andersen Corporation, Bayport, Minnesota)*

in many dwellings. Casement windows usually are installed in pairs, but may be used in a row to create wider windows.

STYLES AND FABRICS

The basic styles of window treatments include panel draperies with cornice, tieback draperies with swag, and tailored, Priscilla, tier, café, and cottage curtains (Figure 18–14). Fabrics for Priscilla and tier curtains usually are sheer and lightweight, as are the variations of these basic styles, such as glass, tieback, and crisscross. Commonly used fabrics include voile, cotton prints, chintz, dimity, dotted Swiss, marquisette, organdy, and lawn, all of which help create a light, airy feeling.

Draw draperies, valances, swags, and cornices are used in more formal settings and are more appropriately made from heavier fabrics such as damask, brocade, antique satin, tapestry, velveteen, monk's cloth, linen, hopsacking, and homespun. Draperies usually are lined, and lining fabrics may be

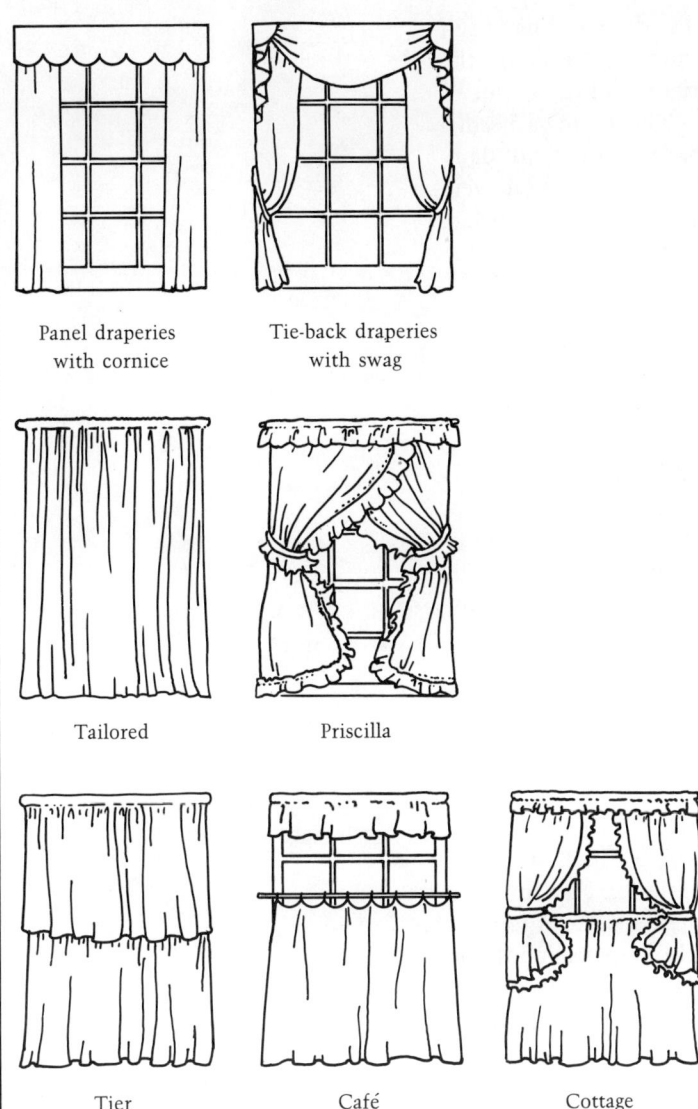

FIGURE 18-14 *The basic styles of curtains and draperies.*

either light or heavy in weight. Sateen is widely used in drapery linings, as are polished cotton and blends.

The energy crisis has made consumers more aware of the need for better insulation in homes, in order to reduce fuel consumption. Many people have found that large areas of glass in windows and sliding doors increase fuel usage for both cooling and heating. Specially treated draperies are used to provide better insulation in both these areas.

In the past, insulated draperies were made of a fabric coated with Milium. These were fairly effective, but the coating tended to wear off after a while, when the draperies had been cleaned several times. Most insulated draperies now on the market are made of foam-backed fabric, which is lighter in weight than the Milium-treated ones. The foam is permanently bonded to the drapery fabric and usually is not damaged during cleaning if the care instructions are followed. Some of these fabrics can be machine washed and dried, but labels should be read carefully and directions followed exactly.

SERVICEABILITY

Curtains and draperies are exposed to long periods of sunlight, and fabrics should be selected for their resistance to color fading and fiber deterioration. Additionally, these fabrics should hold their shape and size, neither stretching nor shrinking. Fibers such as cotton, flax, and rayon absorb moisture from the atmosphere and stretch; manufactured fibers that do not absorb moisture are more stable. Glass and polyester are especially good choices, but cotton and rayon fade and rot comparatively quickly. For safety, both these items should either be made of nonflammable fibers or have a flame-retardant finish.

CARE

Fabrics that resist soil, can be machine washed, and need no ironing make curtains that are the easiest to care for. Both curtains and draperies should be Sanforized if they are to be washed, and any applied finishes should be permanent and durable to cleaning. Draperies and heavier-weight curtains should be brushed or vacuum cleaned frequently, to remove surface dust.

Study Questions

1. What are the general properties that fabrics used in homes should have?
2. What are two major problems for fabric in upholstered furniture?
3. For best service, what characteristics should fabric in upholstered furniture have?
4. What label information should the consumer look for on upholstered furniture?
5. What specific decisions relating to textiles must one make when purchasing floor coverings?

6. What fibers are commonly used in carpets?
7. What fiber characteristics relate to serviceability in carpets?
8. What factors determine quality in carpets?
9. What is the most widely used method of making carpet today?
10. What are other ways that carpet is made?
11. What fibers are commonly used to make indoor-outdoor carpeting?
12. What are the basic differences between curtains and draperies?
13. What are the two styles of window most commonly used in homes today?
14. What are the basic styles of window treatments used today?
15. What basic characteristics should drapery and curtain fabric have?
16. What measurements are needed in order to purchase draperies or curtains?

Suggested Activities

1. Visit a home furnishings or home decorating shop and talk with a merchant about the types of fabrics found in furniture and draperies today. Examine the merchandise being sold and look for marks of quality.
2. Talk with people who have recently purchased carpeting for their home and find out what characteristics they considered most important for the carpeting to have.
3. Arrange an exhibit on the factors influencing a consumer's decisions about carpets, upholstered furniture, and/or draperies.
4. Examine the furnishings in an apartment or dormitory and evaluate them for quality. Suggest changes which you would make if you were selecting them.
5. Offer to assist someone who is purchasing draperies or carpeting by helping to figure the dimensions needed and suggesting factors to consider before making a purchase.

Chapter 19

Household Linens

CERTAIN TEXTILES used in the home still are called "linens," because originally linen was the fiber used to make sheets, pillowcases, towels, and tablecloths. The term has remained in use, although it is incorrect in the 1970s. Linen has limited use in luxury sheets, tablecloths, and in some towels, but cotton and manufactured fibers are the rule today.

These household products are subjected to hard use in the home, both in wear and in laundering. Current decorative trends and the addition of color and pattern complicate selection, but a very wide range of merchandise is available. The cost of these items amounts to a sizeable sum, so the consumer should look for durability and quality construction. Sleazy fabrics and poor construction cannot be expected to stand up to the wear given to these items in everyday use.

Bedroom

SHEETS

Bed sheets, flat or fitted, are made in standard sizes to fit standard-sized mattresses, called twin, double, queen, and king. Table 19-1 shows these sizes for both flat and fitted sheets. Since mattresses may be anywhere from four to seven inches thick, the sheet size needed must be determined after the mattress is measured in length, width, and depth.

TABLE 19-1 *Standard Sizes for Mattresses and Sheets*

Type of bed	Standard mattress size (inches)	Sheet sizes (in inches)	
		Flat	Fitted bottom
Standard twin	39 × 75	75 × 108	39 × 75
Standard double (full)	54 × 75	90 × 108	54 × 75
Queen size	60 × 80	90 × 120	60 × 80
King size	77 × 80	108 × 120	78 × 80

Source: Spring and Summer Catalogue, J. C. Penney Co., New York, 1974, p. 982.

SHAPE AND SIZE Usually, the size given on the label refers to the torn length of the sheet before it is hemmed. The sheet actually is several inches shorter, and the finished length depends on the width of the hems. A bottom sheet should be long enough for the five-inch tuck-in at the bottom and an eighteen-inch foldback over the blanket at the top. Both sheets should have sufficient width for tuck-in or hang-over at the sides. Usually, the size for the top sheet is used for all sheets for a particular bed. This allows the sheets to be alternated in use, for better wear. Many people also reverse sheets occasionally for better wear, putting the top hem, which usually is wider than the bottom hem, at the foot of the bed. Sheets with equal-width hems are automatically reversed in use. The edges of flat sheets, the selvages, may be plain or tape. Tape selvages are much sturdier and resist tearing longer than plain.

Fitted sheets are made to fit the mattress, sliding over corners and fitting snugly. Bottom sheets fit over all four mattress corners, while top sheets fit two corners only. Standard sizes for these sheets also are shown in Table 19-1. The depth of the corners of fitted sheets should be checked before purchase, to be sure they will go over the mattress. Fitted sheets usually are more expensive than flat sheets, because more workmanship and material are used to produce them.

FABRICS Sheets are available in both woven and knitted fabrics of natural and manufactured fibers. Woven linen sheets are so high-priced that they are luxury items. All cotton sheets, knitted sheets of nylon tricot, and woven sheets of polyester are available, but the majority of sheets are made of blends of cotton and polyester. This combination produces sheets that are durable and launder well. A popular blend is 50 percent cotton and 50 percent polyester (Figure 19–1). Another popular blend seems to be 65 percent cotton and 35 percent polyester.

Cotton sheets are either muslin or percale. The difference is a matter of the thread count and the type and size of yarn used. As was mentioned in Chapter 8, thread count means the number of threads per square inch of fabric. A thread count of 140 would usually indicate a fairly thick, carded yarn, and a heavy muslin. Muslin sheets have lower thread counts and heavier weights than percales because of their coarser yarns.

Percale generally is made of yarn that is combed as well as carded. Since the yarns are finer and smoother, percale sheets are lighter in weight than muslin and they have a more luxurious feeling. Percale thread counts vary from about 170 to 200. Because of the weight difference, percale sheets sometimes are preferred. They are easier to handle in home laundering, and cheaper if done by commercial laundries that charge by weight. However, a sheet made of a good muslin is both durable and economical.

The thread count of cotton-polyester blends depends upon whether the sheet is muslin or percale. Table 19–2 gives information on differences among the types of sheets available.

FIGURE 19-1 *A crisp, small print with solid-color borders, in a 50 percent cotton/50 percent polyester blend, with durable-press finish, makes a soft but tailored sheet and pillowcase.* (Courtesy of Cannon Mills, Inc.)

TABLE 19-2 *Kinds of Sheets Most Commonly Available*

Fiber content	Sheet type	Characteristics	Thread count
Cotton	Muslin	Heavier, longer-wearing, coarser than percale	Lower count than percale (128–139 threads per inch)
Cotton	Percale	Soft, luxurious, fine-textured	Higher count than muslin (180–188 threads per inch)
Polyester/cotton	Muslin blend	Longer-wearing, stays smooth on the bed; no-iron finish eliminates ironing if tumble dried	Same as for muslin above
Polyester/cotton	Percale blend	Luxurious, long-wearing, soft, wrinkle-free appearance; no-iron finish eliminates ironing if tumble dried	Same as for percale above

Source: Spring and Summer Catalogue, J. C. Penney Co., New York, 1974, p. 982.

Most families find that sheets in the 133 to 145 thread count range are the most economical buy. A count of 140 usually will give about 25 percent more wear than a 128 count, and in recent years the price difference has not been sufficient to warrant buying sheets under a 133 count.

The consumer can judge strength of sheets by the following simple test. Hold the sheet to the light so the threads

FIGURE 19-2 *An overall floral pattern in sheets and pillowcases.* (Courtesy of Wamsutta/Pacific Home Products)

can be seen. Lengthwise and crosswise threads should be of a uniform thickness, evenly woven in straight lines. Any unevenness in the weave may indicate weak places that will wear out before other sections of the sheet.

Consumers who prefer decorator colors and designs in sheets can expect to pay more for them (Figure 19-2). Although reputable manufacturers use good dyes, some fading in color is usual during the life of a sheet. Trims such as embroidery and lace also add to the cost of the sheet and because they are more delicate than the basic sheet fabric add to the care.

PILLOWCASES

Pillowcases also are sized before hemming and are available in a similar range of sizes. Table 19-3 shows the standard sizes now in use. Pillowcases are made in the same variety of fabrics discussed for sheets.

MATTRESS COVERS AND PADS

Mattress covers encase the mattress and are zippered closed. They are made in a range of standard sizes, of woven polyester-cotton blends, all-cotton, or of knitted manufactured yarns. Some covers have a vinyl lining for moisture resistance.

Pads are either flat or fitted. Both types are made in standard sizes. They consist of a layer (or pad) of filling, covered by fabric; the two thicknesses are stitched together to form the finished product. Most fillings are made of manufactured fiber. The top may be a cotton-polyester blend or a knit nylon or acetate. Some pads, particularly those used in cribs, have a vinyl or film backing for moisture resistance.

TABLE 19-3 *Standard Sizes for Pillows and Pillowcases*

Type of pillow	Standard size (inches)	Pillowcase size needed
Standard	20 × 26	42 × 36
Queen	20 × 30	42 × 40
King	20 × 36	42 × 46
Bolster	20 × 36	42 × 46
	20 × 44	42 × 54
	20 × 62	42 × 72

Source: "Sheets and Pillowcases," *Consumer Buying Guide*, J. C. Penney Co., Inc., Educational Relations, New York, 1971.

Fitted pads have an elasticized skirt that covers the mattress sides and fits under the bottom edge. Flat pads have tapes at the corners, to hold them on the mattress. There are also flat pads made with electrical wiring, like blankets. These must be laundered very carefully, according to label instructions. The label should be checked to be sure it carries the Underwriters' Laboratories (UL) symbol for safety.

Labels on mattress pads should be read very carefully before purchase. If 100 percent cotton is used in a pad, it should be labeled Sanforized; shrinkage in a fitted pad can make it unusable. All stitching should be even and firm. The edges of flat pads should be bound with sturdy tape. Elastic used in fitted pads should be firmly woven and well stitched to the skirt of the pad. Mattress pads take hard wear; purchasing a good-quality product is advisable, particularly for a child's bed.

BLANKETS

A blanket is expected to deliver good service for a number of years. In some respects, blankets receive even harder wear than sheets, especially if they are used on children's and adolescents' beds. Good-quality blankets deliver maximum value for the consumer's dollar (Figure 19–3). Like clothing, blankets keep people warm by acting as insulators. They both hold the warmth of the individual in the bed and keep the cold air from reaching through. Therefore, nap and thickness are much more important for warmth in a blanket than are weight and fiber content.

SIZE   Blankets are made in a wide variety of sizes. They should be large enough to allow a minimum of six inches for tuck-under at the foot and sides. Blankets that are too small are subject to excessive stress as the sleeper tries to keep covered.

FABRICS   Wool, with its long, fluffy nap, makes the warmest blankets. However, wool blankets must be laundered or dry cleaned with care, to prevent shrinkage and matting of the nap, and must be protected from attack by moths and other insects during summer storage. Since they may be bulkier than other blankets, they do take up considerable storage space. However, with the proper care, good-quality wool blankets can last a lifetime, which makes them a good investment in cold climates. Moth-resistant finishes are applied to some wool blankets and must be repeated after cleaning. Care instructions on labels must be followed exactly.

Cotton blankets are light and durable and make excellent summer coverings or year-round coverings, as the case may be. Laundering and storage present no problems. Manufactured materials, especially acrylic and polyester, are widely used for blankets, and they make attractive, durable products. Laundering is easy, insects do not attack them, but their bulk takes up storage space. Blends such as wool and cotton, cotton and rayon, and so on, also are used for blankets. They are serviceable but generally not as durable as all-wool or all-cotton blankets.

Thermal blankets, purposely constructed to have many air spaces for insulating, are widely used. In cool or cold weather, a second, light covering must be used over them, to add to their insulating ability. Thermals usually are made of cotton, but some are available in wool. Care and storage depend on the fiber.

Electric blankets, usually made of manufactured fibers, are popular because only one is needed for each bed, storage is not a problem, and they can be dial-set for the desired temperature. But because the wiring is delicate, these blankets should not be folded, sat on, or lain upon. They must be cleaned very carefully, according to the label instructions.

FIGURE 19-3 *Matching design in fabrics for bedroom and bath in sheets, pillowcases, and towels. Coordinating solid colors in towels and blankets are also available. The blanket shown in the illustration is made by laminating nylon scrim between two layers of foam. Colored adhesive is then applied to both sides of the foam and nylon fibers are flocked onto the surface.* (Martex—courtesy of West Point Pepperell)

Flammability and long-range durability should be considered before purchase. The consumer should make sure that the blanket carries the symbol of the Underwriters' Laboratories (UL), which indicates that the design and safety have been checked.

Flammability is a factor to consider when any blanket is purchased. All tags and labels must be checked carefully for information on flame-retardant finishes. This is especially important for cotton-rayon blends, since both rayon and cotton burn very readily.

BINDINGS Blankets usually have a wide, satin-finish blanket binding stitched over the ends. Bindings of nylon or other manufactured fibers are desirable, since rayon often wears out and must be replaced. Any binding should be firmly stitched to the blanket and the edges finished, not just tucked in.

The selvage edges of a thermal blanket should be solidly constructed to resist tearing. Blankets of nonwoven construction generally have binding on all four sides, since they have no true ends or selvages.

COLORS AND PATTERNS Blankets range from plain, solid colors, through plaid, striped, and floral patterns, to fashion designs. The consumer may need to consider both color and pattern in relation to bedroom decor, before buying.

BEDSPREADS

Spreads and other coverlets usually are selected for decoration or for durability. Durability would be the first consideration for a teenager's bedspread; decoration probably would dictate the choice for his parents' room (Figure 19-4).

Bedspreads are available in a very wide range of fabrics, finishes, colors, patterns, sizes, and styles. The consumer's best course is to determine size, color, and style desired, and then check a number of stores for available items. All labels should be read with care and selection made after consideration of all factors wanted. Good bedspreads are not inexpensive, so long-range, satisfactory service should be the primary factor.

COMFORTERS

A bed comforter consists of a layer, or bat, of insulating material, usually cotton or manufactured fiber, covered on

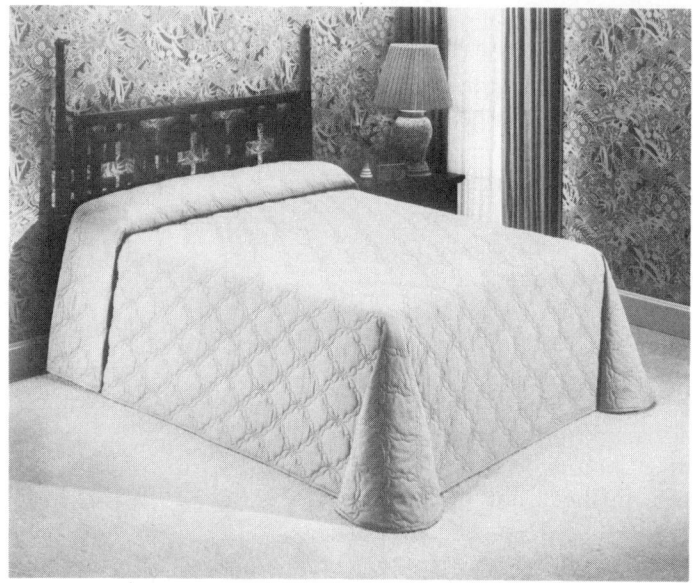

FIGURE 19-4 *A luxurious effect and easy-care characteristics are provided by this quilted bedspread, made of 100 percent bonded polyester fill, with the front and back of a 50 percent polyester/50 percent cotton fabric.* (Courtesy of Cannon Mills, Inc.)

both sides with colorful fabric. Fibers and fabrics vary, and the considerations given for bedspreads also apply to comforters.

As a rule, comforters covered with slippery fabrics such as taffeta or smooth nylon tend to slide off the bed and prove very annoying to the sleeper. Covers made of a slightly rough fabric, or one that has an unevenness in weave, often are more satisfactory.

Bathroom and Kitchen

TOWELS

Towels make up an important part of the linen closet, and they add color and design to both bathroom and kitchen. Included on the towel list are bath and hand towels, washcloths, glass and dishtowels, and dishcloths.

SIZES Bath towels are made in a standard range of sizes, from 20 × 40 to 27 × 50 inches. Even larger sizes (36 × 70 inches), called bath sheets, are enjoyed by many people. Hand towels range in size from 15 × 25 to 16 × 32 inches, and washcloths (face cloths) usually are 12 or 13 inches square. Glass and dishtowels run from about 16 × 27 to 18 × 34 inches. Dishcloth dimensions vary but they are either square or rectangular.

FIBER Until very recently, towels were almost always made of cotton. However, bath towels of a 65 percent polyester/35 percent cotton blend are now on the market, and it is thought that the addition of the stronger polyester fiber will be desirable. Bath towels invariably show breaks in the selvages as the first signs of wear, and the strength of the polyester should prolong selvage durability and extend the serviceability of the towels. Also, manufacturers of these blended towels state that less shrinkage can be expected, absorbency is not reduced, and dyeability is not impaired.

CONSTRUCTION Two construction methods are used for towel fabric, looped and the usual flat weaves.

Terry cloth, woven by looping yarns on a firm groundwork, is used for bath, hand, and face towels. A firm twill-weave groundwork is desirable in this type of fabric, to hold the loops firmly in place. Loops may be made of single thread, but double thread makes a more absorbent, long-wearing towel. Loops vary in height and density, and a height of about one-eighth inch is considered the most satisfactory. Density increases absorbency, and towels with many loops placed close together are more satisfactory than those with fewer, sparser loops. The most absorbent towels are densely constructed of long-looped, low-twist cotton yarns. If the loops are sheared, the towel is called "plush" or "velvet." Shearing adds to the cost, as do extra height and density of loops.

 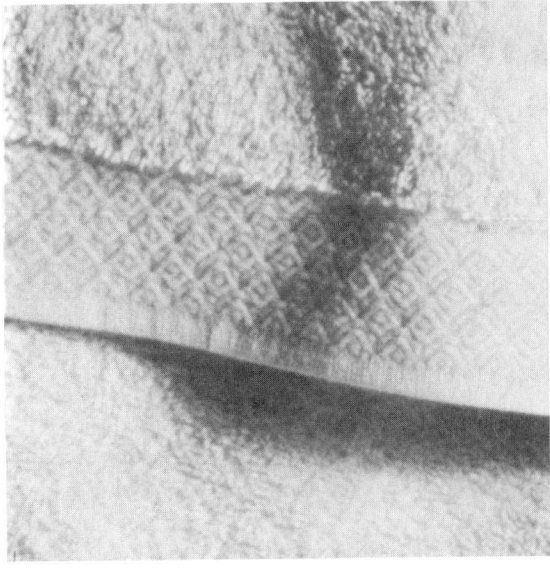

FIGURE 19-5 *Details of towel selvage and hem. Selvages should be firmly woven and hems firmly stitched. Weak selvages will tear and poorly finished hems will fray, shortening the serviceability of the towel. (Courtesy of Cannon Mills, Inc.)*

FIGURE 19-6 *Floral-patterned and plain-colored towels add to the decorative effect in a bathroom. They are of all cotton, for absorbency and durability.* (Courtesy of Cannon Mills, Inc.)

Bath towels and bath sheets are made of terry cloth; hand and face towels are also available in terry cloth, as are washcloths. (Knitted washcloths are produced, also, which are smoother and softer than terry, but they stretch and do not hold their shape.)

Flat fabrics are woven with or without patterns, with a slightly rough surface, in huck hand and face towels, or with a smooth surface for glass towels. Typical fabrics for these items are huck and crash, made from linen or cotton, or blends.

Towels receive very hard wear, yet they are expected to last a long time. To be sure of long service, the consumer should check all hems for even, solid stitching and well-fastened corners. Terry towels should have solid, firm selvages, with filling yarns that go out and around the edges (Figure 19-5). Patterns and borders should be woven in smoothly but loosely, to prevent puckering after use. Terry washcloths should be well stitched on all edges and corners, to prevent raveling. Fabric in glass and dishtowels should be closely and evenly woven of strong yarns.

COLORS AND PATTERNS Because cotton and linen fibers are easily dyed, towels are available in nearly every hue in the rainbow. A wide range of designs—plaids, stripes, and florals—may be purchased to fit the decor of individual rooms (Figure 19-6). The consumer should check labels to be sure of colorfast dyes, but some fading is to be expected.

BATH MATS OR RUGS

Manufactured fibers, such as nylon or polyester, and cotton are used for bath mats or rugs. Many have nonskid backs for safety. The materials used for this safety backing are not always satisfactory, since some substances tend to crack and fall off in small, grainy pellets after several launderings. Sizes, textures, colors, and patterns vary very widely, and selection depends on decor and personal preference.

SHOWER CURTAINS

Nowadays these important items are made primarily of manufactured films and thus are not true textiles. However, they are necessities and are mentioned briefly here. These curtains must be large and full enough to keep water inside the tub or enclosure. They should be long enough to hang inside a tub for six or eight inches; in an enclosure, the curtain should touch the floor. Extra thickness is required at the top, to hold the hangers without tearing.

Mildew is a common problem on shower curtains, particularly at the bottom edge. Leaving the curtain spread out to dry helps prevent this condition, though ventilation in bathrooms without a window is not always satisfactory. Soaking in a household cleaner that is safe for use on plastic films often will clear up the areas affected.

Dining Room

Many kinds of covering are used on dining tables today. While linen damask, fine linens, and laces may be used for very festive or formal occasions, most families have shifted to fabrics that require a minimum of care. Coverings may be made of the traditional natural fibers, treated for wrinkle and soil resistance and soil release, or be fabric imitations of manufactured fibers, in good design and appearance. The main considerations in purchasing tablecloths, placemats, and napkins are size, purpose and suitability of fabric, color and design, and durability.

SIZES

Tablecloths are made in various sizes, and Table 19-4 shows the standard range. As a rule, a tablecloth should hang over the table edge for at least twelve inches. This hang-over

TABLE 19-4 *Standard Sizes for Ready-made Tablecloths*

Table type	Size (in inches)
Card	36 × 36
Dinette	54 × 54
Dinette with extended leaves	54 × 72
Regular dining	64 × 72
	72 × 90
	90 × 108
Round	48 to 68 in diameter

Source: Dorothy Stepat-Devan, *Introduction to Home Furnishings*, 2nd ed., Macmillan, New York, 1971, p. 354. Copyright © 1971 by Macmillan Publishing Co., Inc. Used by permission of the publisher.

often is a matter of family preference. Households that include small children may prefer smaller cloths to avoid accidents. For very festive meals, a deeper hang-over adds an elegant look to most tables. When in doubt about the size of cloth needed for a particular table, a little experimentation with a folded bedsheet often can settle the question.

Placemats vary widely in size and shape. The basic rule is that a placemat should be big enough in proportion to the table and should provide a frame outside the place setting of flatware, glassware, and dishes needed for the meal.

Napkins range in size from twelve-inch squares, for tea or lunch, to twenty-four- or thirty-inch squares, for formal dinners. Rectangular napkins are commonly found in a similar size range.

PURPOSE AND SUITABILITY

For informal indoor meals, fabrics are selected according to individual preference. Tablecloths and napkins are available in plain or patterned fabrics of natural fibers, blends of natural and manufactured, or all manufactured fibers. Selection will depend on budget, decor, and facilities for care. Terry cloth is generally used for outdoor meals, but a busy mother of several young children might prefer terry placemats for family dining, as a precaution against overturned beverage glasses.

The consumer's best course is to consider the type of meal service used, color and design preferences in relation to the dining space and tableware, and time available for care. Brightly patterned tableware shows best against a solid-colored cover; solid-colored tableware is attractive on a patterned cloth. Napkins, in solid colors or patterns, may match, contrast with, or complement cloths.

DURABILITY

Tablecloths made of natural fibers wear best when they are evenly and firmly woven. Crash (cotton or cotton-linen blends) makes a very serviceable tablecloth. Cotton and rayon blends make attractive cloths, but the rayon tends to wear out before the cotton. Manufactured fibers, used alone or combined with natural fibers, prolong the serviceability of table covers and napkins. Such products usually are easier to care for than the natural-fiber items.

Trims, such as embroidery, fringes, hemstitching, and lace, increase the attractiveness of tablecloths and napkins, but they add to the cost and usually require careful handling in laundering and ironing. Most people prefer to use these more decorative items only for entertaining. These cloths and napkins are more likely to be made of linen; if so, they should be rolled up for storage, not folded, to prevent fiber damage.

Fabrics used in tablecloths and napkins should be colorfast, especially if they are patterned. All hems should be evenly and neatly stitched, particularly at the corners.

Study Questions

1. What two styles of sheets are available on the market? What sizes are available?
2. What fabrics are used to make sheets?
3. What are the differences between muslin and percale sheets?
4. What does "thread count" mean?
5. What features should the consumer look for in mattress covers and pads?
6. What fibers are used to make blankets?
7. What does the UL symbol on an electric blanket mean?
8. What care should be given an electric blanket?
9. What fibers work best for towels? Why?
10. What construction methods are used for making towel fabric?
11. What features should the consumer look for in towels to be sure of long service?
12. What fibers wear best for tablecloths?
13. About how much hang-over should a tablecloth have?
14. What sizes do napkins usually come in?

Suggested Activities

1. Visit a household linen department in a store and study the quality, kind, style, and range of selection of merchandise available.
2. Visit both a household linen specialty shop and a discount store and make a comparison of the merchandise available in the two stores. Consider points such as price range, quality, and selection.
3. Make a consumer opinion survey concerning factors considered when purchasing household linen. A single item such as sheets, blankets, towels, or tablecloths may be selected.
4. Arrange a display on points to be considered when buying household linens for the home.

Bibliography

Part One: Textile Elements

American Fabrics Magazine Editors. *Encyclopedia of Textiles.* Prentice-Hall, Englewood Cliffs, N.J., 1972.

American Home Economics Association. *Textile Handbook,* 5th ed. AHEA, Washington, D.C., 1974.

Cowan, Mary L., and Martha E. Jungerman. *Introduction to Textiles,* 2nd ed., Appleton-Century-Crofts, New York, 1969.

Dan River, Inc. *A Dictionary of Textile Terms,* 11th ed. Dan River, Inc., New York, 1971.

"Fabric Finishes—What They Mean to You." *Better Homes and Gardens* (May 1973), 14ff.

Federal Trade Commission. *Care Labels Can Save You Money and Trouble.* Buyer's Guide No. 10. U.S. Government Printing Office, Washington, D.C., n.d.

Hollen, Norma, and Jane Saddler. *Textiles,* 4th ed. Macmillan, New York, 1973.

Joseph, Marjory L. *Introductory Textile Science,* 2nd ed. Holt, Rinehart and Winston, New York, 1972.

Joseph, Marjory L., and Audrey G. Gieseking. *Illustrated Guide to Textiles.* Plycon Press, Fullerton, Calif., 1971.

Labarthe, Jules. *Elements of Textiles.* Macmillan, New York, 1975.

Man-Made Fiber Producers Association, Inc. *Guide to Man-Made Fibers.* Man-Made Fiber Producers Association, Inc., Washington, D.C., 1973.

———. *Man-Made Fiber Fact Book.* Man-Made Fiber Producers Association, Inc., Washington, D.C., 1974.

Perry, Patricia, ed. *The Vogue Sewing Book.* Vogue Patterns, New York, © 1970 by Butterick Division, American Can Co.

Richardson, Byron L. "Guide to Textile Finishes." *Textile World* (December 1973), 45.

Stout, Evelyn E. *Introduction to Textiles,* 3rd ed. John Wiley & Sons, New York, 1970.

Wingate, Isabel B. *Textile Fabrics and Their Selection,* 7th ed. Prentice-Hall, Englewood Cliffs, N.J., 1976.

Part Two: Care

American Home Economics Association. *Textile Handbook,* 5th ed. AHEA, Washington, D.C., 1974.

"Apparel Makers Test New Flammability Law." *Textile World,* 123 (December 1973), 22.

Bush, Sharon. "Fabrics and Fire: What You Don't Know *Can* Hurt You." *What's New in Home Economics,* 35 (April 1971), 29–30.

Celanese Fibers Marketing Company, Consumer and Retail Information Department. *Guide for Permanent Care Labeling.* Celanese Corporation, Washington, D.C., 1971.

"Children's Sleepwear Code a Hot Issue." *What's New in Home Economics,* 37 (October 1973), 47.

Drake, George L., Jr., and Leon H. Chance. "Flame-Retardant Fabrics Safeguard Your Life." *Science for Better Living,* The Yearbook of Agriculture 1968. U.S. Department of Agriculture. U.S. Government Printing Office, Washington, D.C.

Federal Trade Commission. *Look for That Label.* FTC Buyer's Guide no. 6. Federal Trade Commission, Washington, D.C., n.d.

———. *Rules and Regulations under the Flammable Fabrics Act,* as amended on May 4, 1967. Federal Trade Commission, Washington, D.C.

———. *Rules and Regulations under the Textile Fiber Products Identification Act,* as amended to November 3, 1969. FTC L-5031. Federal Trade Commission, Washington, D.C.

———. *Rules and Regulations under the Wool Products Labeling Act of 1939,* as amended through June 20, 1964. L-4453 rev. Federal Trade Commission, Washington, D.C.

Frigidaire, a division of GMC. *Important Washing Tips on the Proper Use of Your Frigidaire Jet Action Washer.* Frigidaire, New York, n.d.

General Services Administration, Consumer Product Information. *Clothing and Fabric Care Labeling,* 7700–108. General Services Administration, Washington, D.C., Fall 1972.

Hollen, Norma, and Jane Saddler. *Textiles,* 4th ed. Macmillan, New York, 1973.

Journal of Home Economics (September 1973), 47.

Labarthe, Jules. *Elements of Textiles.* Macmillan, New York, 1975.

Learn, Jean. *Lots about Laundering.* Procter & Gamble Co., Cincinnati, Ohio, 1970.

Lever Brothers Company, Public Relations and Educational Service. *Stain Removal Chart.* Lever Brothers Company, New York, 1965.

Man-Made Fiber Producers Association, Inc. *Guide to Man-Made Fibers.* Man-Made Fiber Producers Association, Inc., Washington, D.C., 1973.

———. *Man-Made Fiber Fact Book.* Man-Made Fiber Producers Association, Inc., Washington, D.C., 1974.

Mauldin, William L., and Marianne S. Beeson. "Reading the Labels on Apparel and Household Textiles." In *Handbook for the Home.* The Yearbook of Agriculture 1973. U.S. Department of Agriculture, U.S. Government Printing Office, Washington, D.C., 1973.

National Retail Merchants Association. *A Voluntary Industry Guide for Improved and Permanent Care Labeling of Consumer Textile Products.* National Retail Merchants Association, New York, 1971.

Purex Corporation, Ltd. *How-to-Do's for Stain Removal.* Purex Corporation, Ltd., Lakewood, Calif. (August 1960).

Richardson, Byron L., associate editor. "Guide to Textile Finishes." *Textile World,* 123 (December 1973), 45–63.

Sears, Roebuck and Co. *Your Guide to Brighter Wash Days.* Sears, Roebuck and Co., Chicago, n.d.

U.S., Congress, House, Committee on Government Operations. *Phosphates in Detergents and the Eutrophication of America's Waters: Hearings before a Subcommittee,* 91st Cong., December 15–16, 1969. U.S. Government Printing Office, Washington, D.C., 1970.

U.S., Congress, House, Committee on Interstate and Foreign Commerce, and U.S., Congress, Senate, Committee on Labor and Public Welfare. *Compilation of Selected Public Health Laws.* U.S. Government Printing Office, Washington, D.C., 1973.

U.S., Department of Agriculture. *Removing Stains from Fabrics, Home Methods.* Home and Garden Bulletin 62. U.S. Government Printing Office, Washington, D.C., 1964 (revised).

U.S., Department of Commerce. *Report to the Congress, A Metric America.* U.S. Government Printing Office, Washington, D.C., July 1971.

U.S., Department of Health, Education, and Welfare. *Studies of Deaths, Injuries and Economic Losses Resulting from Accidental Burning of Products, Fabrics or Related Materials through June 1970.* U.S. Government Printing Office, Washington, D.C., 1971.

U.S., Environmental Protection Agency. *Technical Evaluation of Phosphate-free Home Laundry Detergents.* Water Pollution Control Research Series 16080 DVF. U.S. Government Printing Office, Washington, D.C., February 1972.

———. *Water Quality Standards Criteria Digest, A Compilation of Federal / State Criteria on Phosphates.* Environmental Protection Agency, Washington, D.C., 1972.

Part Three: Selection

Alexander, Patsy Ruth. "Problems and Practices of Rural and Urban Homemakers in Clothing Construction and Buying, Bossier Parish, 1964." Master's thesis, Louisiana State University, Baton Rouge, 1965.

American Home Economics Association. *Textile Handbook,* 5th ed. AHEA, Washington, D.C., 1974.

Congressional Quarterly Service. *Congressional Quarterly Almanac.* Congressional Quarterly Inc., Washington, D.C., 1973.

Congressional Quarterly Service. *Congressional Quarterly Almanac.* Congressional Quarterly Inc., Washington, D.C., 1975.

Congressional Quarterly Service. *The 18th Annual CQ Almanac.* Congressional Quarterly Service, Washington, D.C., 1962.

Cowan, Mary L., and Martha E. Jungerman. *Introduction to Textiles,* 2nd ed. Meredith Corporation, New York, 1969.

Federal Register, Weekly Compilation of Presidential Documents. U.S. Government Printing Office, Washington, D.C., 1962.

Frame, Thelma. "In Choosing Values Today's Children Need Practice." *The Delta Kappa Gamma Bulletin* (Fall 1969), 33–36.

"Giant Burlington Faces Trying Times for Textiles." *Business Week* (March 2, 1974), 45–49.

Hollen, Norman, and Jane Saddler. *Textiles*, 4th ed. Macmillan, New York, 1973.

Joseph, Marjory L. *Introductory Textile Science*, 2nd ed. Holt, Rinehart and Winston, New York, 1972.

Labarthe, Jules. *Elements of Textiles*. Macmillan, New York, 1975.

Man-Made Fiber Producers Association, Inc. *Man-Made Fiber Fact Book*. Man-Made Fiber Producers Association, Inc., Washington, D.C., 1974.

Mansfield, Edwin. *Micro-Economics*. W. W. Norton & Company, New York, 1970.

Margolius, Sidney. *The Consumer's Guide to Better Buying*, rev. ed. Pocket Books, a division of Simon & Schuster, New York, 1972.

Maslow, A. H. *Motivation and Personality*. Harper and Brothers Publishers, New York, 1954.

"New GATT Textiles Arrangement Aims at Orderly Trade Expansion." *Commerce Today* (February 4, 1974), 4.

Rescher, Nicholas. "What Is Valuing?" *Forum*, J. C. Penney Company, Inc., New York (Spring/Summer 1972), 3.

Rice, Ann Smith. "Where Are We in Consumer Education?" *What's New in Home Economics*, (January 1971), 35.

Stout, Evelyn E. *Introduction to Textiles*, 3rd ed. John Wiley & Sons, New York, 1970.

Textile Organon (December 1973).

Troelstrup, Arch W. *The Consumer in American Society*, 5th ed. McGraw-Hill, New York, 1974.

Turner, Harvey S. "Miracle in Mexico." *American Fabrics and Fashions*, no. 99 (Winter 1973), 31–35.

Unity Buying Service, American Consumer's Guide. *How to Get More for Your Money*. The Benjamin Company, New York, 1973.

U.S., Department of Agriculture. *A Place to Live*. The Yearbook of Agriculture 1963. U.S. Government Printing Office, Washington, D.C., 1963.

———. *Power to Produce*. The Yearbook of Agriculture 1960. U.S. Government Printing Office, Washington, D.C., 1960.

U.S., Department of State. *General Agreement on Tariffs and Trade*. U.S. Government Printing Office, Washington, D.C., 1949.

Wingate, Isabel B. *Textile Fabrics and Their Selection*, 7th ed. Prentice-Hall, Englewood Cliffs, N.J., 1976.

Part Four: Family Clothing

Alexander, Patsy Ruth. "The Blind Learn Sewing Skills." *What's New in Home Economics* 32 (February 1968), 76–77.

———. "Problems and Practices of Rural and Urban Homemakers in Clothing Construction and Buying, Bossier Parish, 1964." Master's thesis, Louisiana State University, Baton Rouge, 1965.

Baker, Marjorie Y. *Clothing for the Elderly*. Publication E-811. The Oklahoma State University Cooperative Extension Service, Stillwater, Okla., November 1969.

Bare, Clari, Eleanor Boettke, and Neva Waggoner. *Self-Help Clothing for Handicapped Children*. The National Society for Crippled Children and Adults, Inc., Chicago, 1962.

Brockman, Helen L. *The Theory of Fashion Design*. John Wiley & Sons, New York, 1965.

"Boys' Jeans." *Consumer Reports*, 39 (May 1974), 415–417.

California State Department of Education. *Teachers' Guide to Education in Early Childhood*. California State Department of Education, 1956.

Chambers, Helen G., and Verna Moulton. *Clothing Selection*, 2nd ed. J. B. Lippincott Company, New York, 1969.

Cookman, Helen, and Muriel E. Zimmerman. *Functional Fashions for the Physically Handicapped*. Institute of Physical Medicine and Rehabilitation, New York University Medical Center, New York, 1961.

Economic Report of the President. Transmitted to the Congress, 1973.

Eicher, Joanne B., and Eleanor A. Kelley, with Betty Wass. *A Longitudinal Study of High School Girls' Friendship Patterns, Social Class, and Clothing*. Research Report 222, Home and Family Living. Michigan State University Agricultural Experiment Station, East Lansing, 1974.

Erwin, Mabel D., and Lila A. Kinchen. *Clothing for Moderns*, 5th ed. Macmillan, New York, 1974.

Gray, Helen M. "How to Select Clothing for Children." *What's New in Home Economics*, 33 (November 1969), 34–39.

Hollen, Norma, and Jane Saddler. *Textiles*, 4th ed. Macmillan, New York, 1973.

Horn, Marilyn J. *The Second Skin*, 2nd ed. Houghton Mifflin, Boston, 1975.

Hosiery, Consumer Buying Guide. J. C. Penney Co., Inc., New York, 1969.

"If the Shoe Fits—." *What's New in Home Economics,* 33 (September 1969), 60.

Jarnow, Jeannette A., and Beatrice Judelle. *Inside the Fashion Business,* 2nd ed. John Wiley & Sons, New York, 1974.

Kelley, Eleanor A., Caroline W. Daigle, Rosetta S. LaFleur, and Lenda Jo Wilson. *Clothing Acquisition and Use Practices of Early Adolescents.* Home Economics Research Report No. 2. Louisiana State University and Agricultural Experiment Station, Baton Rouge, June 1973.

Labarthe, Jules. *Elements of Textiles.* Macmillan, New York, 1975.

"Lingerie Follows the Fashion Lead for Fit and Fun." *What's New in Home Economics,* 32 (December 1968), 15-16.

Margolius, Sidney. *The Consumer's Guide to Better Buying,* rev. ed. Pocket Books, a division of Simon & Schuster, New York, 1972.

May, Elizabeth, Neva Waggoner, and Eleanor Hotte. *Independent Living for the Handicapped and the Elderly.* Houghton Mifflin, Boston, 1974.

Morton, Grace M. *The Arts of Costume and Personal Appearance,* 3rd ed., revised by Mary E. Guthrie, Viletta Leite, and June Ericson. John Wiley & Sons, New York, 1964.

Perry, Patricia, ed. *The Vogue Sewing Book.* Vogue Patterns, New York, ©1970 by Butterick Division, American Can Co.

Roach, Mary Ellen, and Joanne Eicher. *The Visible Self.* Prentice-Hall, Englewood Cliffs, N.J., 1973.

Roark, Fae, Bobbie L. McFatter, and R. Elizabeth Williams. *Shopping for Shirts.* Publication no. 1397. Lousiana State University Cooperative Extension Service, Baton Rouge, 1971.

Rosencranz, Mary Lou. *Clothing Concepts: A Social-Psychological Approach.* Macmillan, New York, 1972.

Scott, Clarice L. *Clothes for the Physically Handicapped Homemaker.* U.S. Department of Agriculture, Home Economics Research Report no. 12. Agricultural Research Service, U.S. Government Printing Office, Washington, D.C., 1961.

"Sweater Sense," *Forecast* (December 1971), 82.

Tate, Mildred Thurow, and Oris Glisson. *Family Clothing.* John Wiley & Sons, New York, 1961.

U.S., Department of Agriculture. *Consumers All.* The Yearbook of Agriculture 1965. U.S. Government Printing Office, Washington, D.C., 1965.

U.S., Department of Commerce, Social and Economic Statistics Administration, Bureau of Economic Analyses. *Survey of Current Business,* 54 (February 1974).

Williams, R. Elizabeth. *Smart Shoppers for Smart Clothes.* Cooperative Extension Publication no. 1499. Louisiana State University Cooperative Extension Service, Baton Rouge, 1971.

———. *Sweater Shopping Guide.* Cooperative Extension Publication no. 1232. Louisiana State University Cooperative Extension Service, Baton Rouge, 1965.

Williams, R. Elizabeth, and Celia Hissong. *Foundation Garments.* Cooperative Extension Publication no. 1502. Louisiana State University Cooperative Extension Service, Baton Rouge, 1967.

Williams, R. Elizabeth, Fae Roark, and Celia Hissong. *What Is a Good Shoe?* Cooperative Extension Publication no. 1303. Louisiana State University Cooperative Extension Service, Baton Rouge, 1970.

Wingate, Isabel B. *Textile Fabrics and Their Selection,* 7th ed. Prentice-Hall, Englewood Cliffs, N.J., 1976.

Part Five: Textiles in the Home

American Consumer's Guide. How to Get More for Your Money. Unity Buying Service, Hicksville, N.Y., 1973.

"Bright News in Carpets." *News Notes for the Home Economist.* Hercules Incorporated, Wilmington, Del. (Fall–Winter 1973).

Brown, Jan. "Buy It Right, Quality, Construction and Fabric Guidelines for Buying Upholstered Furniture." *What's New in Home Economics,* 38 (May/June 1974), 38.

Consumer Reports. The 1974 Buying Guide Issue. Consumers Union of United States, Inc., Mount Vernon, N.Y., 1974.

Dieffenderfer, Ruth. "Consumption and the Home Furnishings Industry." *Forecast for Home Economics,* 19 (September 1973), F-108 to F-109.

"Indoor-Outdoor Carpets." *Consumer Buying Guide.* J. C. Penney Co., Educational and Consumer Relations, New York, 1968.

Kinder, Faye. *Meal Management,* 4th ed. Macmillan, New York, 1973.

Know Your Upholstery Fabrics. R. G. Culp Associates, Inc., High Point, N.C., October 1972.

Kumbier, Maridel. "How to Buy a Carpet or Rug." *Consumers' Research Magazine*, 57 (March 1974), 23–27.

Labarthe, Jules. *Elements of Textiles*. Macmillan, New York, 1975.

Margolius, Sidney. *The Consumers' Guide to Better Buying*, rev. ed. Pocket Books, a division of Simon & Schuster, New York, 1972.

Schneider, Rita Marie, ed. "Carpet Developments Offer Wide Choice." *What's New in Home Economics*, 32 (May–June 1968), 29–31.

"Sheets and Pillowcases." *Consumer Buying Guide.* J. C. Penney Co., Educational Relations, New York, 1971.

Spring and Summer Catalogue. J. C. Penney Co., New York, 1974.

Stepat-DeVan, Dorothy. *Introduction to Home Furnishings*, 2nd ed. Macmillan, New York, 1971.

"Towels." *Consumer Buying Guide.* J. C. Penney Co., New York, n.d.

Wingate, Isabel B. *Textile Fabrics and Their Selection*, 7th ed. Prentice-Hall, Englewood Cliffs, N.J., 1976.

Williams, R. Elizabeth, and Verna D. Guillory. *Upholstered Furniture*. Cooperative Extension Publication no. 1546. Louisiana State University Cooperative Extension Service, Baton Rouge, 1970.

Williams, R. Elizabeth, Verna D. Guillory, and Celia S. Hissong. *Rug and Carpet Fibers*. Cooperative Extension Publication no. 1595. Louisiana State University Cooperative Extension Service, Baton Rouge, 1970.

Trade Associations

Textiles

American Printed Fabrics Council, 909 Third Avenue, New York, N.Y. 10022

American Textile Manufacturers Institute, 1501 Johnston Building, Charlotte, N.C. 28202

Cotton Incorporated, 350 Fifth Avenue, New York, N.Y. 10001

Fur Information & Fashion Council, 101 W. 30th Street, New York, N.Y. 10001

International Silk Association, 299 Madison Avenue, New York, N.Y. 10017

Irish Linen Guild, 641 Lexington Avenue, New New York, N.Y. 10022

Man-Made Fiber Products Association, Inc., 1150 17th Street, N.W., Washington, D.C. 20036

National Cotton Council, 1918 Parkway, Memphis, Tenn. 38112

Tanners Council, 411 Fifth Avenue, New York, N.Y. 10016

Textile Distributors Association, 1040 Avenue of the Americas, New York, N.Y. 10018

Textile Fabrics Association, 36 E. 31st Street, New York, N.Y. 10016

Wool Bureau, Inc., 386 Lexington Avenue, New York, N.Y. 10017

Apparel

American Apparel Manufacturers Association, 2000 K Street, N.W., Washington, D.C. 20006

American Cloak and Suit Manufacturers Association, 450 Seventh Avenue, New York, N.Y. 10001

American Footwear Manufacturers Association, 1611 N. Kent Street, Arlington, Va. 22209

Boys' and Young Men's Apparel Manufacturers Association, 10 W. 33rd Street, New York, N.Y. 10001

Clothing Manufacturers Association of the United States, 135 W. 50th Street, New York, N.Y. 10020

Corset and Brassiere Association of America, 220 Fifth Avenue, New York, N.Y. 10001

Greater Clothing Contractors Association, Inc., 100 Fifth Avenue, New York, N.Y. 10011

Lingerie Manufacturers Association, 41 East 42nd Street, New York, N.Y. 10017

National Association of Glove Manufacturers, 52 South Main Street, Gloversville, N.Y. 12078

National Dress Manufacturers Association, 570 Seventh Avenue, New York, N.Y. 10018

National Knitwear Manufacturers Institute, 350 Fifth Avenue, New York, N.Y. 10001

Merchandising

Association of General Merchandise Chains, 1441 Broadway, New York, N.Y. 10018

International Council of Shopping Centers, 445 Park Avenue, New York, N.Y. 10022

Mail Order Association of America, 612 N. Michigan Avenue, Chicago, Ill. 60611

Mass Merchandising Association, Inc., 100 Merrick Road, Rockville Center, N.Y. 11570

Menswear Retailers of America, 1290 Avenue of the Americas, New York, N.Y. 10019

National Outerwear & Sportswear Association, 347 Fifth Avenue, New York, N.Y. 10016

National Retail Merchants Association, 100 W. 31st Street, New York, N.Y. 10001

Shoe Retailers League, 60 W. 32nd Street, New York, N.Y. 10001

Miscellaneous

National Association of Furniture Manufacturers, 8401 Connecticut Avenue, Chevy Chase, Md. 20015

Index

Acetate, 6–7, 13, 16–19
Acrylic, 7, 11, 13, 16–19
Adolescents, clothing needs of, 219–223
Adults, clothing needs of, 224–227
Anidex, 7, 11, 13
Apparel
   care labeling, 95–97
   Consumer Care Guide, 96–97
   see also Clothing
Aramid, 7, 11, 13
Asbestos, 6
Axminster carpet, 317
Azlon, 7, 11, 13

Bath mats, rugs, 335
Batik, 74
Beauty, and consumer satisfaction, 139–142
Bedspreads, 331
Bindings, 331
Blankets
   bindings, 331
   care, 329–330
   colors, 331
   electric, 330
   fabrics, 329
   flammability, 331
   size, 329
   thermal, 330
Bleaches, 107
Blending, fiber, 18–20
Blind, clothing needs of, 231–232
Blouses, 286
Bonding, 46
Bouclé, 25, 28
Boys, *see* Men and boys
Braiding, 33, 47
Broadloom, carpets, 315
Burning test, 17

Carding, yarn, 22–23, 144
Care
   of blankets, 329–330
   and consumer satisfaction, 152–154
   of curtains and draperies, 322
   and fabric construction, 83–86
   and fabric storage, 148, 152
   and fiber properties, 79–81
   and finishes, 86–89
   of manufactured fibers, 80–81
   of natural fibers, 80
   of rugs and carpets, 317
   and shopping awareness, 89
   of upholstery, 312
   and yarn structure, 79, 82–83, 153
Care labeling
   apparel, 95–97
   Consumer Care Guide for Apparel, 96–97
   permanent care, 94
   piece goods, 95, 97
   upholstery, 97–98
Carpets
   care, 317
   construction
      Axminster, 317
      chenille, 317
      indoor-outdoor, 318
      level loop, 317
      plush, 317
      random shear, 317
      shag, 317
      tufting, 317
      velvet, 317
      Wilton, 317
      woven, 317
   fibers, 315
   quality, 316
Charge accounts, 177. *See also* Credit
Chemicals, household, 17–18
Chenille, 317
Children, clothing of, 234–240
   fabrics in, 235–237, 240–241
   needs, 216–217
   ready-made, 235–244
Clothing
   basic needs, 214–216
      of adolescents, 219–223
      of adults, 224–227
      of blind persons, 231–232
      of children, 216–217
      of elderly persons, 227–229
      of physically handicapped persons, 231
   leather, 261–262

Clothing (*continued*)
  ownership determinants, 203
  preferences, factors influencing, 197–203
  quality construction in, 187–189
  recycling, 133
  restyling, 136
  safety, 230, 232, 235–237, 241
  values, 204–209
    identification scale, 205
Coats
  men and boys, 247–254
  women and girls, 272–279
Color
  application, 64–65
  of blankets, 331
  and fabric finishes, 74–75
Combing, yarn, 22–23, 144
Comfort, and fabric finishes, 148–151
Comforters, 331–332
Consumer
  care awareness, 89
  clothing preferences, 197–203
  fiber/fabric preferences, 128–129
  protection, 91–102
  satisfaction, 139–154
Consumer Care Guide for Apparel, 96–97
Consumer Credit Protection Act, 178–179
Consumer Product Safety Commission, 102
Consumption
  of manufactured fibers, 123–124, 132–133
    Qiana nylon, 123
    rayon, 123
  of natural fibers
    cotton, 123, 131–132
    flax, 123
    silk, 123
    wool, 129–130
Cotton, 5, 11, 16–19
  consumption of, 123, 131–132
  usage changes, 131
Credit, 176–178
  Consumer Credit Protection Act, 178–179
  determination of need, 177
  truth-in-lending law, 178–179
  types of, 177–178
Creepers, 236

Cross-dyeing, 65
Curtains, draperies, 318–322, 335

Decision-making process, 182–185
Denier, yarn, 25
Department stores, 168
Design
  and fabric finishes, 74–75
  structural, 68
Diapers, 235
Discount stores, 171
Dope dyeing, 65
Double cloth construction, 46, 48
Draperies, *see* Curtains
Dresses, 281–284
Dyeing Methods, 65, 140

Elderly, clothing needs of, 227–229
Electric blankets, 330
Embroidery, 74

Fabric finishes, 58
  applied design, 68
    batik, 74
    embroidery, 74
    flocking, 74
    printing, 68–69, 70
    quilting, 74
    tie-and-dye, 74
  care characteristics, 86–89
  color and design terms, 74–75
  color application, 64
    cross-dyeing, 65
    dope dyeing, solution dyeing, 65
    piece dyeing, 65
    yarn dyeing, 65
  and comfort, 150–151
  general or routine, 58–59
  and sewing, 159
  special or functional, 59–64
  structural design, 68
Fabrics
  in clothing
    children, 235–237, 240–241
    men and boys, 247, 253, 257, 260, 262, 265
  shoes, 236

women and girls, 276–277, 280–281, 286–288
construction methods, 47–48, 140, 148, 149
   bonding, 46
   braiding, 33, 47
   double-cloth, 46, 48
   felting, 31, 47
   knit-sew, 43, 48
   knitting, 35, 47
   lace making, 34, 47
   laminating, 46, 48
   leno weave, 42, 48
   multilayer, 45–46
   nonwoven, 33, 47
   plastic film, 45
   pile, 43
   quilting, 46, 48
   tufting, 43, 48
   woven, 37–42, 47–48
from fibers, 31
in furnishings, 312, 315, 320–322
glossary of names, 48–56
grainline, 160
   bias, 161
   interfacings, support fabrics, 164
   knit construction, 164
   "off-grain" finish, 161
   "on-grain" construction, 161
   woven construction, 161
for home furnishings, 309, 312, 315, 320
in household linens, 325–337
laundry products for, 106–108
and patterns, 157
pressing of, 165
quality, 185–187
raveling of, 162
sewability of, 162, 164
from yarns, 33
Federal Trade Commission, 7
Felting, 31, 47
Fiber blending, 18–20
Fibers
  care characteristics, 79–81
  cellulosic, 5
  consumer preferences, 128–129
  content labeling, 93
  definitions of, 3

dyeing of, 65, 140
filaments, 18
flammability of, 16–17
general characteristics, 3–6
generic names, 7, 10–11
glossary, 20–21
and household chemicals, 17–18
identification techniques, 16–18
manufactured
   characteristics of, 10, 12–15
   consumption, 123–124, 132–133
natural, characteristics of, 5–6
protein, 5
requirements for textiles, 4
safety of, 98–102, 147
tradenames, 11
Filaments, 18
Finishes, see Fabric finishes
Fit, 210–212
Flammability, 16–17
  labeling laws, 98–102
Flax, 5, 11, 16–18
  consumption of, 123
Flocking, 74
Fur, labeling of, 92–93
Furnishings, home, 307–322
  care of, 313, 317, 322
  construction details, 310, 317–318
  curtains, draperies, 318
  fabrics, 307, 312, 315, 320
  indoot-outdoor carpeting, 318
  quality, 308, 316
  rugs, carpets, 315
  selection of, 307, 319
  styles, 315, 317–318, 320
  upholstered furniture, 309–313

Girls, see Women and girls
Glass, 7, 11, 13
Grainline, see Fabrics

Hand, 144–145
Handicapped, clothing needs of, 231

Hosiery
   men and boys, 263–264
   women and girls, 290–292
Household linens, *see* Linens
Hydrophilic, 20
Hydrophobic, 12, 21
Hygroscopicity, 5, 21

Ideals, 183
Indoor-outdoor carpeting, 318
Infants, apparel for, 235
Interfacing, 164
International Trade Organizations, 125–126

Jackets, 247, 254
Jeans, 259–261

Knit construction, fabrics, 164
Knit-sew construction, 43, 48
Knitting, fabric construction, 35, 47

Labeling, 91–98
Lace making, 34, 47
Laminating, 46, 48
Lastrile, 7, 11, 13
Laundering
   products, 106–108
   stain and spot removal, 110–114
   temperatures
     drying temperature, 110
     water temperature, 108–109
   water pollution, 114–116
Leather
   clothing, 261–262
   shoes, 302–303
   terms, 302–303
Legislation
   consumer credit, 178–179
   labeling laws
     flammability, 98–102
     fur products, 92–93
     permanent care, 94–95
     textile fiber products identification, 93–94
     wool products, 91–92

Leno weave, 42, 48
Linens, 325–328
Luster, 140

Mail-order houses, 171
Manufactured fibers, 10, 12–15
   consumption of, 123–124, 132–133
Mattress covers, pads, 328–329
Men and boys, clothing of, 247–265
   coats, 247–254
   fabrics in, 247, 253, 257, 260, 262, 265
   pants, 251, 259
   ready-made, 247–265
Metallics, 7, 11, 13
Metric measurement, 192–193
Microscope test, 18
Modacrylic, 7, 11, 14, 17, 19
Multilayer construction, fabrics, 45–46

Natural fibers, 4–6
Needs, Maslow's theory relating to, 184
Nightclothes, 265, 290
Nonwoven construction, fabrics, 33, 47
Novoloid, 7, 11, 14
Nylon, 7, 11, 14, 17, 19
   Qiana, 123
Nytril, 7, 11, 14

"Off-grain" finish, 161
Olefin, 7, 11, 14, 19
"On-grain" construction, 161
Overalls, children's, 236
Overcoats (topcoats), 253–254

Pajamas, 265
Pants
   men and boys, 251, 259
   women and girls, 259, 284, 286
Patchwork, 136
Permanent care, 94–95
Piece dyeing, 65
Piece goods, care labeling of, 95, 97
Pile, 43

Pilling, 140
Pillows
   cases, 328
   sizes, 328
Polyester, 7, 11, 14, 16, 19
Polypropylene, *see* Olefin
Printing, fabric finish, 68–70
Protection, consumer, *see* Consumer

Qiana, *see* Nylon
Quality
   construction in clothing, 187–189
   in fabrics, 185–187
Quilting, 46, 48, 74
Quilts, *see* Comforters

Rayon, 6–7, 11, 15, 17, 18–19
   consumption of, 123
Ready-made clothing
   for children, 235–244
      costumes, 237
      creepers, 236
      diapers, 235
      overalls, 236
      shirts, 235
      shoes, 236
      snowsuits, 236
   fit, 210–212
   for men and boys, 247–265
      jackets, 247, 254
      jeans, 259–261
      leather, 261–262
      overcoats (topcoats), 253–254
      pajamas, 265
      shirts, 256–259
      slacks, trousers, 247, 251–252
      socks, 263–264
      suits, 247–252
      sweaters, 262–263
      underwear, 264–265
   size standards, 212
   for women and girls, 280–292
      blouses, 286
      coats, 276–279
      dresses, 281–284
      foundation garments, 287–290
      hosiery, 290–292
      nightclothes, 290
      pants, 284–286
      suits, 280–281
      sweaters, 286–287
Recycling
   clothing, 133
   textiles, 133, 136–137
Restyling, clothing, 136
Rubber
   manufactured, 11, 15
   natural, 6, 11
Rugs, *see* Carpets

Sales, 174–176
Saran, 7, 11, 15
Satisfaction, consumer, 139–154
Serviceability, 322
Sewing, home, 156–165
   and fabric finishes, 159
Sheets, 325–327
Shirts, 256–259
   children, 235
   men and boys, 256–259
Shoes
   care, 301–302
   children, 235–244
   fit, 298–300
   leather, 302–303
   manufacturing of, 296-298
   materials, 298
   parts of, 294–295
   quality, 300–301
Shower curtains, 335
Silk, 5, 11, 17, 18
   consumption of, 123
Sizing, apparel, 212
   children, 235
   men and boys, 247
Slacks, 247, 251–252
Snowsuits, 236
Soaps and detergents, 106
Solubility test, 17
Solution dyeing, 65
Spandex, 7, 11, 15

Specialty shops, 168
Spinning, yarn, 23–24, 144
Starch, 108
Stores, types of, 168–173
Suits
    men and boys, 247–252
    women and girls, 280–281
Sweaters
    men and boys, 262–263
    women and girls, 286–287

Tablecloths, 335–337
Tables, sizes, 336
Textiles
    consumption, 121, 128
    developments, 20th century, 122
    in home, 305–322
    technology, 124
    trade, 124
    usage changes, 129–136
Thermal blankets, 330
Thermoplasticity, 10, 21
Thread, 28–29, 162, 164
Tie-and-dye, 74
Toddlers, clothing for, 235
Towels, 332–334
Trade associations, 344
Trademark, 189–191
Triacetate, 7, 11, 15
Truth-in-lending law, 178–179
Tufting, 43, 48
Twisting, yarn, 23–25, 144, 147, 149, 152–153

Underclothing
    men and boys, 264–265
    women and girls, 287–290
Upholstery, 312–313
    care labeling of, 97–98

Values, 183–185
Variety stores, 170
Velvet carpets, construction, 317
Vinal, 7, 11, 15
Vinyon, 7, 11, 15

Water temperature, 108–109
Wilton carpet construction, 317
Women and girls, clothing of
    coats, 272–279
    fabrics in, 276–277, 280–281, 286–288
    hosiery, 291–292
    pants, 259, 284, 286
    ready-made, 280–292
    underclothing, 287–290
Wool, 5, 11, 16–19
    consumption of, 129–230
    labeling of, 91
    usage changes, 129
Woven fabrics, 37–42, 47–48

Yarn
    bouclé, 25, 28
    consumer satisfaction, 140, 144, 147, 149
    definition, 21
    denier, 25
    dyeing, in fabric finishes, 65
    fabrics from, 33
    glossary, 28–29
    hand spun, 140
    knotted, 27
    looped, 26
    metallic, 140
    novelty, 25, 28
    nubbed, 27
    ply, 24, 28
    simple, 25, 28
    size, 24–25
    slubbed, 26
    spiral, 27
    textured, 27, 29
    thread, 28–29, 162, 164
    twist, 23–24
    types, 25–27
    woolen, 23–24, 29
    worsted, 23, 29
Yarn processes
    carding, 22–23, 144
    combing, 22–23, 144
    spinning, 23–24, 144
    twisting, 23–25, 144, 147, 149, 152–153